For Birgit

CONTENTS

'How football has changed! Everything has become more complicated – and more beautiful.'

Xabi Alonso

INTRODUCTION

I've always looked up to Christoph Biermann: he's very tall, and I'm not. But his physical height, by my cautious estimate, is only 4.83 per cent of the reason why he's considered one of the outstanding writers of his generation in Germany. If not the greatest.

Born in 1960 in Krefeld, Biermann lost his heart to unfashionable VfL Bochum, the kind of side Germans sneeringly refer to as *graue Maus* (grey mouse) while studying German and History at Bochum University. For 25 years, he went to see almost every home game of the self-proclaimed 'Unrelegatables' – they're more like the 'Unpromotables' now, having been stuck in Bundesliga 2 since 2010 – but the rather mundane fare on show at the Ruhrstadion didn't put him off football for the rest of his life. On the contrary, Biermann has found himself hooked on the mystical grandeur and strong sense of meaning the sport radiates, especially in the (post-industrial) heartland of the game. 'We can find the whole world in football, and it's easier to do so in the Ruhr area than in any other place in Germany,' he wrote in *Wenn wir vom Fußball träumen (Dreaming of Football)*, the most personal of his nine exceptionally brilliant, and multiple award-winning books to date.

Before starting to write about football, Biermann became music editor for a Bochum-based magazine and later recorded a seven-inch single in honour of his favourite team. The self-deprecating track ('Deutscher Meister wird nie der VfL!', 'VfL will never be champions') was once played over the stadium tannoy, albeit in its even more absurd B-side version which replaced the lyrics of the chorus with an overly optimistic 'Only VfL will be champions!' line.

His journalistic exploits were a lot more sound. After some well-received freelance work, Biermann was hired to adorn the pages of many highbrow publications such as *Süddeutsche Zeitung*, *Der Spiegel* and *11FREUNDE* magazine with his original take on the game, cast in carefully crafted sentences coloured by affection. An unwillingness to look past football's multitude of ills has made him no less entranced by the enduring magic of the game, by its archaic emotionalism and by its history and its stories. He's got a very fine sense of humour, too. Especially for a German.

But more importantly than that, Christoph is one of those rare writers who is unerringly honest with his readers and with the subject he covers. You'll never find him smooth over all the countless incongruities until his account fits a pre-conceived, simple notion as snugly as a goalkeeper's glove or attempt to extract significance where there isn't any. The football he describes is never just one thing, but the real thing – a barely comprehensible melee of incredibly sophisticated ideas and clumsy inadequacies, of epic sensations and soggy banalities. Biermann lays bare the game's internal contradictions, and with it, the fault lines in his own arguments.

In *The Undoing Project*, Michael Lewis' gripping tale of two Israeli economists who detected the systemic flaws in people's reasoning, we meet Daryl Morey, the general manager of the NBA's Houston Rockets. Morey, Lewis writes, had 'an understanding of how hard it is to know anything for sure. The closest he came to certainty was in his approach to making decisions. He never simply went with his first thought. He suggested a new definition of the nerd: a person who knows his own mind well enough to mistrust it.' Biermann's approach to writing about football, three decades into the job, is rather similar. He opens a door on his doubts, and his views are only all the more convincing and reliable for it.

This book, his first but surely not last to appear in English, profiles the loose network of data renegades obsessed with rendering football into a series of convention-defying numbers. I suspect he was partially drawn to their ingenious efforts because he has already mastered the game's translation into words himself. But he'd be far too humble to admit to that.

Football Hackers is ostensibly about codes, algorithms and statistical models, but ultimately, like all of his work, it is really about love. His love for football, to be sure, but more than that: Biermann is driven by the thrill of edging a little closer to knowing what might be going on in this simple, tangled, crazy game, and by the even deeper satisfaction that comes from sharing his wondrous discoveries.

Raphael Honigstein

PROLOGUE
THE ADVENTURE BEGINS

On an early summer's night in 2011, I sat at Wembley with tears in my eyes. The magnitude of the moment had overwhelmed me. Four decades after entering a stadium for the first time in my life, a realisation had grown stronger with every passing minute of the Champions League final: I had never seen a better football match in my life. Manchester United, managed by Sir Alex Ferguson at the time, were very good against Pep Guardiola's FC Barcelona, but they didn't stand a chance. The Catalans had fantastic players, first and foremost Lionel Messi, the man of the match. Manchester United had some fine players of their own, but the artistry of individuals took a back seat to the beauty of Barcelona's collective splendour. They transformed the biggest games of the season into a demonstration of football that had reached a new level of evolution. Pep Guardiola brought out the genius of his players with an elaborate plan of unprecedented perfection. Manchester United might have only lost 3–1 on the night, but in truth, they had been hopelessly inferior.

Although planned, Barça's football was free and easy, playful and elegant. It didn't cram their players into a tight corset, but gave them a framework for their creativity instead. It looked brand new, but it had deep roots going back to the Netherlands of the 1960s, when Johan Cruyff was first taught *Totaalvoetbal* at Ajax Amsterdam and later became its greatest catalyst. Influenced by those fundamental ideas, Cruyff had arrived in Barcelona where he developed his footballing principles further and had a decisive influence on the club's youth development.

In the summer of 2017, I was back in London, this time not in a stadium packed with ecstatic, cheering people, but in a conference room of a co-working space overlooking the Thames. Around me, young people were working on digital projects, careful to look both terribly earnest and conspicuously relaxed. The coffee was good, it was free, and I soon looked at a computer screen to witness a great marriage of sorts. I was able to watch a football match from various camera angles; it was almost as if a broadcasting van had been shrunk into the laptop. Alongside the footage, you could pull up different data extracted from the match, provided by spotters from data companies or by the thermal imaging cameras of the tracking systems. Every event on the pitch, every move and every run had been measured and counted. Video and data were joined up more seamlessly than I had ever seen before in football.

This software had initially been developed for Formula 1 by a company called SGB who work with half of the teams. Formula 1 is the most technologically advanced sport on the planet. There are dozens of sensors built into a car, every race produces 10 terabytes of data. On race days, 200 specialists interpret the flow of information; every manoeuvre on the track has been calculated and analysed in advance. In autumn of 2014, SGB had given a demonstration of the software at the Abu Dhabi Grand Prix to the Emirates' rulers, who also own Manchester City. When they said they wanted a similar program for football as well, SGB set about working on the software I was now looking at in transfixed amazement in a windowless conference room.

Eight years ago, I wrote 'football has become a game of numbers', in *Die Fußball-Matrix*, the German precursor of this book. It had looked that way back then, but it wasn't right. Not yet. I had fallen prey to that illusion when I had first sat in front of numerous pages filled with the stats that top-level football games had started to produce. Every shot was counted, every pass, every sprint and many other things. But there was a problem: the numbers and the game did not correlate.

But that day in London I realised that the revolution was now truly happening. Not only had the amount of data grown, but also the ability to make sense of it, thanks to computer scientists and statisticians tearing into it with guidance from football experts. It's not quite packaged into a finished, mainstream article yet but the knowledge is available, it's out there. If you ignore it, you've only got yourself to blame. Whether we like it or not, the game has reached its digital tidal point.

In spring 2017, I took a ferry from the Icelandic mainland across the rough North Atlantic to the island of Vestmannaeyjar, to meet with Heimir Hallgrímsson, the national manager of the least-populated country ever to qualify for the World Cup finals. Hall-grímsson's tired old laptop didn't have any modish analysis tools on its whirring hard drive like those I would later see in London. Most of his players were not playing at glamorous clubs and didn't feature in the Champions League. The national team flew economy to away games. Hallgrímsson showed me around his little island where he still worked as a dentist then, time permitting. (He also scraped off some tartar from my teeth, but that's a different story.) The next day, we drove around the capital Reykjavik to watch some youth teams in action. Hallgrímsson can teach you as much about football as Pep Guardiola, but in a different way. Having to make do with less talented players and far inferior resources in Iceland, he knew how to manage scarcity. He was mindful of the tiniest advantage he could obtain for his team.

The national manager found an advantage that would prove decisive for his team, as it turned out. He joins the ranks of the other unusual heroes of this book. There's a professional gambler who has bought his childhood club and a German-American psephologist who became a general manager in football; a Northern-Irish bank employee who penned a brilliant analysis of Borussia Dortmund and the unkempt, unshaven scout of the Bundesliga club who later joined Arsenal FC for a seven-figure fee. You will meet a somewhat erratic coach, whose football beats the statistics, and two former Bundesliga professionals who became football scientists.

I didn't set out to find these exceptional, headstrong and zany characters; it was almost inevitable that I would meet them on a journey through terrain that remains largely uncharted. You recognise them easily. They are the ones who have more questions than answers and don't want to explain how things work to you but understand them themselves first. They are all adventurers and the adventure is only starting. All of them are motivated by the same quest Heimir Hallgrímsson has dedicated himself to. They all seek an edge. The difference is that they attempt to find it in the data and in the opportunities of digitalisation.

High-end football, like the type Barcelona showcased in 2011, still has a spellbinding effect on me, at times, and I'm drawn to the sparkling promises of the digital age, too. But in truth, I've always been more interested in the underdogs, and especially those who take to their role with cunning verve. They are the ones who subvert the system and try to beat it – the hackers of football.

Without really knowing it at the time, I was looking for these disruptors when I travelled to the world's biggest conference for Sports Analytics in Boston, and to a tiny club in Denmark where I met with an employee of an energy provider in Hamburg, who had managed to take a little information and turn it into staggeringly precise evaluations of players.

Eight years ago, I also wrote: 'Data is part of an ongoing evolution that changes football from a game of opinions into one of knowledge.' That sentence expressed a hope, more than anything. Opinions got on my nerves even then. They were so arbitrary and interchangeable. But I had little idea at the time of the absurd ways us humans arrived at our verdicts – in football and beyond. That's why this book is also about the possibility of changing and improving the way of thinking about the game, for us as fans but also club officials.

The future of football will not simply belong to those with the best data, but those who draw the best conclusions from the information at their disposal. Football is no different in that regard to other walks of life.

This book was first released in spring 2018 in Germany. For its English version, it was updated and new chapters were added. The fact it needed substantial modifications is down to the lightning speed of change in this particular field. Football's hackers are here to stay.

Berlin, March 2019

WHY OPINIONS ARE ANNOYING AND VERDICTS ARE WRONG

Two professional footballers feel they're being wrongly evaluated. They find a new way to look at the game. And: why we're all prone to confirmation bias and overrate the importance of results.

JUSTICE FOR VEDAD IBISEVIC

I first met Stefan Reinartz on a Monday night in the autumn of 2011. He was 22 years old at the time, a midfielder at Bayer 04 Leverkusen in the Bundesliga, and even by Germanic standards of punctuality, he had arrived a little earlier than necessary. We were due to go live on a radio show together, in Cologne. But he wanted to show me something first.

Reinartz often has an unsettling effect on those who don't know him well. He can look at you completely devoid of any expression.

It's only once one of his eyebrows is slowly arching that you begin to suspect that there's possibly a very humorous, perhaps even downright funny person hiding underneath the blank facade. But I didn't know that at the time. This rather tall man stood in front of me like a prosecutor in front of the accused. In his hand, he held a bill of indictment: a folder filled with clips of player ratings from Bundesliga games, just like the ones that appear in newspapers and on websites every weekend the world over.

Adopting a tone of quiet indignation, he fished out a few pages and arranged them neatly on the table. *Kölner Stadt-Anzeiger*, a Cologne-based daily, had rated Renato Augusto, Reinartz's Brazilian team-mate at the time, 2 out of 6 for his game against SC Freiburg. (In Germany, football ratings follow school marks, with 1, 'very good' being the equivalent of 'A', the best in class and 6, 'inadequate', the absolute worst, like an 'F' in the UK.) *Kicker,* Germany's oldest and most respected football magazine as well as national tabloid *Bild* had both awarded Augusto a 5, however: 'flawed'. As a schoolboy, his progress to the next form would have been in severe danger.

On the whole, there was a large range of differing verdicts on his performance:

Kölner Stadt-Anzeiger	Sport1	Rheinische Post	kicker	Bild
2	2.5	4.5	5	5

It had been a similar story for striker Vedad Ibisevic that very same weekend. His game for TSG 1899 Hoffenheim against Werder

Bremen had split the opinion of media observers. Some felt it had been pretty good, others thought he'd been rather awful.

Westdeutsche Zeitung	Sportal	Sport1	kicker	Bild
2	3	3.5	4	5

Reinartz offered a few more examples in the same vein. They all begged one simple question, and he was keen to ask it, in the name of many of his puzzled colleagues. 'How did those ratings come about?'

That was the opening line for his, the prosecution's, case. I wasn't entirely sure if he didn't actually know the answer to his query all along. Many journalists have to start writing their match reports while the game is still in full swing, I explained, defensively. They couldn't be expected to appraise every detail correctly. If they were also tasked to write the ratings, in addition to their main pieces, they were only really judging players on one or two big moments they had witnessed or perhaps seen as replays on the TV monitors. And even if they had more time to file, how were they supposed to arrive at appropriate marks for 22 players? Since none of the writers were privy to the pre-match team talk, they had no idea whether a full-back was rarely involved in attack because he was out of form or if he was in fact following a strict instruction from his manager to stay in his own half. I also told him that some reporters relied on the wisdom of crowds in the press box, conducting straw polls along the lines of 'Reinartz: 3 or 4?'

One couldn't fully discount the possibility that a reporter had simply no idea, of course. And some could be following their own secret agenda: they were generous to those who tipped them off about the happenings in the dressing room or punished those who didn't play ball or – worse – preferred to talk to another journalist. Those things were not nearly as prevalent as they used to be. But they did still happen.

On the whole, I pleaded mitigating circumstances on behalf of my co-defendants. Reinartz appeared understanding, if not really satisfied. Interestingly, he didn't disagree with the general idea of player ratings. On the contrary, he considered being evaluated a natural part of professional life. He had joined Leverkusen as a ten-year-old and played in all the national team youth sides from age 16 to 21. Young players had to handle assessment every single day. Had he trained well enough to get picked at the weekend? Did his performance warrant making the step up to the next, older group of players? Countless times he had seen team-mates discarded for being too slow, too small, technically deficient, for lacking tactical nous or being mentally too weak. Even some of the players he had played with in the U20s and U21s of the national team didn't make it into the top flight.

And then, things only became more difficult as a professional. Was he better than his rival for the same position in his Bundesliga team? Was he maybe stronger than most German players in that position and therefore a contender for the national team? Or was it better for him to move from midfield into defence instead?

Reinartz had no problem at all with any of that. His complaints about the media marks were motivated by something else entirely. If he was to be constantly judged, objectivity and fairness were all he wanted. As it turned out, he had made both his calling.

There was no point denying that journalists were by and large guilty as charged. The grades they were handing out had no objective basis, and therefore couldn't be said to be fair. Luckily, Reinartz proved a prosecutor of the forgiving kind.

We kept in touch, spoke on the phone from time to time, and bumped into each other in strange places: footballers don't usually frequent sports analytics conferences, not even former footballers.

Two years after our meeting on the radio show, Reinartz contacted me once more. Could they meet me for a coffee and ask something? 'They', it transpired, were Reinartz and his former Leverkusen teammate Jens Hegeler, who played for Hertha BSC at the time and would move to Bristol City in 2017. Reinartz, too, had just moved clubs, from Leverkusen to Eintracht Frankfurt. We met on a cold winter's day in a cafe in Berlin. The conversation soon took an unexpected turn, with both of them interrogating me at length about the use of game data in football. Most importantly, they wanted to know whether there was any specific data set that reliably predicted results. Did those who ran more, sprinted more times, passed the ball better or shot at goal more frequently win more games?

Reinartz and Hegeler had often heard managers talk about those factors in their team talks. They had implored the players to remember that 'winning more tackles than the opponent' was the key requirement for three points or emphasised the all-important need to run more, run faster or move the ball quicker if the players wanted to win the match.

All I could do was to tell them what they knew all along. There was, to be sure, nothing wrong with running more, passing better and shooting more often than your opponent, but as far as I knew, none of those parameters were statistically proven to guarantee any wins. Any manager telling them otherwise was therefore talking nonsense.

Reinartz and Hegeler were happy with that answer and slowly began to explain why they had asked me all this in the first place. Both had come to a simple conclusion about this whole business of football and stats. If the existing data said nothing about a team's propensity to win a game, new and better data needed to be found. Their idea was, on the face of it, a simple one: they added up the number of bypassed players during a game. Preliminary findings were in the process of being evaluated by a sports scientist, in a study they both had personally funded. As we are about to see, this novel concept would evolve into a pretty big thing.

I thought it fascinating that two active football professionals had dedicated themselves to revolutionising the analysis of the game with the help of new data. I also had to think back to Reinartz's complaint about the marks. The amount of energy and time they both dedicated to finding a better way to evaluate players' performances was driven by a quest for more justice.

They were also fed up with all the stupid things managers were often telling them. Stefan and Jens seemed to belong to a rather small group of players who not only want to play the game as well as possible but also truly understand it. Some were destined to become managers or technical directors after their active careers, but I had never met any active footballers taking a deep interest in analytics before.

During Euro 2016, TV viewers got to see what Reinartz and Hegeler had explained to me in broad strokes three years earlier and had since developed into a functioning model. They had come up with a way to assign a numerical value to effective passing and dribbling by counting the number of opponents – specifically defenders – taken out by a completed forward move of the ball. They named their new metric 'Packing' – an English-German hybrid term that played on the verb *packen*, and its colloquial use in sporting contexts as a synonym for beating somebody.

Out of the blue, TV pundit Mehmet Scholl confronted millions of people with a new Packing metric. Scholl, a former Germany international and Champions League winner with Bayern Munich, was deeply impressed with the concept and leaned very heavily, if not say a little clumsily, on it in an effort to give his on-air analysis of matches at the European Championship in France a statistical grounding. It didn't quite work. Scholl had simplified the concept to the point where it no longer provided insight but mere banalities. Maybe the underlying principles should have been explained in more depth. In any case, Packing left most of the audience puzzled and bemused, which was a shame as there is much to be gained from its proper use. But for many traditionally-minded football fans, Scholl's ill-fated attempt to make sense of an outcome by way of some weird passing numbers was merely another illustration of the wider, regrettable trend that has seen pompous know-it-alls add unnecessary layers of complexity to a simple game.

One of the most appealing aspects of football lies in the fact that everyone is allowed an opinion. Or to put it slightly differently: football thrives on all of us being able to pass judgement on games and players. The reason player ratings are so popular is because they offer us the chance to compare them to our own observations. We are all members of the jury these days, forever rating people and their performances on reality TV or social media. You can't move for polls and requests for audience feedback. Everybody is interested in everybody else's views on literally everything. Facebook, Twitter and Instagram are virtual courthouses, presiding over public opinion, 24/7.

Football, a game made of emotions, is rarely prone to too much rational discourse; arguments are mostly informed by feelings rather than facts. There's a natural tendency to lionise those who score the winning goal for our teams and to curse those who make costly mistakes. But football isn't just a wonderfully simple, emotionally-charged game. It's also highly complex, becoming only more complicated on closer inspection.

Over the course of time, I've found it only harder to properly evaluate players and matches, rather than easier. The opposite should have been true, really, as I've been privileged to attend hundreds of games at the highest level, and met many fascinating coaches, great sporting directors and interesting players. I've witnessed close up how the knowledge of football has continuously grown wider and deeper. You get the sense that everyone's constantly learning new things about the game and trying to understand it better. The pivotal question: what do we do with all of that knowledge?

THE WONDERFUL WORLD
OF COGNITIVE BIASES

Jörg Schmadtke has been one of the Bundesliga's most successful operators over the last decade or so – provided one is prepared to look beyond silverware and positions in the table. Since first getting appointed in his role at second division Alemannia Aachen in 2001, the former Borussia Mönchengladbach goalkeeper has never seen one of his teams win the championship or the DFB Pokal German Cup. His work has nevertheless been extraordinary, as he's routinely overachieved everywhere.

He led heavily indebted Aachen not only into the UEFA Cup/ Europa League, courtesy of reaching the domestic cup final, but also saw them promoted to the top flight for the first time in 30 years in 2007. During his reign at Hannover 96 (2009–13), the Lower Saxons twice qualified for Europe and played their best-ever season in the Bundesliga. And in 2017, Schmadtke managed to guide 1. FC Köln, one of Germany's most storied but also most temperamental clubs, into the Europa League after a 25-year absence.

There are many different definitions of a sporting director's role in the Bundesliga. For Schmadtke, the scouting of players has always been a key part of his work. Often, he effectively served as the chief scout and travelled the world in search of new recruits, picking up a high number of very good strikers along the way. Without spelling it out explicitly himself, Schmadtke has had to deal with one of scouting's biggest problems – the propensity for systematic errors in judgement. Or, as psychologists call it: cognitive bias.

'I used to send my scouts to games not telling them which player I was interested in,' he told me in London, shortly before Köln's first international game in 25 years, against Arsenal. Keeping his employees in the dark was not meant as a weird test of their capabilities or a mean trick to unsettle them. 'I wanted them to watch the game with fresh eyes, free of any suppositions. Ideally, they would like the very same player I found interesting.' Schmadtke refrained from narrowing his scouts' focus. He widened it. By doing so he instinctively tried to avoid a phenomenon that behavioural economists call confirmation bias. Once a scout is aware that his supporting director has his eye on a specific player, he might regard him differently; thus, judging him objectively becomes more difficult. We tend to filter out information that doesn't chime with pre-existing notions.

But that's only one variant of a bias that comes in many guises. Scouts who like dynamic, physical players might overlook technical deficits or a lack of footballing intelligence, or consider those flaws of lesser importance. Those with a penchant for elegant technicians, conversely, are perhaps more lenient when it comes to judging a player's ability to recover the ball.

'When I get cold sitting in the stands, things get difficult,' Schmadtke said, admitting that getting grumpy in the stadium could also negatively influence a scout's verdict on a player who might have received a much better report on a balmy summer's night. How many talent spotters will have faced similar issues on a rainy afternoon in eastern Europe or on a freezing-cold evening in Scandinavia? Shivering and in a foul mood, they might have missed the sophisticated build-up play of a full-back or the penetrative power of a centre-forward, players who ended up moving to a rival club whose scouts had seen a game of theirs on a sunny and pleasant day. There's a danger of the opposite happening, too. Players who perform in a nice, comfortable stadium packed with enthusiastic fans might get overrated because the scout is enjoying the spectacle too much.

The importance of cognitive biases has received much attention over the last few years, not least due to the seminal work of Israeli economist Daniel Kahneman, a Nobel Prize winner for his findings in this field. His book *Thinking, Fast and Slow* has become an international bestseller. Kahneman and other academics have discovered 188 different forms of cognitive bias that are in part related or connected. All of them have their cause in the brain's tendency to get things wrong when it is forced to think quickly, as opposed to calmly and analytically. Judgements made in haste are often faulty, as we vastly overestimate our own abilities to make the right call in a short space of time. It is those types of fast, half-baked verdicts and evaluations that also lie at the heart of the problems that Stefan Reinartz and Jens Hegeler have encountered, and encouraged them to develop their own football data in response.

Data doesn't necessarily lead to better analysis by itself, however. On the contrary, numbers can easily give rise to more cognitive bias. There's a huge temptation to cherry-pick stats that confirm a preexisting view of a player and to dismiss those that present a conflicting picture. Managers are prone to doing just that when they sometimes shake their head looking at the poor 50/50 numbers of a player who they had already suspected of not having won enough tackles, while simultaneously ignoring the fact that he made more sprints than usual to close down opposition passing lanes.

As a football fan, you immediately understand what Swiss novelist Max Frisch meant when he said that 'we try on stories as we try on clothes'. Football is a giant narrative factory, with each season unfolding like a new series of a soap opera called 'Premier League', 'Champions League' or 'World Cup'. They each have their own, unscripted plot, delighting the audience with unforeseen twists and turns. Rank outsiders rise up from the depths of despair to become heroes. Every competition, league and club has their own story. Who could fail to fall in love with the fairy tale of Leicester City, winners of the Premier League in 2016 as the biggest underdogs in the history of English football? And how can you not marvel at the fantastical career trajectory of the Foxes' Jamie Vardy, the mercurial striker who used to play for a non-league side with an electronic tag underneath his sock, having been sentenced to house arrest after dark for grievous bodily harm?

But there are also clubs who suddenly find themselves in an unexpected crisis. That's what happened to Köln upon their return to European football, and that's why Schmadtke ended up leaving them later that season. Max Frisch's aphorism rang true once more. The story of the headstrong but brilliant sporting director with a genius' eye for talent no longer fit the external circumstances. Köln's tale was now being told very differently – it was that of a sporting director who had become too intransigent and in the process lost his touch in the transfer market.

We understand how that sort of highly selective and flexible storytelling works when it comes to ourselves. We, too, attempt to forge many moments and singular life events into a somewhat coherent tale. But the narrative is constantly evolving. Almost no one keeps telling themselves the same autobiographical story they have told themselves ten years earlier. Other issues have taken on more importance as we have moved further along life's path, and things look widely different in hindsight. This is not necessarily a form of lying to ourselves or wilfully bending the facts. There is a deep-seated human need to mould everything into one sweeping, seemingly coherent narrative. Story bias, social psychologists call this trait.

Have a look at the different stories that are being rolled out when coaches make many tactical changes or rotate their personnel – or both – from one game to the next. In Pep Guardiola's case, his high-frequency interventionism has become an integral part of the 'genius' narrative, hailing a coach who keeps pushing the envelope of football, in theory and on the pitch. That positive perception owes much to Guardiola's teams winning most of the games they play in. But there could be a more banal explanation: money. Guardiola has so far either coached the most expensive or the second-most expensive teams in the league, sides who were financially clearly stronger than most of their rivals. In Barcelona, Munich and Manchester, he has had the best players at his disposal. They had been mostly winning in the years before his arrival and continued mostly winning once he was gone. Those teams would have probably won a majority of games without any sophisticated tactical decisions, too.

Coaches who try to be tactically versatile in charge of non-elite clubs, and therefore end up losing quite often, are conversely in danger of being saddled with a different story. They're being quickly accused of 'not knowing their best XI' or having 'a lack of identity' by pundits and fans alike. People deride them as tinker men, forever in search of a winning formula that keeps eluding them.

Until he sensationally won the Premier League with Leicester City to become briefly labelled a genius and have a statue built in his image, Claudio Ranieri was known as one of the most infamous tinker men. He won the title fielding almost the same XI in every game for the Foxes, playing a smaller total number of players during the course of the season than most other sides in the league. But when his team had to contest matches in the Champions League in the following season, he altered his line-ups to allow for the increased workload und unsurprisingly lost a few more games. Soon, he was regarded as tinkering too much for the team's good once more. There was no escaping that narrative. There is no escaping from narrative, period. Humans are hard-wired to make sense of things by telling stories, even if that's rarely the most helpful way to analyse problems and arrive at solutions.

Cognitive biases are prevalent in all walks of life. At work, in relationships or in the interpretation of political events. Football, too, is riddled with them. The so-called clustering illusion, to take another example of faulty thinking, has us seeing supposed patterns in the accumulation of events. A team conceding goals from dead balls in two consecutive games immediately invites a discussion about their weakness from corners and free-kicks. And another side conceding a few late goals unerringly leads to experts talking about a team's physical condition. In both cases, those could actually be correct observations rather than mere coincidence. But there's no way to know with any certainty. The sample size is just too small.

One of football's most popular cognitive mistakes is hindsight bias. After the event, people convince themselves they had known the outcome all along. A team surprisingly getting sucked into the relegation zone, another one making an unexpected bid for the title. It doesn't take much to think: 'I had a feeling that might happen.' (That's also down to us constantly overestimating our own ability to make informed judgements.) We always knew one specific player would make it! Or not. Granted, nobody might be bold enough to pretend they had predicted the miracle of Leicester or Jamie Vardy's rise. But we all tend to misremember our football forecasts as much more accurate than they were at the time. That's why noting down one's predictions ahead of a season and checking up on them later is a very useful exercise in humility.

As a low-scoring game, it is in football's nature to produce singular events that get lodged in the memory. In people's perception, it's a game of decisive moments. We recall the fantastic last-ditch tackle, the deadly pass and, most of all, the 25-yard screamer into the top corner. Those moments get retold over and over until they become mythology. They determine how we see and understand the game.

But there is a problem. The term 'availability heuristic' describes our mind's flawed presumption that things that are memorised are also important. This leads to us unfairly thinking of certain strikers solely in relation to some high-profile misses we happen to remember, or have perhaps been reminded of thanks to social media spewing out the footage again and again. Every football culture has its own special memories that fall into the 'he's missed a sitter!' category. Germans forever think of Frank Mill, the Borussia Dortmund striker who didn't just bear down on goal completely by himself, but also expertly rounded the Bayern Munich keeper Jean-Marie Pfaff, only to then hit the post of an empty goal from five metres out. In England, Liverpool FC forward Ronny Rosenthal will never live down his miss against Aston Villa. 'My granny would have scored that one,' the cry goes.

In high-scoring games such as basketball or baseball, there are of course particular moments that have decided championships and have become memorable as a consequence, as you would expect. But how can a single shot come to define the story of a run-of-the-mill basketball game that ends 102–93? The lesser importance of singular events automatically makes high-scoring games appear more structured and more complex than football. In football, we focus on decisive moments and interpret the game backwards from there. US sports don't work like that. Statistical analysis is much more prevalent there.

One could reasonably argue that it's precisely the critical importance of isolated actions that makes football so enjoyable, for fans in particular. But there's a problem if important, costly decisions – on the future of a manager or the transfer of a player – are made on the basis of cognitive biases; if sporting directors, coaches or other key figures prefer trying out different stories to carefully analysing a situation. If they think fast, not slow.

That's especially true in relation to the mother of all cognitive errors in football: the so-called outcome bias. It denotes our unfortunate tendency to construe judgements that take the result as their starting point, rather than a coach's intentions and strategies. To put it simpler: if the outcome is positive, we assume that his plan or pre-game decisions were right. If the result is negative, however, we are quick to believe that his tactics must have been bad. Thinking that way is especially widespread in football, as each game comes with a result measured in simple numbers. Criticism of the players' performances and of a manager's tactics tend to be much more severe for the losing side than for those who won. You might say that's only right and logical. But that would disregard the next, really big problem we're faced with in football: there's often quite a gap between performances and results.

THE POWER OF COINCIDENCE

Luck plays a much greater role in football than we would like to admit: it's even quantifiable. If Jürgen Klopp had known as much, he might have never become coach of Liverpool FC.

HE HAS TO SCORE!

On 15 April 2015, Borussia Dortmund manager Jürgen Klopp, CEO Hans-Joachim Watzke and Sporting Director Michael Zorc stepped into the press room of Dortmund's stadium and announced the most heartfelt of goodbyes: Klopp was to leave the club at the end of the season, after seven (mostly) golden years, two championships, one DFB Pokal win and a run to the final of the Champions League. During the bespectacled Swabian's reign, the club had been transformed; Borussia, barely solvent in 2008, had become a financial powerhouse and widely admired around the globe for their thrilling football.

Watzke, his voice trembling, declared his 'eternal gratitude' to the manager and hailed their personal friendship. Both got up for a brief embrace. Then Klopp took the microphone. 'For me, one thing was certain all along: the moment I was no longer the perfect manager for this extraordinary club, I'd say so. I wasn't sure that I was no longer the right manager. But I couldn't unequivocally say that I was, either.'

BVB were placed tenth in the league as the end of an era was proclaimed. Before the start of the season, Klopp had had to endure Robert Lewandowski, the league's top goalscorer and most important player, leaving for Bayern Munich. Dortmund hadn't even received a fee for the prolific striker, as Lewandowski had run down his contract. The Polish forward had been replaced with Ciro Immobile, the best striker in Serie A that year. The Colombian Adrian Ramos had also been brought in from Hertha BSC, and fan favourite Shinji Kagawa had returned from Manchester United, where the Japanese midfielder had been unable to make a lasting impression. On top of that, Dortmund had bought defender Matthias Ginter, a highly talented youngster, from SC Freiburg. All in all, the club invested €50m in the new recruits, a huge sum by Bundesliga standards at the time.

The season had started in spectacular fashion, albeit not to Klopp's liking. On match day 1, on a fine Saturday in August, visitors Leverkusen took the lead after a mere nine seconds; the fastest goal in Bundesliga history. Dortmund went on to lose 2–0. Things only got worse in the following months. At the end of a horrible first half of the season, the Black and Yellows hit rock bottom. They lost 2–1 at Werder to go into the Christmas break in 17th place in the table. If they had conceded one more goal, they would have found themselves last, having played Dortmund's worst first half of a campaign in almost three decades. 'We look like complete idiots,' Klopp lamented.

But Colin Trainor did not agree. During the winter break, he published a groundbreaking analysis of Dortmund's travails on statsbomb.com. Trainor, a bank auditor, lived in County Armagh, Northern Ireland. He had no inside knowledge, nor was he a fan of BVB. He hadn't even seen a single game of theirs. Dortmund's fall from grace, however, had piqued his interest. How was it possible, he wondered, that one of Europe's best teams would suddenly stoop so low as to get mired in a relegation battle? To make sense of it all, he decided to take a closer look at their match statistics in the league.

'The use of analytics can help us begin to make assessments about whether certain results have arisen from great skill or were possibly due to some combination of 'fortuitous circumstances', Trainor wrote in his blog. In Dortmund's case, he found the numbers pointed towards a random sequence of bad luck. They had created enough good goalscoring opportunities to finish the year with 25 goals instead of 18. At the other end of the pitch, their defence hadn't been quite as bad as 26 conceded goals suggested, either. They should have only conceded 17, he claimed. Taking both numbers together, Dortmund should have had a goal difference of +8 rather than -8, and many games should have finished with more positive results as a consequence. Extrapolating 'Expected Points' (xP) from those figures, Trainor calculated that Dortmund should have amassed a tally of 30 as opposed to the meagre 15 they actually ended up with. The difference made for a huge swing in the table: with the greater number, Dortmund would have sat in fourth place at the winter break.

Position	Team	xPts	Points	Deviation
1	Bayern München	41	45	4
2	VfL Wolfsburg	30	34	4
3	Bayer 04 Leverkusen	30	28	-2
4	Borussia Dortmund	30	15	-15
5	Eintracht Frankfurt	26	23	-3

Source: statsbomb.com

But what exactly led Trainor to make the bold claim that the table was essentially wrong?

In order to understand his method, it's first important to realise that football is a game of probabilities. Every football fan has cried out 'He has to score!' at one point or another, witnessing a striker heading towards goal unimpeded from only six yards out or being faced with the seemingly simple task of passing the ball into a deserted net, just like Frank Mill or Ronny Rosenthal. We react a little differently, however, when a forward attempts to find the top corner with an angled shot from the edge of the box. The reason for that is probability; we instinctively assign a lower rate of success to a much more speculative attempt and are likewise less disappointed if there isn't a goal at the end of it. The weighing up of chances in such a manner forms the basis of much of the post-match discussions in the pub. 'Of course we should have won the game – we had much better opportunities,' and so on and so forth.

Our attempts to explain what should have happened to ourselves are not systematic, however. No one tries to quantify a goalscoring opportunity in precise figures sitting in the stands. But doing just that is in fact possible, thanks to the proliferation of match data.

Let's take a relatively straightforward situation: penalties. In the Premier League, the odds for a penalty being scored are 76.83 per cent: from its inauguration in 1992 to the 2017–18 season, 1,079 attempts from the spot yielded 876 goals. Nearly a quarter of kicks were saved, missed or only converted on the rebound. The same proportion, with only minimal deviation, can incidentally be found in most professional leagues. It's thus fair to say with a high degree of confidence that the average success rate for penalties is three out of four.

This type of statistical analysis can be extended to other types of shots – as long as we know where they have been taken on the pitch and in what specific context. It naturally makes a difference if shots result from open play or from free-kicks, to name just one distinguishing factor. The ubiquitous collection of data in most professional leagues enables us to collate tens of thousands of shots from thousands of games, see where they have occurred on the pitch and find how many of them have found the net. This triangulation provides us with a map of the playing field that can fairly precisely predict the probability of any given shot from any given position going in.

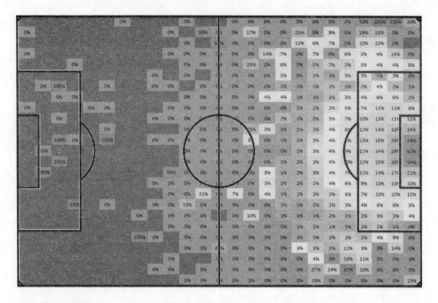

Source: 21st Club

This map is still a rough one. It contains the odd random wonder goal from close to the touchline, for example, far away from the box. These wonder goals show up as high probabilities as almost no one ever shoots from those positions in the first place. But some goals have been scored that way. Arsenal FC supporters will wince at the memory of Real Zaragoza's Nayim lobbing David Seaman from near the halfway line in the 1995 Cup Winners' Cup final, for example.

In and around the box, as Andy Townsend likes to say, the picture becomes more realistic, however. There's no need to crunch the numbers to understand that there must be better and worse positions for taking shots, simple experience tells you as much. Every football fan instantly felt that Marco van Basten scoring the second goal for the Netherlands in the 1988 European Championship final was a one-in-a-million goal, as the striker had taken aim with a volley from a seemingly impossible angle, close to the touchline outside the six-yard box. Van Basten made the improbable look easy, but the odds for this type of shot had been very slim. Nowadays, we can put an exact figure on it: 2 per cent. If van Basten had taken the same volley 50 times, he would have scored only once, statistically.

Taking all shots by a team in the course of the game and looking at the probabilities gives you an overall score called 'Expected Goals' (xG). Van Basten's shot would add 0.02 to the calculation, a penalty 0.75. To make xG more meaningful, the context of the shot is taken into account as well. Shots from 12 yards out are more likely to yield goals than headers, for example, as are shots from counter-attacks – the opposition defences tend to be more disorganised then. Attempts from dead-ball situations come with specific probabilities, too. The situational context of a shot has a marked effect on its odds of going in, as this table from the Premier League shows.

	Open Game	Counter-Attacks	Corners	Free-Kicks
Attacks/Goals	6467/534	1116/166	1115/100	539/26
Success rate	8.26%	14.87%	8.97%	4.82%

Source: STATS

As we will see in more detail later, the amount of defenders who are positioned between the attacker and the goal plays a role, too. Complex mathematical models are necessary to add granular detail to the calculations.

But can there ever be a number that fits every player? Surely Cristiano Ronaldo, Lionel Messi or Harry Kane taking aim have a much better chance of scoring than others boasting far less talent? The argument has some merit, but the differences between players at the top level are surprisingly small. English football analyst Omar Chaudhuri, who produced the shot map above, has taken a closer look at Cristiano Ronaldo's numbers to prove the point. Part of the British consultancy firm 21st Club, he analysed 1,490 shots taken by the Portuguese forward from 2010 to 2017 for Real Madrid in the Spanish league, penalties excluded. A total of 13.3 per cent of Ronaldo's attempts were successful, an increase of just over 2 per cent on the league average, 11.1 per cent. Chaudhuri concluded that one of the best strikers of his generation was scoring between one and two goals more per season due to his special talent.

Cristiano Ronaldo can therefore not be said to be an amazingly good finisher; he's extraordinary in a different sense. He shoots much more frequently on goal than all other strikers; on average almost seven times per game, which is an incredibly high figure. More importantly, still, he often shoots from promising positions on the pitch, comprising high xG values. Ronaldo is helped by his very good team-mates in that respect, no doubt, but he has a strong sense of taking up dangerous positions as well. Maybe someone once told him that he's more likely to score from certain positions, but having an instinctive feel for goal-worthy situations is probably a huge part of his talent. Chaudhuri found that Ronaldo was scoring eight to ten more goals than the average striker per season, simply by taking up better shooting positions. The numbers for other top strikers follow a similar pattern. They're top because they shoot often, and from positions with high probabilities of success.

Until a few years ago, there was insufficient data and no mathematical concept to assemble such findings. 'Expected Goals' was invented by the Englishman Sam Green, who first described the idea in 2012. Green was working at data service company OptaPro, in the department that provided club analysts with information that went beyond the stats regularly published by the media. OptaPro's remit included finding new performance metrics; Expected Goals quickly became recognised as a very helpful tool. A small but global band of bloggers devoted to data analysis in football instantly then began to build their own models for xG or to come up with interesting variants.

FORCING DESTINY'S HAND, WITH LUCKY PANTS AND HOLY WATER

Colin Trainor has his own xG model, too. Applying it to Borussia Dortmund in the winter of 2014 left him shaking his head. He had never seen a deviation between expected and actual goals that was this pronounced. He predicted that Klopp's team would soon see better results again. 'Even if their performances didn't improve on what they have exhibited to date I see only a small chance of them being in relegation trouble at the end of the season,' Trainor wrote. Dortmund, he claimed, had simply been very unlucky, for a fairly long period of time stretching back half a season. But with football not being a game of chance, their bad run was bound to end. The only question was when.

It would be a mistake, however, to see Expected Goals as the 'true' result of a game. It's not that simple. Expected Goals represent a mathematical approximation, based on an algorithm. An 'algorithm' is one of those mysterious terms of the digital age that are hard to grasp for laymen; something to do with data and computers, impressive and frightening in equal measure. But algorithms are nothing but instructions, designed to solve a problem. A human interested in the best position on the pitch from which to score a goal writes an algorithm that crunches the data. The reliability of the findings are dependent on the amount and the quality of the data, as well as the design of the algorithm itself. That explains the existence of different ways to calculate Expected Goals, with different if not too diverging results.

There's another factor that must not be overlooked in relation to Expected Goals. Every game has its own story. It's not just the quality and amount of goalscoring opportunities that are decisive but also their timing. Dutchman Sander Ijtsma, a surgeon from Groningen, has developed so-called xGplots to give shape to that phenomenon. These 'Expected Goals Plots', arranged along a horizontal timeline of 90 minutes, illustrate the game's narrative in chronological fashion and add to our understanding of the way Expected Goals are best employed. A few games from the Russia 2018 World Cup are instructive in that respect.

Most (neutral) viewers will likely recall Brazil vs Belgium as the tournament's most spectacular game, finishing in a riveting win by the underdogs. In Belgium, they will probably talk about it for years to come, given that the match paved the way for their best World

Cup finish ever, third place. The fact that the win was very lucky will not feature as prominently in the collective memory, in all likelihood. Those who don't like to talk of luck and bad luck when it comes to such momentous results can, with the help of data, put it in more prosaic terms: according to Belgium's quality of goalscoring opportunities, they had a 4 per cent chance of winning in regular time. If the game had been played in exactly the same way 100 times, the Red Devils would have expected to win four of those matches, lose 84, with 12 draws. They had benefited from an early own goal by the Brazilians and a counter-attack strike from Kevin De Bruyne. In the second half, Roberto Martínez's men only created one small goalscoring opportunity themselves and spent most of the time defending the *Seleção*'s many and in part promising attempts that led to one solitary goal.

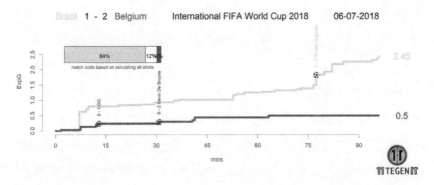

Source: 11tegen11

Senegal vs Colombia in the group stage made for an extreme companion piece to that dramatic quarter-final. The South Americans had to win the game to advance whereas the Africans would have gone through with a draw. Senegal did well to nullify Colombia's attacking game right until 15 minutes from time, when they conceded from a corner and failed to create any promising shots at goal themselves. They were eliminated on account of the fairplay rule after finishing level on points and goals with Japan in their group.

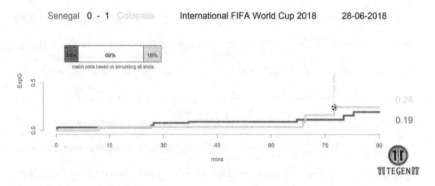

Senegal 0 - 1 Colombia   International FIFA World Cup 2018   28-06-2018

Source: 11tegen11

England needed a last-minute header from Harry Kane to secure a win in their opening game against Tunisia but everyone who had seen the entire match would have felt that the victory had been well deserved. The Expected Goals Plots confirms that impression: Tunisia had only created one big goalscoring opportunity, courtesy of a dubious penalty after Kyle Walker was adjudged to have pulled back Fakhreddine Ben Youssef. England, by contrast, had amassed opportunities throughout the game, even if they hadn't been of the same high quality after the break.

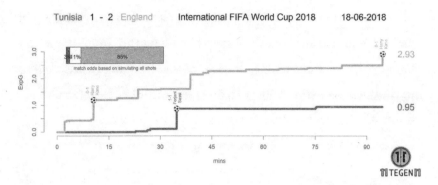

Source: 11tegen11

The last 16 tie against Colombia will chiefly be remembered for England's first-ever win in a World Cup penalty shoot-out. But it didn't have to come to that. Gareth Southgate's team had deservedly led 1–0 until the end of regular time in light of their high-quality attempts at goal. Colombia had equalised in the 93rd minute after a corner.

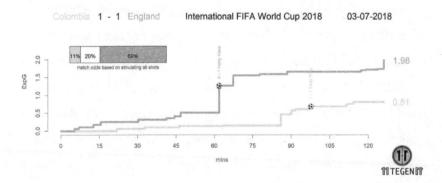

Source: 11tegen11

England seemed to hit their glass ceiling in the semi-final against Croatia, despite taking an early lead thanks to Kieran Trippier's free-kick. There were chances at both ends of the pitch after that, but Croatia equalised and had marginally better chances by the time 90 minutes were over. But in the second half of extra-time, Croatia pulled clear of England's young team as far as chances created were concerned.

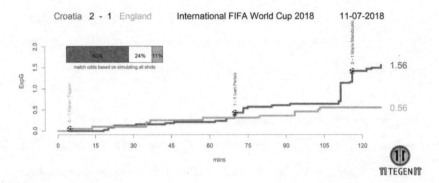

Source: 11tegen11

The xGplots show that goals and goalscoring opportunities relate to each other. By and large, they conform to the way we intuitively experience the game – as neutrals. Supporters often tend to see games very differently, in line with those who are actively involved on the pitch. Sander Ijtsma has noticed something remarkable in that specific context. He told me he enjoyed listening to the coaches' evaluation of a game and comparing them with the goalscoring opportunities captured by his Expected Goals Plots. 'Coaches are usually spot on when it comes to assessing their own team's chances but they're not nearly as precise when it comes to the opposition's opportunities.'

To be sure, totting up Expected Goals tells us nothing about other aspects of coincidence that play their part in the outcome of a football game. Looking at Croatia vs France in the final in Moscow, for example, it seems as if the result was in tandem with the story of the game. But *Les Bleus* took advantage of their opponents, scoring the first-ever own goal in a World Cup final, and both the preceding free-kick and the referee's decision to award a penalty were rather questionable. If we discount both these incidents of random good fortune for the French, Croatia would have actually been ahead in the xGs.

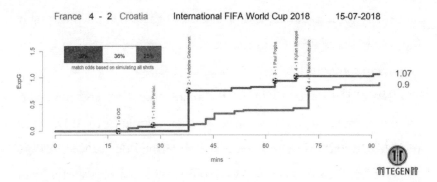

France 4 - 2 Croatia   International FIFA World Cup 2018   15-07-2018

Source: 11tegen11

Expected Goals don't show the 'true' result. But they provide a clearer view of the game. As we all know, the better team loses quite often, as Brazil did against Belgium. That's what distinguishes football from other team sports involving a ball, due to the afore-mentioned relatively low number of goals.

In the Premier League, 2.68 goals on average were scored per game in the 2017–18 season. Most professional leagues average just below three goals per match as well. In a basketball game, by contrast, there are often more than 100 successful baskets, and in rugby, scores average 50 points. Individual points are of lesser importance. But in football, matches have a habit of unfolding in mysterious ways. A far superior side can find itself besieging the opposition goal without scoring and fall prey to the underdogs' one, decisive foray into their box. These are fateful moments of almost poetic quality. Sometimes, the gods of football seem to tap teams gently on the shoulder. Sometimes, they point at them in anger. Cup competitions, in particular, owe much of their magic to fate's capricious mood, and football's popularity has, one suspects, not least grown on the back of its in-built propensity for unpredictable outcomes. But there's an uncomfortable flip side to all of this. Performance and results are much less closely aligned in football than in basketball or rugby.

That might explain why professional footballers and managers are much more superstitious at work than people in most walks of life. Would you ever pay attention to entering your office with the left foot first in the morning? Or would you insist on wearing your colleague's underwear during difficult meetings? That's what Gerrie Mühren did. The Ajax icon – this is true – made a point of wearing the pants of his team-mate Sjaak Swart for tricky games.

Football's history is full of similar anecdotes. Gary Lineker would change his shirt at half-time if he hadn't yet scored. Former Germany international Mario Gomez has worn the same pair of shin pads for 16 years. Bastian Schweinsteiger hasn't changed his either since his days as a youth player. (Shin pads, that is, not underwear.) Giovanni Trapattoni even sought divine help in charge of Italy's national team. He sprinkled holy water onto the pitch at the 2002 World Cup. His sister, a nun, had given him the flask as a good luck gift.

Footballers also often like to repeat the same things they did when they were successful. Bruno Pesaola, while coach of ACF Fiorentina, once travelled 500km back to the team's home town on the eve of an away game – to fetch a record. He had played it to his side before winning the previous match. When Sergei Rebrov was in charge of Dynamo Kiev, he also tried to replicate exactly what he did before a win. He got up at the same time of day, ate the same things and talked to the same people.

Superstition has led to some players developing very bizarre rituals. Former England goalkeeper David James used to spit at the wall of the toilet in the dressing room. Not only if he was alone. Kolo Touré, the ex-Ivory Coast international and Arsenal defender, was obsessed with stepping onto the pitch as the last player of his team. In one Champions League game, at AS Roma, Touré stayed off the pitch after the break as he was waiting for William Gallas, who was receiving treatment in the dressing room. Arsenal restarted the game with eight outfield players, and Touré was then shown a yellow card for running back onto the pitch without the referee's permission.

These examples from the colourful world of rituals and lucky charms show how much effort is being made by players to curry fate's favour. But at the same time, nobody really wants to admit the importance of coincidence. The idea that everything happens for a reason is deeply rooted in the human psyche. Why would we otherwise seek to identify patterns in lottery numbers? Before picking six numbers from 59, we look at numbers that haven't been drawn for a while and believe that they're due to come up. But numbers that haven't been picked for a while of course don't enjoy a higher probability of getting picked next time. The machine picking them doesn't memorise previous results. There's also no objective reason to suggest that a combination of 9, 17, 24, 31, 32 and 57 is more likely to be drawn than 1, 2, 3, 4, 5 and 6. The probability is the same for all combinations: 1 in 32,468,436.

Football is not a lottery, though. Not everything is at the whim of random occurrence. It helps if players are versed in passing and controlling the ball, and if they're fit and strong enough for the entire game. Their coach should develop a playing strategy that's in line with their abilities and ideally take into account the opponents' strengths and weaknesses as well. But what do you do if having done all that, you still get unlucky?

THE TABLE DOES LIE

People tasked with self-evaluating their own performance are prone to a cognitive error named self-serving bias. In short, we are likely to ascribe success to our own skills and actions but prefer blaming failure on uncontrollable external factors such as bad luck or coincidence. In football, this phenomenon takes on an interesting contrarian guise. There's almost something like an unofficial ban on blaming failure on anything but your own performance. All coaches know of the power that randomness exerts over the game, but to openly bemoan bad luck is seen as something of a taboo. Explanations that hint at the role of fate always have to come with an admission of guilt. 'We were unlucky in front of goal but should have been more determined,' a manager might say. It's okay to mention being on the wrong side of coincidence quietly, but a strong dose of self-criticism has to follow to make it palatable.

One might conclude that people in professional football are inherently resistant against self-serving bias but that would be doubly wrong. Coaches might not talk of unlucky defeats, but they won't talk much of lucky wins either. It's extremely rare for a player to say 'we won today because we got lucky'. Diego Maradona once claimed that 'success has nothing to do with luck'. Instead, rather puzzling, contradictory lines such as 'we made our own luck today' get trotted out routinely.

In the course of my research for this book, I have tried to talk about luck as an important factor in football with many players, coaches and technical directors. It would be wrong to say I came up against a wall of denial, but almost all of them cut short the discussion before it had even started in earnest. Their reason for doing so was simple. Talking about luck and bad luck, they felt, would lead to nothing but people making excuses and making less of an effort. Coincidence is football's elephant in the room. It's there, without question, but no one wants to acknowledge it. Everybody prefers to believe that wins, draws and defeats happen for a reason instead.

In the summer of 2017, I met with Peter Krawietz, a long-term member of Jürgen Klopp's coaching staff who has accompanied him to Liverpool. When I asked if they had been aware that Dortmund had been extraordinarily unlucky in that first half of the 2014–15 season, he replied with an interesting line. It plays on the act of a German comedian, who once joked that Lukas Podolski regarded football as 'a game like chess, but without dice'.

'I would actually flip that on its head,' Krawietz said. 'Football is like chess, but with dice.' It's a strategic game, in other words, but one in which random events can put paid to best-laid plans. Beyond that very original and elegant response, Krawietz was unwilling to say much more about the subject, however. He went into great detail about the BVB coaching staff's attempts to become successful again during that winter break but ignored all requests to discuss the role of good or bad fortune.

Krawietz's reluctance is emblematic of the attitude of the whole of professional football. It allows one of the game's biggest untruths to continue to flourish: the idea that 'the table does not lie'. You hear this phrase all the time, in all footballing nations. Players, coaches or club officials repeat the mantra, convinced that good luck and bad luck in front of goal, wrong refereeing decisions or the absence of key players end up evening themselves out at the end of the season, and that the table paints an accurate picture of performances. This belief corresponds neatly to our strong need for explanations and rationality, but it's wrong nevertheless. More often than not, the table is a shameless liar.

Firstly, it's simply nonsense to suggest that refereeing mistakes even themselves out in the course of a campaign. It's far more likely that one team ends up with a few points too many or with too few points. Those couple of points either way could easily be the ones that make the difference between relegation and staying up or between winning the league as triumphant heroes and finishing as runners-up who bottled it.

A closer look at the discrepancy between performances and results leads us to fascinating phenomena such as the story of Newcastle

United in 2011–12. The Magpies, coached by Alan Pardew at the time, surprisingly finished all the way up in fifth place that season. Newcastle fans will look back with fond memories on their best campaign in 15 years and on the miraculous emergence of Papiss Cissé who joined in January 2012 from SC Freiburg and scored 13 times in 14 games. This is how the final table looked:

Team	Games	Goal difference	Points
1. Manchester City	38	64	89
2. Manchester United	38	56	89
3. Arsenal	38	25	70
4. Tottenham	38	25	69
5. Newcastle	38	5	65
6. Chelsea	38	19	64
7. Everton	38	10	56

Newcastle's relatively poor goal difference immediately jumps out. They only scored five goals more than they conceded. Usually, teams that win more often than not have better goal differences. That's self-evident. The side with the best goal difference tends to win the championship, the one with the worst often gets relegated. Placing high up in the table with a low positive goal difference, on the other hand, can be an indication that the team in question had fate on their side.

A second sign that points to the football gods having lent a helping hand is the distribution of goals. Every season, the Premier League stages 380 games that see roughly 8,800 shots fired and 1,000 goals scored. But not every goal is of equal value. The fourth goal in a 4–0 win isn't as important as the fourth goal in a 4–3 win. Following on from that, a GD of 0 can mean a number of very different things. A series of seven games resulting in 0–1, 0–1, 0–1, 6–0, 0–1, 0–1, 0–1 would deliver only three points from a possible 21. But seven games ending 1–0, 1–0, 1–0, 0–6, 1–0, 1–0, 1–0 would come with a very different bottom line: 18 points on the board.

Newcastle had a very efficient goal distribution that year. Eight games were won by one goal, nine by a margin of two. They also suffered a few big defeats, among them a 2–5, 0–5 and 0–4.

Goal difference and goal distribution don't necessarily signify that teams might have overachieved points-wise in relation to their performance. But a look at Newcastle net shots on target – the number of their shots on target minus the number of shots on target from opposition teams – suggests they did, with Pardew's team ranking the sixth-worst side of the league.

Team	Home	Away	Total
1. Manchester City	12.3	5.3	8.8
2. Manchester United	8.5	–1.2	3.6
3. Arsenal	9.5	3.1	6.3
4. Tottenham	10.4	2.1	6.2
5. Newcastle	3.5	–6.3	–1.4
6. Chelsea	8.8	2.8	5.8

Source: Ankersen, Hunger in Paradise

After receiving plaudits for a great season, Newcastle crashed down to 16th spot in the following campaign. They barely survived relegation. Alan Pardew would keep his job for another 18 months but the way he and his team were viewed had changed completely. One story about Newcastle was mothballed and hung back into the wardrobe, and another one was tried on for size. In their successful season, there had been much talk about the side's attractive play and Pardew's courage to play youngsters. Now, they said his style was too gung-ho and that there was a lack of experience in the side. Many commentators were affected by outcome bias, the tendency to judge efforts on their results. They were sure that good results were underpinned by good performances and that bad results were the consequence of bad performances. Newcastle's case was especially bizarre, however, since both assumptions were wrong. According to their Expected Goals and the resulting distribution of points, their performances in both seasons hardly differed.

	Points per game	Points total	xPts per game	xPts total
2011–12	1.72	65	1.22	46
2012–13	1.07	41	1.16	44

Source: Ankersen, *Hunger in Paradise*

In both campaigns, Newcastle had created and conceded a similar amount and quality of goalscoring opportunities. But they won 19 points more than expected in the first season, and three fewer than expected in the following one. One season, they made it to the Europa League, the next one, they were battling against the drop. One year, they were hailed for their performances, with Alan Pardew signing an eight-year deal, and in the next one, they were heavily criticised. To put it bluntly, they were applauded for getting lucky and blamed for being unlucky.

Small deviations can have big effects in football. A team drawing only two games that they had really deserved to win and losing two games they should have drawn will be short of six points at the end of the season, even if all other games have finished perfectly in line with the balance of chances.

A multitude of examples show the extent of the repercussions. In 2015–16, fairy-tale champions Leicester City won 12.06 points more than expected, runners-up Arsenal 6.01 points fewer. In terms of pure probability, Arsène Wenger's team should have lifted the trophy. It was a similar case one year later, when Chelsea won 17.26 points more than expected and Manchester City 7.41 points fewer. Pep Guardiola really should have won the title in his first Premier League season instead of finishing third. West Bromwich Albion were hit much harder, however. They should have won 11.96 points more than they did, which would have seen them placed 13th, not 20th. For most of that relegation season, Alan Pardew had been in charge at the Hawthorns, incidentally. He seems a magnet for either very good or very bad luck.

In other leagues, plenty of clubs can feel hard done by as well. Taking Expected Goals into account, SSC Napoli should have won the Scudetto in 2015–16 and again two years later ahead of Juventus. But they didn't, of course. Expected Goals don't make it onto the scoreboard, only actual ones do. But they can offer important insight, nevertheless – they can provide an internal sense of direction amidst all the noise and hype that football generates.

This is not about making it easier to bemoan bad luck or look for excuses. One shouldn't claim that Chelsea merely got lucky before looking much closer at all those numbers, either. They don't make for an alternative reality. But for those in charge of making decisions in football, it's often difficult to keep a clear view of a team's perform-ance levels due to the immense amounts of pressure. Are they achieving the results their showings on the pitch deserve? Do they get less or perhaps even more? These questions are too important to rely solely on results that can be quite misleading for the answers.

Take Juve in the aforementioned 2015–16 Serie A season. Italy's record champions only won three of their first ten games that year, scoring 11 goals and conceding nine in the process. The goal differ-ence of Expected Goals told a very different tale, however; it had Juventus on +14, with 19 goals scored, five conceded. It's easy to forget that top teams can get unlucky, too. Juve's bad spell of results soon gave way to normal service again. They went undefeated in the following 15 games and won another championship. Gaining 12.26 more points than expected saw them leapfrog unlucky Napoli.

Statistical outliers are inevitably followed by the regression to the mean. That's what happened to Borussia Dortmund in 2014–15 too, just as Trainor had foreseen. Without making any significant changes in personnel, BVB scored 29 goals, conceded only 16 and won 31 points – almost exactly the same tally they should have had in the first half of the season in Trainor's calculations. 'We left no stone unturned, trying to eradicate the causes of our bad results,' Krawietz told me. But maybe he and Klopp wouldn't be at Liverpool today if they had been aware that it was possible to measure the influence of coincidence back then. As it was, they only learnt about it when they arrived at Anfield and were shown those highly unusual numbers by Liverpool's analytics team.

In spring 2015, Liverpool's Head of Research Ian Graham was invited by the German FA to give a lecture to Bundesliga analysts in Frankfurt. Borussia Dortmund were slowly moving out of the relegation zone at the time, and the audience were astonished when Graham told them his model rated Klopp's team as the second-best of the league. Most of them hadn't heard of Expected Goals, let alone of his model's ability to identify lucky or unlucky runs.

A few months later, it became obvious that Graham had had an ulterior motive for looking into Dortmund's troubles: Liverpool had started considering Klopp as a contender to succeed Brendan Rodgers. 'We really thought that Dortmund had had bad luck,' Graham said at an OptaPro conference in March 2019. 'It wasn't anything to do with systematic problems with the players and the coach. That is really important because one of the biggest strategic decisions a club has to make is hiring a new manager. If we wanted to hire Jürgen Klopp as our new manager, we had to understand if there was something wrong with Dortmund. And the statistical analysis said very clearly and very strongly: no.'

When Klopp was indeed appointed manager at Anfield, Graham showed him his findings and how the stats deviated from the results, game by game. Klopp said, 'Did you see that match? We destroyed them, and then he went through it, chance by chance. He did the same with the next matches I showed him.' Klopp assumed Graham had taken the trouble to watch all the games back. 'I said I hadn't seen them – but that I had just produced the statistical analysis,' Graham explained.

Coaches in top leagues only stay between one and two years at any club on average, and their reigns become ever shorter still. It's a ridiculously short time for any executive, even more so for the supposedly most important figure in the club. Much has been written about the game's propensity for short-termism; studies have also shown that a change of manager has mostly very little lasting impact. But there has rarely been an attempt to systematically evaluate whether a coach is lucky or unlucky before he is dismissed.

Often enough, getting rid of a manager follows an archaic logic: as the phrase itself spells out, axing the coach of an unlucky team becomes a symbolic human sacrifice, foreshadowed by a public baying for blood. Supporters moan, jeer and demand the man on the bench should be ousted. The media slam him for his inept handling of the team and are sure to find a fitting narrative as to why things have gone awry. At some stage, the club fires their most important figure to appease the angry gods of football and pray that good fortune might return.

There is another way though. Ben Olsen, manager of D.C. United in Washington, benefited greatly from his club turning to Expected Goals after the start of the 2017 season had gone very badly. Olsen's side had not found the target in four of their opening six games and had only scored four goals in total but Stewart Mairs, D.C. United's

Director of Soccer Strategy and Analysis, declared that there was no need to panic: the team's Expected Goals pointed to much better performances than the naked results suggested. Olsen even told his players: 'Don't worry, things will fall in line.' Unfortunately, he was mistaken, however. United kept conceding too many goals and scored too few, relative to their Expected Goals, throughout a rotten campaign that saw them finish second from bottom in the Eastern Conference. Maybe the MLS club would have taken a different stance if they had been threatened with relegation, like European or South American clubs. Everybody is still learning how to handle the new Expected Goals metric. But one thing is obvious: it provides us with far more interesting observations about team performances than the still widely used possession and shot statistics. That explains why xG has outgrown its birthplace, the nerdy underground of bloggers and analysts, and has made its first forays into the mainstream. In 2017, the BBC started using it discreetly, posting the numbers on the screen without comment on its flagship show *Match of the Day*. *The Times* introduced a league table made up of Expected Points for the 2018–19 season. Sky's *Monday Night Football* references Expected Goals, too, as a matter of course.

Considering what we have learned about the game so far, understanding it more fully is being complicated by an enormous dilemma. In this world of constant pressure and tension, secure judgements would be extremely helpful in making the evaluation of one's own game or of players a more cogent process than that employed at one's rivals. But in reality, the path towards such an enlightened process doesn't just come with a series of obstacles made up of cognitive biases. Football is, unfortunately, also a game in which a good performance doesn't inevitably lead to a good result. And the result is, at the same time, still widely seen as the only thing that truly matters. That state of affairs can be disheartening. But it can also force us to draw the necessary conclusions. Doing so opens a door to a new way of looking at the game. As it happens, those who gamble on football games for a living have already walked through it.

RISE OF THE
OUTSIDERS

Professional football gamblers become trailblazers for analytics, the German-American pollster Chris Anderson takes over a club and Rasmus Ankersen changes Danish football.

BEATING THE BOOKIES

I first met Matthew Benham in 2008, researching an allegedly rigged Bundesliga game. He opened my eyes to a world that I couldn't even have imagined existing. The things he told me then changed my view of the game far beyond the subjects of betting and match fixing. In November 2005, unknown people had put an unusually large amount of money on 1. FC Kaiserslautern losing heavily at Hannover 96. I sought out Benham, a professional gambler, to gain an understanding of the betting market's workings and the possibility for corruption. Professional gamblers hate fixed matches: they're set to lose a lot of money if manipulation brings about unpredictable results. Benham and his ilk should not be confused with shady fortune hunters chomping on big cigars. They are better understood as engineers of probabilities.

Benham, in his early forties at the time, came across like a highly gifted nerd. He was pale, spoke quickly and threw in the odd 'yo' for effect. I could hardly believe what I was hearing. It took me a while to comprehend what it was they were doing in that non-descript industrial space in North London. Benham had his desk in a glass cubicle, right in the middle of an open plan office. Above the working spaces, TV monitors were showing football games, but most seats were empty: we met at lunchtime on a weekday, so there weren't many games on.

In an adjoining room, satellite decoders from all over Europe and South America made it possible to see games from Germany, France, Italy, Spain, Scandinavia and all sorts of other leagues. Young men sat in front of the screens and noted down goalscoring opportunities. They had firm instructions to assign them to specific categories. A huge opportunity was called an 'Oooh!', named after the collective sigh inside a ground when a team misses a sitter.

Benham had studied physics and worked as a derivatives trader in the City. In finance, he had learnt how to exploit inefficient markets, and he would employ the same principle in football betting, starting in 2002. His old job had him seeking out undervalued positions before selling them on at a profit. Football betting was no different, really. The point was to be smarter than the bookies. If he could calculate the outcome of games more precisely than them in more than half of all games, there was money to be made.

Placing high stakes had become possible in the new millennium, as globalisation fuelled the betting market. Benham no longer bet with traditional companies in England but with bookies based in the

Philippines, in Thailand or Singapore. Asian firms charged smaller commissions and allowed bigger bets. Thanks to the volume they offered, he was able to build up a veritable betting factory, where serious money was being put on games in almost 40 leagues. His company, Smartodds, advised a syndicate of gamblers who would regularly stake six and sometimes even seven figures on a single game on a weekend that could easily see hundreds of individual bets.

The most frequent form of bets placed was called Asian Handicap. The favourites – jollies, in betting parlance – are saddled with a numerical handicap, a bit like racehorses who have to carry extra weight. The most interesting part of Asian Handicap, however, is the fact that it discounts draws and thus makes it easier to determine the probabilities.

To gain an edge over the bookies, Benham had become a sort of football scientist. 'I never bet for fun or the thrill, we are all about calculating probabilities with the help of mathematical models,' he told me. At the time, I was surprised to learn that he paid little attention to the previous results of a team when it came to evaluating their chances; whether they went into the next game on the back of a comfortable 3–0 win or a narrow 2–1 didn't really matter to him. 'Results are not completely irrelevant. But they are mostly noise,' he said.

Those who scour data sets for relevant information distinguish between 'signal' and 'noise'. The signal is substantive, useful information. Noise is the opposite – data that doesn't tell you anything but can drown out the signal. The trick is to filter out the truly relevant bits from among all the hum and the whirr. Believing a team was in good shape after winning 2–1 away in the previous week could be noise. Maybe they had simply been lucky. Benham was the first person I ever heard insist that the table was lying. To underline his argument, he pointed to the outcome of two recent Bundesliga title races. According to his calculations, the 2007 championship had been won by the fourth-best team that season, VfB Stuttgart. And two years later, VfL Wolfsburg, the third-best side, had won the league, and he added. 'I don't mean to say these teams played beyond their means or utilised their potential more fully than their rivals. No. Their performances – evaluated by us in pretty precise manner, we'd like to think – made them third- or fourth-best. The rest was luck.'

Look at the contrasting fortunes of England and Germany in big tournament shoot-outs, he said, in a further example of the difficulty of separating signal from noise. England had lost six out of seven times in spot-kicks before the World Cup in Russia, including twice against Germany. The Germans, on the other hand, have won all shoot-outs bar the final of the Euros in 1976 vs Czechoslovakia. Various studies have sought to explain those sequences, citing national character or footballing education. But Benham didn't think much of that. 'If games were still decided by a coin flip instead of penalties, like they were in the old days, we might have seen a similar series of results. I wouldn't assume England's chances vs Germany for the next shoot-out to be 50–50 but they won't be far off.'

Getting to a precise evaluation of performance was at the core of everything Smartodds did. A special importance was afforded to categorising goalscoring opportunities with maximum precision, thanks to so-called watchers taking notes during games. The idea applied the general logic of Expected Goals; in fact, it preceded it. It's not a coincidence that Colin Trainor concerned himself with the same kind of questions. He bets on games as well, albeit with much smaller stakes. Many members of the global analytics community who blog about football data are either professionally or personally involved in gambling. But even in 2008, Benham's methods of working out football's probabilities were more advanced than Expected Goals are today. Having young people from all over the world sit in front of screens and keep account of goalscoring opportunities from hundreds of games yielded the best possible approximation of events. Expected Goals, you will recall, relies on statistical simulation. The output from Benham's betting factory was more sophisticated.

Goalscoring chances were not the only factor determining his calculations. To this day, he employs highly qualified IT specialists, mathematicians and statisticians; many of them have PhDs or degrees from top universities. His team is always on the hunt for information with 'predictability', as he calls it. A deeper dive into the chance statistics had them identify the impact of specific players on a team's performance. If an important player was out, they could downgrade the probability of a win with a certain degree of confidence, or upgrade it upon his return.

Benham's team also discovered that a team's chances for an away win were slightly raised if they had a shorter journey to the game. Contrary to perception, there's a better chance of winning local derbies than away games that take place at the far side of the country. Such observations have been incorporated into a mathematical model that has grown ever more complex over the years. In addition, a network of international informants supply 'soft' information that can play a part as well. Is there dressing-room strife or a conflict inside the club that might have a negative impact on performance?

Previous head-to-head results, on the other hand, are readily dismissed as noise by Benham. They have nothing to say about the probability of a specific outcome in the next game, he maintains. The much-cherished idea of a bogey team is no more a signal than Germany's fabled superiority from the spot. The sample size is too small to rule out mere randomness.

Benham isn't the only gambler who puts this much effort into predicting outcome. Perhaps he is not even the biggest one. Just down the road from Smartodds' offices in Kentish Town, in Camden Town there's another company called Starlizard, named after its owner, Tony Bloom. Bloom, born in 1970, became famous playing poker and was nicknamed 'the lizard' by his competitors. He doesn't talk to journalists, but he and Benham reportedly used to work together before falling out and each going their separate ways.

Starlizard was founded in 2006, two years after Smartodds. Both firms work with high-stake syndicates, and both their founders have become very wealthy in the process. They have one more thing in common, in fact: both have bought the clubs they respectively supported for their whole lives. In 2009, Bloom became the majority shareholder of Brighton & Hove Albion, where his grandfather had been a vice president and his uncle a director. He built a new stadium for the club and led them into the Premier League in 2017.

Benham has been going to see Brentford FC play for over four decades. He was 11 years old when he attended his first Bees home game, in 1979. In 2006, he first became financially involved, as a sponsor. Brentford, one of London's less glamorous clubs, was then a financially stricken side stuck in the third division. Having grown frustrated with spending substantial sums without having any control, Benham bought the majority of the club in 2012.

Griffin Park is a lovely old ground, famous for having a pub on each of its four corners. There's a directors' box in the main stand that's smaller than the VIP lounges of most German third division sides. A glass box houses a hotchpotch of curious exhibits. There's a porcelain cup in commemoration of lunch with Stoke City's president in 1937, and also pennants from East German sides Lok Leipzig and Erzgebirge Aue. The terrace is kitted out with foldable wooden seats and the rows are so close to each other that the knees of tall fans could cover the ears of those sitting in front of them.

Taking his seat, Benham's gaze firmly rests on the pitch. He doesn't like talking during a game. 'It might sound arrogant, but people do talk a load of rubbish in the stadium. If the opponent ventures forward once or twice after we have dominated for five minutes, someone immediately will say, "They want it more than us!"'

Cognitive biases and the wrong judgements that result from them are one of his favourite topics. Smartodds employees are given Kahneman's *Thinking, Fast and Slow* book and are encouraged to read it, too. But Benham himself is not immune from walking into the ubiquitous traps. 'We are all telling ourselves stories, and sometimes I'm stuck in that pattern of thinking, too. The other day we had a very bad game. If it hadn't been my team, I might have been moved to downgrade Brentford from the sixth-best to the seventh-best team of the league. But as a fan, I thought, "Fuck. We're the seventeenth-best side, we're going down..."

Buying his favourite team put Benham into an interesting position. All of a sudden, he could put years of observations and conclusions into practice. He would make a conscious effort not to fall prey to cognitive biases and try to utilise the enormous amount of knowledge he had built up as a gambler, in his effort to translate football's secrets into reliable numbers. He had already built a model to identify the most useful players; now was a chance to make it work on the pitch. Matthew Benham didn't put it that way, but wasn't he ideally placed to adapt the ideas described in the book and feature film, *Moneyball*, to football? Would he live the dream that so many others had – that of being Billy Beane?

THE MAN WHO WANTED
TO BE BILLY BEANE

Chris Anderson has been living in the United States and in England for the last three decades but he still talks German with a slight Rhenish accent that gives away his family background. He was born in 1966 in the Eifel, a low mountain range south of Cologne, the son of a German mother and a US soldier stationed in the area. Shortly after his birth, his father was sent to Vietnam. When he returned, Anderson's parents split up. He was four years old. His father moved back to the States, settled down with a new family, but kept in touch. 'It was all relatively normal,' Anderson says.

For a long time, he had no idea he was a US citizen thanks to his father. But the matter became important when he started studying. Anderson had read politics, history and English literacy in Cologne. Afterwards, a student exchange scheme brought him to Virginia. The idea had been to do a Masters in politics and then return to Germany but the plan changed when he met the well-known German pollster Hans-Dieter Klingemann on campus. 'Because of him, I developed a passion for polling,' Anderson says. Polling is a specialist discipline of the Americans. They developed it and continue to dominate the field to this day, thanks to having the smartest academics. Anderson understood he had to stay in the US if he was serious about immersing himself further in the subject. As a US citizen, he had no problems doing so. He moved to Washington University in St. Louis for a PhD. He then became assistant professor at Houston and moved on to different colleges from there. Anderson conducted many studies and won a few scientific awards. 'Everything was wonderful. I had a great, very satisfying career.'

And that's how things were, for more than two decades. But then, in 2009, a book changed his life. Anderson's wife, an economist, had brought it home with her. It was called *Moneyball*, and she had been using it in class to teach her students 'evidence-based decision-making', hoping they would be more receptive than usual because the subject matter was baseball. In it, the American author Michael Lewis told the story of Billy Beane, the managing director of a baseball club who was able to overcome the constraints of his lowly budget by using data in a clever way.

Moneyball, published in 2003 and later made into a feature film with Brad Pitt in the leading role, is probably the most influential sports book ever written. Most clubs in Major League Baseball have taken inspiration from the pioneering work done by Beane at Oakland Athletics in the early 1990s, relying on data in their search for players. Most importantly, they have dedicated a lot of work to finding new sets of data with even stronger significance. In hindsight, it's not a surprise the data revolution in ball sports started with baseball, where most plays are static; a bit like a football game, consisting solely of corners.

For his new approach, Beane recruited an employee from the niche community of Sabermetrics, made up of baseball fans and nerds intent on extracting knowledge from game data. Together, the two of them managed to leave teams with much higher playing budgets in their wake. The influence of the concept of Moneyball soon went beyond baseball. Club bosses, technical directors and coaches in American football, basketball and (to a lesser extent) ice hockey started wondering how a competitive edge could be gained with the assistance of data.

Today's sporting landscape in the US has changed beyond recognition. All big clubs have dedicated analysis departments crunching the numbers. In 2017, the 30 clubs in Major League Baseball employed 250 analysts. Most of them have an academic background or PhDs in mathematics, statistics or IT. Other team sports are heading in the same direction.

After Anderson had read *Moneyball* in 2009, he asked himself: 'Where was football's Billy Beane?' His own interest in football had lessened somewhat after moving to the States in the late 1980s. As a child, he had played football in the Eifel, like all the kids there, and he had been a fan of Borussia Mönchengladbach, without being especially passionate. In the US, football hadn't mattered all that much to him; the beautiful game only crept up on him again in 2006. Anderson was on a sabbatical in Oxford with his family at the time, his oldest son was four and had started kicking a ball, and the World Cup in Germany rekindled his interest. Upon the family's return to the States, Anderson started coaching his sons. He found increasing pleasure in managing their clubs' U6s, U7s and U8s teams. He was one of the few parents who had at least a vague conception of the game and could play a little bit himself.

Still in the thrall of *Moneyball*, Anderson started to search for freely available game data on the internet. He downloaded the numbers into Excel sheets and probed for correlations. In his blog, soccerbythenumbers, he posed the kind of questions a pollster would have investigated and sought to prove or disprove certain hypotheses. How often do you have to shoot at goal to score a goal? Are corners important? How big is the disadvantage of a team with a player on a yellow card?

At first, it was just a bit of fun; the hobby of a forty-something man who had achieved what he wanted in his academic and personal life. Only a handful of people were interested in his empirical analysis. But then he collated historical tournament data to predict who would win the 2010 World Cup and how many goals would be scored in the group phase. 'I would spend more and more time on the sofa with the laptop. My wife was laughing at me, and the kids said: "Look, dad is doing his football stats again."' He enjoyed it, however, and so did his rapidly growing audience. They shot up from a dozen or so a day to about a hundred.

People working in professional football were now among his readers. In 2011, he met the technical scout of Fulham FC at an event. They both had a passion for data and talked for hours. Anderson was subsequently invited to Craven Cottage to work on a couple of small projects for the Premier League side. 'Here they were, all those guys I had only ever seen on television, live and in colour,' he laughs.

In the meantime, he had started talking about his interest to a colleague of his wife, David Sally. Sally, a former college basketball player at Harvard, was an economist and shared Anderson's interest in sports data. They joined forces to write a book based on the blog. Anderson was worried that no one would take two US American academics writing about football seriously, however. He told Sally of his fears. But he just looked at Anderson and asked him very calmly: 'What is it you actually want?' The way Anderson tells the story, you imagine the moment as the dramatic twist in a film. The main protagonist is faced with truth, some roaring music kicks in and a string crescendo delivers the epiphany. 'I said: "I want to be Billy Beane. Basically."'

Anderson and Sally are men with a good sense of self-deprecating humour. They knew full well that they, two grown men successful in their specific fields, were behaving like teenagers chasing a dream.

Of course it was absurd to believe, even for a moment, that they could turn the business of football on its head. They had no background in the game, no direct experience, almost no contacts. They were living in Ithaca, a university town in the state of New York, with its picture-postcard campus of red-brick buildings, manicured lawns and ancient trees. A place of nobility and class no doubt, but hardly the natural base to launch a football revolution. If Chris Anderson was to become the beautiful game's answer to Billy Beane, they needed a damn good plan.

They thought carefully about what it would take to get a foot in the door. The way they saw it, two factors were decisive. They needed to be taken seriously. And they had to come up with something that would be a real game changer, disruptive and impressive enough to make potential clients pay good money for it. The book they were planning to write was going to help them do just that in two different ways. 'It would become our Trojan horse. Firstly, it allowed us to conduct extensive research, enabling us to better understand the industry, its people and its dynamics. And it also gave us a chance to prove to those people that numbers could show very interesting things.'

They began by begging sports data companies such as Opta or Prozone for the free use of their very expensive data, promising to namecheck them in the book in return. But they didn't just crunch the numbers. Anderson and Sally went to clubs in Germany and England to find out how they were using data. 'We weren't competition. Everyone saw us as two naive village idiots and opened their doors to us,' Anderson says. They visited Chelsea, Liverpool,

Everton, 1. FC Köln and many more. All of them happily explained their way of working with data to them.

When their book was finished, Anderson and Sally made sure *The Numbers Game* was first published in England. It had a better chance of being taken seriously than a book on soccer from the US. Released in 2013, it became a big success, finding many readers in Britain, the States, in Scandinavia and a few Asian countries. The first part of their plan had worked out. People did take them seriously, and their research had led to a network of useful contacts.

But they had also found that analytics departments had a hard time getting appreciated by their own clubs. 'There is a lot of interest for these new technologies, but it's not a grass roots movement,' Anderson says. 'Nothing really grows or thrives there; a lot of it is just being left alone to die a slow death.' He and Sally determined that many of the bigger clubs, especially in the Premier League, had indeed invested in technical scouts or data analysts. But many of them only seemed to have been hired because their bosses didn't want to be accused of being old-fashioned. When it came to decisions processes, the work of those people at best played a minor role. 'All sports who use analytics successfully do so because the clubs see it as part of the management strategy. If that doesn't come from the very top, nothing happens.' Billy Beane had only been able to implement his plan by being in a position of power at the Oakland A's.

That realisation led Anderson and Sally to reach a radical conclusion. There was no point trying to convince club bosses to adopt their ideas. They had to find investors willing to buy a club and have it managed differently from the outset. 'When I say, "I want to be

Billy Beane," what I'm really talking about is approaching football differently,' Anderson says. As two Ivy League professors, they used their contacts to pitch their vision to high net-worth entrepreneurs from the Middle East, Russia and of course from the US, too.

There had been a few American takeovers of Premier League clubs already. The Glazers at Manchester United, Randy Lerner at Aston Villa, Ellis Short at Sunderland, Stan Kroenke at Arsenal, John W. Henry at Liverpool. A consortium of investors were willing to back Anderson and Sally and buy a Championship club, with a view to getting promoted with the use of fresh ideas. They nearly pulled off a move for Charlton Athletic and got close to buying Reading, too, but both deals fell through at the last minute.

Things seemed to be going nowhere when another US-based investor appeared on the scene and was prepared to take a shortcut: he wanted to buy a team in the top flight straight away. The project's parameters changed; it's about ten times more expensive to buy a Premier League club than a championship side. The man who wanted to be Billy Beane found himself going to dozens of lunches in the best and most expensive restaurants in London's exclusive Mayfair neighbourhood, talking to American billionaires about how many hundreds of millions of pounds they were ready to spend on a football club. It was a hugely exciting time but a complicated and drawn-out process, too.

Buying a football club is not exactly a fail-proof proposition; there are many easier ways to get a return on your investment. The Americans Anderson spoke to were aghast to find that English football came with a thing called 'relegation', the very real danger to lose not just your place in the Premier League but a ton of money, with no guarantee to get back in. Owning a club also brings with it huge visibility. That's part of the attraction, without a doubt. But nobody wants to embarrass themselves on the global stage, either. Moneyball sounded sexy enough but there was a clear reputational risk for anyone prepared to spend a fortune and put a cherished sporting and social institution into the hands of two US academics without any footballing experience.

The people Anderson and Sally had negotiated with ended up buying a majority in Crystal Palace but Anderson was no longer involved when the deal went through in December 2015. The takeover had taken so long that he had run out of patience and accepted the offer to become the Managing Director of Coventry City, then in the third division. He was tempted by the big opportunity to gain some practical experience in leading a football club. 'I wanted to serve an apprenticeship,' he says, looking back.

The Sky Blues have only ever won one trophy in their history, the FA Cup in 1987. But between 1967 and 2001, the Midlands side had been consistently playing in the top flight for more than three decades. Life in the third division was seen as an affront by everyone in town. On top of that ignominy, a change of ownership and row over the stadium rent had seen the club forced to play in exile for more than a season, in Northampton. There were no two ways about it: Anderson was put in charge of a club in crisis.

Any high-flown fantasies of becoming Billy Beane in Coventry did not survive a first brush with reality. 'I had a good theoretical understanding of football and read everything. I knew people in the business. But I had no idea how it felt living and breathing the game 24/7. After a week or so I understood: this job was the opposite of being Billy Beane.' Anderson's daily routine as the boss of a third division team included looking after ticket sales and making sure the stewards turned up for the game at the weekend. He had to see to it that the driver of the team bus was getting paid and that there was enough detergent to wash the whole kit.

Anderson worked alongside Coventry's Technical Director Mark Venus. Venus had turned professional footballer aged 16 and finished his career 21 years later, after more than 500 league games. Football was his world; he was football. 'He had that instinctive feel for saying and doing the right thing to get the desired effect. That's something I could never have. Unlike me, he has spent 20 years in dressing rooms with players,' Anderson says. Venus knew what a player really wanted when he asked a question; he could look at him and see whether he was happy or secretly troubled. 'I knew that I'd need someone like him to make it in football. You can't walk around the place like a general, barking orders. You need a trusted lieutenant who knows how to get things done on the ground.'

Getting to grips with ticketing, washing powder and other mundane matters still left time for Anderson to understand why working in a football club was both fascinating and very difficult. 'Everything is done manually, and an intellectual approach is almost frowned upon. You have to get your hands dirty or have people who will do that for you. The people you work with need to fulfil three criteria. They have to be competent, totally trustworthy and they have to believe in the mission.'

At Coventry, not everybody did. Anderson took over in autumn 2015 and the club finished the season in eighth place. The following summer, problems arose – problems Anderson felt he couldn't fix and wouldn't discuss because of contractual agreements. In October 2016, after little more than a year in the job, he decided to throw in the towel and leave the club.

You might think that was the end of Chris Anderson's story, and that of his quest to become football's Billy Beane. He was no longer an American Ivy League professor with a comfortable life and secure income – he had given up his academic career to embark on an adventure in football. 'I've had some wonderful experiences but also some bad and stressful ones. I would have never encountered them as a professor, and I'm grateful for that. It doesn't really matter whether I will still turn into Billy Beane because the experience has been interesting enough.'

Did he fall prey to the allure of money, dining in those fancy restaurants, arranging the potential takeover of clubs? 'Never. You do get swept along in a current, and it's not easy to get out again. But I'm not motivated by money.' He doesn't consider his time at Coventry a failure, and the bruising experience hasn't disabused him of the notion that there should be a place for outsiders like him in football. On the contrary: Anderson is still convinced that there's much to be said for not being a proper football man. 'The academic in me is an incorrigible know-it-all, and football is an industry that's not predisposed to thinking too deeply about things.'

Anderson has found that innovation in football has been solely driven by insiders until now. 'I'm motivated by the idea that innovation can come from the outside, too. I want to see if the outsider can win as well. I find that notion very romantic.' Before trying his hand at Coventry, he had set up a consulting firm, Anderson and Sally, to advise investors in football clubs on economic and financial matters, not least in the hope that one of those investors might be bold enough to put his money on an outsider succeeding.

In spring 2018, he took up an offer from Warwick University, however. The man who wanted to be Billy Beane returned to academic life as a professor for economics and politics. But he still does some consulting for football clubs on the side. And maybe, just maybe ... the dream could still come true one day.

THE WORLD'S MOST MODERN FOOTBALL CLUB

In the spring of 2015, I drove to Herning in Denmark to visit the most modern football club in the world. That's how it felt to me in any case.

It's almost always windy here, in the centre of Denmark, miles away from everything. And when there's no wind, there's a storm. Gusts strafed FC Midtjylland's training pitch with incessant salvos. The club's pros were training on a bumpy lawn, in between trees with bird houses and scrawny hedges that had long given up any pretence of keeping out the draught. The wind couldn't blow away the sharp taste of slurry in the air, only the ball. At times, it almost seemed to stop in mid-air, as if wondering whether this, here, was really the team on the lips of many of football's most clued-up people.

The blue-eyed coach shouted encouragingly at his men, his windcheater zipped up all the way to his chin. He was charged with putting into practice all the weird and wonderful ideas of his then only 31-year-old, ponytailed club boss Rasmus Ankersen who had devised them in tandem with Sporting Director Claus Steinlein and Matthew Benham. The three of them had made this provincial Danish club into a football laboratory for mathematical models, algorithms and maverick innovations.

I was rarely welcomed as openly by a professional football club. For a few days, I was practically embedded – allowed to listen in on team meetings in the mornings, to hang out with the coaching staff and even to enter the dressing room after games. My whole time there was marked by a palpable sense of excitement that had engulfed the whole club: Midtjylland were heading towards their first-ever championship. But on top of that, they were proud of all the cool things they were doing. Their success had even their fiercest critics conceding that there was something very special happening here.

'I'm more the old-fashioned type,' Kristian Bach Bak told me. The then 32-year-old was the captain of the team and the fans' favourite. He hailed from the region and his cropped hair and tattoos made him look like the bass player of a heavy metal band. Most of all, though, he was a tireless worker on the right side of defence, somebody who fought for every inch until the very end, the team's natural leader.

When FC Midtjylland were bought in July 2014 by a new owner who rang in wholesale changes overnight, Bak was alarmed. He grew more worried still upon learning that transfers were being approved by mathematical models and that during half-time in matches, his coach was being sent obscure stats to his mobile phone, numbers that directly influenced his decisions on the touchline. Soon, he found himself sitting opposite a sports psychologist who conducted a personality test on him, and after a while, a neurobiologist from Oxford University became part of the staff, too. 'The brain guy,' everybody at the club called him. 'At first, I was convinced it was all bullshit. Because football is about showing heart,' Bak says.

The full-back had played alongside Rasmus Ankersen in Midt-jylland's youth team and shared a flat with him at the time. But Ankersen's career had been cut short aged 21 after he suffered a bad knee injury. He became a youth coach and started writing books about sporting success.

Ankersen made London his base. He travelled the world to deliver lectures that commanded five-figure fees; companies such as LEGO, Facebook and IKEA paid for his consulting services. In 2013, he met Benham, at a time when his club, Brentford, were an ambitious third division side in the mix for promotion.

Ankersen asked Benham about Brentford's chances of going up. The reply: '42.3 per cent.' 'I instantly knew that he was thinking about football differently than most people in the game,' Ankersen recalls. Benham wasn't being flippant. He had in fact calculated the probabilities. The two men got along straight away.

The Dane explained football to the Englishman from the view-point of someone who had played the game and worked as a coach. Benham, meanwhile, stunned Ankersen with a flurry of novel ideas that took their cue from mathematical calculations. 'He taught me to see football with different eyes,' Ankersen says. I understood exactly what he meant.

Ankersen's voice is very pleasant, warm and soft. It's nice listening to him. His greatest talent is his ability to transform complex thoughts into catchy one-liners. In 2011, he published a book in Denmark that has since been translated into 25 languages. In the course of his research, he had travelled to Kenya, Jamaica, Brazil and Russia, and spoken to the world's best long-distance runners, sprinters, footballers and women's tennis players. *The Gold Mine Effect* tried to explain the role of talent in sports and the reasons for the success of top athletes.

After Benham had taken over Brentford in 2012, he quickly noticed that very few things were actually changing at the club. His thoughts and findings were politely noted by the people in charge of the day-to-day decisions on the sporting side – he was the boss, after all – but they were not really implemented. English football, especially at a lower level, was a very conservative affair then; nobody dared to try out new things.

Benham's attempts to make the Bees into a truly modern club hit a brick wall time and time again. He finally understood he had to go elsewhere in order to put his ideas to the test. Maybe a foreign club would be more open to novel methods?

Initially, Benham had looked at a side in Belgium. But Ankersen put him in touch with his old club. Midtjylland were in financial difficulties, they needed the money and didn't mind that it came with some loopy ideas attached. Everyone was pleased when the deal went through in July 2014. Benham bought three-quarters of the club's shares and appointed Ankersen as CEO. Bak's former team-mate and flat-mate had returned as his boss.

Sitting right behind the bench in the MCH Arena, I watched the defender cover his team's right defensive flank in typically indus-trious fashion, in a game against the league's bottom side. On the stroke of half-time, coach Glen Riddersholm took out his mobile phone. There was indeed a text message from Benham's company from London, and it confirmed the impression from within the ground that Midtjylland had played without much oomph. Ridder-sholm's men had created better chances than their opponents, to be sure, but the difference in quality and goalscoring chances hadn't been nearly as pronounced as the model had predicted in view of the two sides' respective strengths.

In the second half, the league leaders continued to play poorly in the plain environs of the 11,000-capacity stadium, but laboured to a 1–0 win. The crowd were happy regardless. The small groups of hardcore fans behind the goal celebrated wildly, and a bare-chested Kristian Bach Bak was leading the triumphant chants in the dressing room. They had come a little closer to winning the league title.

But it wasn't all good news. A text message from the British capital told the coach that the model had just downgraded his team. Having a computer telling the manager how good his side were straight after an important win sounds cruelly technocratic and cold. But Midtjylland's coach didn't see it that way at all. Riddersholm believed that the strictly analytical appraisal of the performance freed him from the vagaries of good fortune when it came to looking at the quality of his work. Nobody blamed him if a striker missed the goal from five yards out or if opponents snatched a draw with a 25-yard wonder strike. Benham and Ankersen wouldn't dream of axing him in the hope of bringing back good luck, and he would never succumb to the sort of unwarranted self-doubt that had plagued Jürgen Klopp and his staff in their final season at Dortmund. On the other hand, he could expect to face fierce criticism, irrespective of his team winning the game, if they had underperformed in relation to the model's expectations.

'In place of emotions, we now have facts,' he said. 'They give us the confidence to believe that there's nothing at all to be afraid of – as long as we do our work properly.'

The 42-year-old seemed like quite an emotional coach to me, he liked talking and went into great detail about the human and social aspects of his job. Riddersholm had been living in the area for 20 years, mostly coaching FC Midtjylland's youth teams as well as the Danish U17s national team for a spell. He personally knew many famous colleagues such as Arsène Wenger and José Mourinho; he had visited almost all of the big clubs in Europe and South America, too. In other words: Riddersholm had been around the block a few times. And yet, there was no place quite like home to him. 'Considering the resources at our disposal, we're the only club in the world doing what we're doing,' he said. He believed in Midtjylland's experimental ways with the fervour of a recent convert; in his mind, there was no doubt that the information and calculations beamed over from London helped him to do his job better, by introducing a strong element of objectivity that few people in football are able to muster. 'The eyes only see what they want to see,' he said.

Riddersholm evaluated his players in accordance with KPI (Key Performance Indicators), numbers that the eggheads in Benham's office were providing. In addition, they were conducting a study into the shooting positions that afford the highest scoring probability, with a view to directing the team towards moving the ball into those areas. It was Expected Goals, reverse-engineered: if one shooting position was doubly promising than another one, it made sense to figure out how to get there.

Was it a coincidence that Pep Guardiola's record-breaking champions Manchester City did not score a single goal outside the box in the first half of the 2017–18 season? In football, the use of game data is beginning to change the game itself, just as it has already done in basketball, for example. After the Houston Rockets had deduced that the higher reward of three-point-shots was worth the higher risk of missing, they realigned this strategy to take more. Other NBA clubs soon followed their lead.

Benham's stats had convinced Riddersholm that a narrow lead was best defended by going aggressively for another goal; playing not to concede, on the other hand, only decreased the probability of scoring and increased the opposition's chance to find the net. The coach had calmly explained that counter-intuitive rationale to his players. That's why no one got nervous any more when he put on an additional striker ten minutes from time with Midtjylland 1–0 up.

The club were founded in 1999, the result of a merger of two traditionally rival clubs that were no longer viable by themselves. Claus Steinlein was 27 at the time. He's since worked as coach, chairman of the board and as the head of the famous youth academy.

The latter was a first in Denmark when it was set up in 2000, but the football school has since produced more professional players than any other club in the country.

Midtjylland's main domestic rivals are the two clubs from the capital, FC Kopenhagen and Bröndby. Both have budgets twice the size. Steinlein enjoyed getting one over the two top teams with only €7m for wages at his disposal. The collaboration with Smartodds has revolutionised recruitment at the club. For each vacant position in the squad, the London-based analysts send a list of 20 potential candidates. 'We used to have one scout, working part-time,' he said. 'Now we have 200.'

Smartodds' vast database of individual performance profiles put forward affordable players from leagues that Steinlein did not know very well. Extensive study of DVD footage narrowed down the selection to a handful of contenders. Only then did the traditional part of the work begin, with Steinlein contacting agents, scouting in person and talking to possible signings.

Midtjylland were used to going where others wouldn't. In 2004, they founded a football school in Nigeria, one of Africa's more difficult countries to operate in. 'We were well aware of the complexities and dangers. Only madmen like us would do that,' Steinlein told me in his office in the stadium's main stand. The football school in Lagos is run by Churchill Oliseh, brother of former Super Eagles international Sunday Oliseh, who played for Ajax, Juventus and Dortmund. Each year, the best youngsters are sent to Denmark; a few of them have become professionals in European leagues. Those who don't make it in Denmark leave with a pay-off worth two annual salaries to make a life for themselves back home. 'We've always gone down different routes; that's a part of our club's DNA,' Steinlein said.

The streak of innovation runs deep in Herning, a city made up of 48,000 inhabitants, red-brick houses and a pedestrianised centre where shops close at 5:30. It's surrounded by barren moors that made the dogged and obstinate inhabitants turn towards breeding sheep centuries ago. They went from producing wool to making clothes, and the region became Denmark's centre of the textile industry. The underwear Cristiano Ronaldo models for comes from here. A few years ago, Scandinavia's biggest exhibition complex was built right next to FC Midtjylland's stadium in Herning; Katy Perry and Madonna have played concerts there.

After the somewhat fortuitous win over the league's bottom team, Rasmus Ankersen was in a cheerful mood and got downright enthusiastic when I asked him about the club's future prospects. 'To be honest, I don't have a clue how far we will end up going with this, but maybe it is a revolution,' he said. A few weeks later, Midtjylland won their first championship, pipping the storied clubs from the capital to the title. They repeated the feat in 2017–18.

THE LESSON OF DICK FOSBURY

Matthew Benham had taken an instant liking to those Danes from the middle of nowhere. He admired their courage to explore new ground in search of success, going all the way to Nigeria. The way Benham saw it, they had been rewarded for following the pioneering lead of Dick Fosbury.

'In corporate life, there are essentially two models. You can be "best in business" or emulate the American high jumper,' he explained. The first option is to do what everybody else is doing and to try to be the best. The second one is to approach the problem from a completely different angle. That's what Fosbury did, quite literally, when he had the seemingly mad idea of jumping head first with his back arching over the bar. He won gold at the 1968 Olympics in Mexico and the 'Fosbury Flop' revolutionised the sport.

Up until then, athletes had attempted to cross the bar with a straddle, which seemed the more logical choice. Fosbury struggled with that particular technique, however, and experimented with the upright scissor method. His innovation was to run up to the bar in a curve and jump backwards, head first over the bar. Fosbury's technique, first employed at a tournament in 1963, was so novel that rival coaches were looking through the rule book, wondering if it was legal.

The giant leap forward was made possible by advances in technology. Up until the late 1950s, high jumpers were landing in sandpits or piles of sawdust. Clearing a two-metre high pole jumping backwards wasn't safe on such a surface, but the introduction of foam mats greatly lowered the risk of injury and allowed Fosbury to try out an alternative style. The civil engineering student initially called his technique a 'back lay-out' in an interview but changed it to the much catchier 'Fosbury Flop' to make it more interesting to journalists. Today, many track and field athletes no longer know the term because no other style is being used by high jumpers.

As a professional gambler, Benham had tried to follow Fosbury's lead and exploited inefficiencies in the betting markets with the help of data. The plan was to do the same with FC Midtjylland and Brentford, only in real life.

Benham, however, is almost violently opposed to the use of the Moneyball moniker, for two reasons. Firstly, he feels that it invokes the mistaken expectation that it's all about data and some fantastical secret winning formula; an absurd suggestion in light of football's elusive complexity. What's more, the popularity of the Brad Pitt *Moneyball* film has resulted in an inflationary use of the term that has obscured its real meaning. Start-ups, publishing houses, law firms, digital media and a whole range of other businesses now profess a dedication to Moneyball, by which they mean the process of having big data identify unknown correlations and come up with results that change everything. For reasons that will become apparent, Benham doesn't consider it useful to think of innovation in that sense.

REVOLUTION

The world of football is governed by money – but not completely. Going against convention can overcome financial constraints. Also in this section: why the game is changing and dead-ball situations are hugely important.

TO SPEND OR INNOVATE

The story of Dick Fosbury, the high jump revolutionary, is of course a modern-day variant of the David and Goliath tale. In the biblical account, the Israelites are fighting the Philistines, who boast a 3m tall warrior called Goliath. He's a fearsome giant carrying heavy bronze armour, a huge sword and a spear. David, a humble shepherd, doesn't stand a chance in direct combat. But he reaches into his pocket, takes out a sling and fires a rock at him. 'The stone sank into his forehead, and he fell face down on the ground,' it says in the book of Samuel. 'So David triumphed over the Philistine with a sling and a stone; without a sword in his hand he struck down the Philistine and killed him.'

These days, one would call it asymmetrical warfare. An overly powerful opponent cannot be beaten on his own terms, only by the use of different tactics. The world of football, too, has become riddled with asymmetries. Most of them are economic in nature and have vast ramifications.

In 2009, economics professor Stefan Szymanski and journalist Simon Kuper published *Why England Lose*. In the US, it was released under the more apt title of *Soccernomics*: football, analysed through the prism of economics.

Szymanski had been studying the relationship between financial power and success on the pitch for a long time. What was the strongest financial indicator for winning games in football? He looked at the wage costs of the 92 professional clubs in England from 1998 to 2007. Those figures should not be equated with the budgets for the first team – they contained the cost of all staff, including admins and kit men – but they were nevertheless telling. Szymanski ranked personnel costs as multiples of the league average and compared it to average league positions. Manchester United, for example, paid wages that were 3.16 times the Premier League average.

It's remarkable how much the teams in the Premier League have changed over the course of the last ten years or so. Aston Villa, Middlesbrough, Leeds, Sunderland, Blackburn and Charlton have all gone down, into division two or three. Manchester City, on the other hand, have become an elite team thanks to generous investment by their owners from Abu Dhabi. Most interestingly of all is the strong correlation between wage cost and average league position, however. 'The more you pay your players, the higher you'll be in the table,' Szymanski concluded.

His findings directly influenced top European football, as Ferran Soriano revealed in his 2011 book *Goal: The Ball Doesn't go*

Club	Wage spending relative to the average spending of all clubs	Average league position
Manchester United	3.16	2
Arsenal	2.63	2
Chelsea	3.50	3
Liverpool	2.68	4
Newcastle United	1.93	9
Aston Villa	1.34	9
Tottenham Hotspur	1.60	10
Everton	1.41	12
Middlesbrough	1.32	12
Leeds United	1.70	13
West Ham United	1.31	14
Blackburn Rovers	1.48	14
Charlton Athletic	0.98	15
Bolton Wanderers	0.92	16
Fulham	1.24	16
Southampton	0.92	16
Sunderland	1.24	18
Manchester City	1.24	18

Source: Kuper/Szymanski, *Soccernomics*

in by Chance. As Vice President of FC Barcelona, the Spaniard had focused on reducing the financial gap with arch-rivals Real Madrid. Barça duly tripled their turnover from 2003 to 2008. 'If you want to have a team of champions who regularly win titles, you have to consistently make sure that it's a big club, generating high levels of income to sign the best players you can possibly get. Luck doesn't come into it,' Soriano wrote. Today, he works as the Chief Executive Officer of Manchester City. His outlook hasn't changed, presumably.

On a season-by-season basis the relationship between payroll and sporting benefit is less clear-cut, however. The table opposite, based on research by the American website spotrac.com, lists wage costs (in millions), the final league position and the deviation from the wage cost ranking for the Premier League in 2017–18.

'The market for players' wages is quite efficient,' Szymanski's long-term study had found. The final table of the 2017–18 league season would run counter to that; the average deviation from the staff cost ranking was nearly five places. Sean Dyche's Burnley overachieved most spectacularly in that regard. They finished 12 places higher than their position in the wage table. Southampton, by contrast, accumulated the least points in relation to the money they had spent on wages – they were seven places worse off. Saints at least avoided relegation, which was more than could be said for Stoke City.

In a single campaign, money might not be the most decisive factor. But over a longer period of time – a decade, for example – the financial power of teams tends to come to the fore. The more you're able to spend on playing staff, the higher your chance of achieving sporting success.

Club	Annual salaries*	Final table	Difference salaries table / final table
Manchester United	143.7	2	-1
Manchester City	128.4	1	1
Arsenal	117.4	6	-3
Chelsea	110.9	5	-1
Liverpool	81.0	4	1
Everton	77.3	8	-2
Tottenham Hotspur	74.4	3	4
West Ham United	74.3	13	-5
Crystal Palace	64.9	11	-2
Southampton	64.5	17	-7
West Bromwich	57.1	20	-9
Leicester City	56.0	9	3
Stoke City	52.3	19	-6
Newcastle United	46.2	10	4
AFC Bournemouth	43.8	12	3
Watford	43.1	14	2
Swansea City	42.6	18	-1
Brighton & Hove	38.6	15	3
Burnley	34.0	7	12
Huddersfield Town	31.3	16	4

* in million pounds

Source: Spotrac

Paying high transfer fees, on the other hand, is not a reliable indicator of sporting success, as the results of clubs who have been mainstays in the Premier League between 2008 and 2018 underline.

Club	League average 2008–18	Transfer balance
Manchester City	3.2	–1,175
Manchester United	3.1	–652
Chelsea	3.5	–398
Liverpool	5.4	–216
Arsenal	3.8	-214
Everton	7.5	-149
Tottenham Hotspur	4.5	–82

* in million euros
Source: transfermarkt.de

Tottenham's rather small net outlay is especially noteworthy. Ahead of the 2018–19 season, they didn't sign any new players – a first in the history of the Premier League. Clubs such as Stoke City, West Bromwich Albion or Aston Villa spent a lot more on players, on aggregate, but couldn't even stay up. Still, the correlation between net spend and results is stronger in the Premier League than in other European leagues. In the Bundesliga, giants Bayern Munich (net spend: €354m) were the most successful side but runners-up Borussia Dortmund made a net profit of €95m over the course of the same decade. The two dominant sides in La Liga, Real Madrid and FC Barcelona, were also the biggest spenders. By contrast, Sevilla (average league position 5.6 over ten years) made €140m more on transfers than they paid out.

If transfer spend isn't the determining factor for success, clubs might be better off investing in wages rather than fees. The strategy could be to focus on growing revenue to spend more on players, to become more successful, generate more income and spend more on players – and so forth. A virtuous cycle. Alternatively, you can try to beat the system, Dick Fosbury-style, by being smarter and faster than the competition. In order to do that though, you need to be very clear where your club is positioned in the grand scheme of things.

Author Daniel Fieldsend drew up a pyramid of wealth in his book *The European Game* and explained that transfer activities must always be seen in the context of a club's position in the financial hierarchy. His pyramid illustrates the low social mobility in modern football. There are five different types of clubs, with relatively little movement between the levels.

Source: Fieldsend, *The European Game*

The way Fieldsend sees it, super clubs are de facto obligated to buy superstar players in their prime. A classic example would be Real

Madrid buying Cristiano Ronaldo, Luis Figo, David Beckham or Zinédine Zidane. It's a similar case for Barcelona, Juventus, the top sides in England and Bayern Munich. On the rung below those regular Champions League contenders sit the second-tier clubs, the likes of Atletico Madrid, FC Sevilla, FC Porto, Benfica or Borussia Dortmund. Dominant domestically and occasionally successful in Europe, they are much more likely to be developing superstars than being able to hold on to them when they're at their peak.

Udinese Calcio is a textbook middle class side by international standards. The club from northern Italy compensate for their geographical disadvantage – they're based in a town of only 100,000 people, without a wide catchment area – by making extensive transfer dealings. Udinese run a global network of scouts and have repeatedly pulled off real coups such as signing a young Alexis Sánchez, who was later sold to Barcelona for €25m. Udinese's owner, Giampaolo Pozzo, also controls Watford FC in England, which helps him move players between different leagues.

A club's position in football's food chain is not least down to the financial possibilities afforded to them by their league. The Eredivisie has lost a lot of ground in that respect.

Dutch football used to be a launch pad for future South American superstars. Romário and Ronaldo both made PSV Eindhoven their first club in Europe and Luis Suárez started out at FC Groningen. That's almost become unthinkable today. Dutch clubs firmly belong to the category of talent developers. The biggest one of all, in the European context, are Ajax. Almost a third of all professional players in the Dutch top flight are products of the Ajax academy. Christian

Eriksen, Toby Alderweireld and Jan Vertonghen (all Tottenham) and Thomas Vermaelen (FC Barcelona) are the most prominent of the 77 academy graduates who were plying their trade in Europe's top divisions in 2017.

Clubs have adopted many different financial models. The distribution of money has a strong effect on the relationship between leagues, as well as on the clubs inside of them. The crassest example is Paris Saint-Germain's dominance of Ligue 1, thanks to the limitless wealth of their owners, the Qatar Investment Authority. Many smaller football countries, too, have become subservient to an all-powerful club that have used their income from the Champions League to make their position at the top all but unassailable. Switzerland's FC Basel used to be a case in point for a long time; Olympiacos (Greece) as well.

Those who want to get one over on the competition need to first appreciate what's truly possible. Udinese will never win the Scudetto and Dortmund cannot seriously rival the super clubs when it comes to winning the Champions League. The fact that Leicester City managed to break the mould to win the Premier League should not be seen as a benchmark, but as a spectacular one-off event.

As a club, you can either accept the fate determined by the structural imbalance or do anything to raise revenues to bring in better players. Alternatively, you can try out new, revolutionary ideas, as Dick Fosbury did.

Football's complexity offers a multitude of opportunities to seek out an edge. That explains why Matthew Benham is strongly dismissive of a Moneyball narrative that heralds the triumph of smart data analysis. There are many different ways to make up for having less money than your richer rivals, and some of them owe their effectiveness to good old-fashioned work on the training pitch rather than advanced algorithms.

MEET THE RULE BREAKERS

One of the most common cognitive biases is called 'social proof', also known as the bandwagon effect. It leads to people doing things the way they have always been done and because everybody else is doing them, too. Footballers, for example, used to be forbidden from drinking water during the game because the intake of fluids was thought to be detrimental to their performance. Today, everyone knows that dehydration is a health risk; on hot days, there are special breaks for water.

Football is quite conservative and often insular. Since the forces of social proof are stronger than in other walks of life, misguided concepts survive for much longer. In England, Charles Reep's long-ball dogma influenced the game for a number of years even though it was based on the wrongful interpretation of data. Breaking free of conventions and of perceived wisdoms – modernisation, in other words – seems especially difficult in football, where protagonists are subject to the strong influence of supporters and the media. Those who try out new things and don't find success are much more harshly criticised than those who simply follow the herd.

For that reason alone it was rather remarkable that a young German coach was willing to give a lecture at 'The Rulebreaker

Society' in 2012. The Leipzig-based network defines itself as 'a completely new generation of a private, international business club'. Its members are self-professed disruptors: they want to break rules in order to explore new markets, transform industries and become rich along the way. The young coach talking to them was called Thomas Tuchel. He was 39 at the time and in his fourth season as head coach of Bundesliga side Mainz 05.

His appointment alone had broken a number of rules. Christian Heidel, the club's general manager at the time, could easily be described as one of the Bundesliga's great revolutionaries, even if the former car salesman would surely wave away such praise with a bemused shrug.

He didn't just transform a provincial second division side into an established Bundesliga club with the help of a long-term plan, however; his choices of managers were also extremely unconventional. In the middle of a seemingly hopeless Bundesliga 2 relegation battle, he appointed Jürgen Klopp as manager, even though the 33-year-old was still playing as a defender for the side at the time, had never coached a team before and didn't have any formal qualifications either.

After becoming General Director of Schalke 04, Heidel became the first club boss in Germany to pay a transfer fee for a manager, FC Augsburg's Markus Weinzierl. When Weinzierl didn't work out, Heidel didn't opt for a safe pair of hands as his successor but brought in a 31-year-old who had mustered the grand total of 11 games as a professional manager in the second division (at lowly Erzgebirge Aue), Domenico Tedesco. 'Experience is overrated,' Heidel declared.

In his first Bundesliga season (2017–18), Tedesco took Schalke to second spot behind champions Bayern.

The lack of importance Heidel assigned to a coach's CV wasn't just informed by Klopp's great success at Mainz but also by a similarly left-field appointment. Five days before the start of the 2009–10 league campaign, Heidel had fired Norwegian manager Jörn Andersen and given the job to the unknown Tuchel. The unprecedented decision was greeted with disbelief: Andersen had won promotion with Mainz only a few months before. But a defeat in the cup at fourth division VfB Lübeck in the first competitive game of the season had convinced Heidel that the problems he had seen in the way Andersen had worked previously were bound to come to the fore in the top flight. He didn't like the coach's decidedly cold and non-communicative man-management style, not least because he didn't consider it in line with the club's identity as one big family. Andersen later became national team manager of North Korea, incidentally. More surprising than the Norwegian's dismissal, however, was the arrival of Tuchel as his successor.

In 2019 Tuchel was the coach of Paris Saint-Germain, but at the time of his Mainz appointment he belonged to the small circle of Bundesliga coaches who had never played professional football. He had won the German amateur championship as a defender with SSV Ulm but an injury had killed off his career. The truly groundbreaking aspect of the appointment, however, was Tuchel's total lack of practical know-how at this level. Having worked as a youth coach at Stuttgart, Augsburg and Mainz since 2000, he had won the

German youth championship with 05 in June 2001 but had never managed a senior team in his life.

Tuchel was a typical product of the German youth academies that had been installed at the turn of the century. A certification system ensured that the education of youth coaches followed the highest standards; many of them had acquired a much deeper understanding of the ins and outs of the game than professional managers of previous generations. That didn't change the fact that Tuchel was faced with a huge challenge. He had to begin life as a professional coach at the very top, with no history to fall back on.

The recording of Tuchel's speech at the Rulebreaker Society had, at the time of writing, been watched on YouTube more than 370,000 times. That's a remarkable amount of hits, even if the lecture itself is remarkable, too. Tuchel explains how he approached his role and how his work developed in the Bundesliga in humorous, moving, yet always analytical fashion.

Mainz had broken the rules by putting him on the bench, and he, the debutant, followed up by courageously breaking with other classical 'patterns of thought', as he called them. Standard practice was for most teams to concentrate on playing one particular system of football as well as possible. A coach was supposed to choose a formation at the beginning of the season and stick with it until the end. They'd plump for a 4-3-3, a 4-2-3-1 or something else and focus on making the playing processes second nature. Some clubs never varied their formations for years on end.

Tuchel and his staff broke the unwritten rule that a side should have a fixed way of playing. They were motivated by a sense of their own inferiority – most opponents simply had better players in their squads. By sticking with the status quo, tactically, they would lose the majority of their games and go down. Tuchel instead took up a radical course: he wanted to 'mirror' the opposition formations, as he put it. Most of the top teams at the time did the exact opposite. They were – and often still are – fixated on the idea of playing their own game; opponents were supposed to adapt to them, not the other way around. Tuchel, by contrast, consciously exaggerated his side's underdog role by setting up the team completely in relation to the opposition from the outset; not just against superior opponents such as Bayern or Borussia Dortmund, but every single time. Ahead of every game, Tuchel had his players practise the system that he thought best fit his opponents. When a team played 4-2-3-1, Tuchel lined up Mainz in a 4-1-4-1. By doing so, he wanted to get his players into the right spaces. 'We wanted to give players a framework for acting intuitively,' he explained. Ideally, they would get into a 'flow', the state of mind all athletes aspire to – when it just 'clicks' for you and everything seems to come off.

'I remember managerial colleagues calling me after my first half of a season and thanking me for making them think about it [tactics]. We came to realise that the systems aren't really that different from one another; the main differences lie in the spaces that you use in line with your particular strengths and of course [you] defend vigorously.' Tuchel also found that players didn't need to spend a lot of time getting to grips with constant change: 'We were able to explain defensive movement, in particular, with video footage in a wonderfully feasible way,' he later recalled. 'That made us lose any inhibition we might have had about playing a variety of formations.'

Tuchel broke up other patterns of thought as well. Mainz, like many other teams, had historically attacked with long balls from wide positions. The logic behind that was self-evident: playing through the congested centre was much tougher. At the same time, it was more difficult to score from the flanks, which is why defending teams liked pushing attackers wide.

Tuchel, however, had his team attacking the most dangerous area of the pitch – right through the middle. In order to practise these moves, he employed a little trick. He cut off the corners of the training pitch with cones to make the playing field resemble a diamond. Players were thus forced to play through the centre towards goal. What's more, Tuchel crammed the midfield full of players for much of the training sessions. When his men were able to play across the whole pitch at the weekend in the real games, it felt like a huge relief to them.

Another of Tuchel's innovations was to get the reserve players or youth side to act out the tactics of the next opponents as a shadow team. He simulated the coming game by having his B-team act out the 4-2-3-1 of the opponents, to make his A-side experience what they would be up against. Later, at Dortmund, he abandoned those sessions, having come to believe that they were inefficient.

Tuchel, his assistant Arno Michels and video analyst Benjamin Weigelt, dissected their opponents' games in a way that let them come up with a 'match plan' for their own team. Tuchel was the first to use that pseudo-Anglicism in the Bundesliga; 'game plan' would have been a better word. That wasn't the reason some were critical of the term, however. Didn't all coaches go into games with a plan, they wondered?

Probably. But in modern football, plans go far beyond simple orders. The idea is to prepare for specific phases and developments during games, with every player knowing exactly what he is supposed to do at any given moment. At Mainz, Tuchel's plan had him changing more than the basic formation; he constantly changed his personnel, too, in another break with accepted wisdom – fielding a fixed starting XI of players who knew each other well was regarded as a must.

Mainz 05 were phenomenally successful during Tuchel's five-year reign; he even outdid his predecessor Jürgen Klopp, points-wise, before becoming his successor for a second time at Dortmund.

Mainz broke a series of club records with him in charge. They even made it to the Europa League once. Tuchel's biggest achievement, however, was to tear up the old social proof that had existed in the German first division in relation to managers. All of a sudden, all clubs wanted to promote their youth team coaches even though they had no experience. And they all wanted to have their teams playing such flexible football, too. Without the success of Tuchel, the likes of Tedesco, Julian Nagelsmann and Florian Kohfeldt would have found it much harder to get top jobs.

LIQUID FOOTBALL

A year before Thomas Tuchel became a Bundesliga coach at Mainz, Barcelona had taken a somewhat surprising decision, too: they had installed Pep Guardiola as manager. Aged 37 at the time, his only practical coaching experience had been a year in charge of the second team. On the face of it, though, his appointment looked rather old-fashioned. The job had gone to a former hero at the club, popular with the fans and from Catalonia; to a man who had worn the Barça shirt for 11 years and had won all the important trophies in his time at the Camp Nou.

But then something unprecedented happened. In his first season as a head coach, Guardiola won the Spanish championship, the Copa del Rey, the Champions League, the European Super Cup and the Club World Championship. A quintuple.

As if that haul of silverware hadn't been enough of an epic achievement, his team had also played football in a way never seen before. Guardiola, too, was one of football's rule breakers, eager to divert from traditional ways of doing things. Starting from the 'total football' premise of his mentor Johan Cruyff, he imposed his own rules, redefining the beautiful game in the process.

In the years that were to follow, first at Barcelona, then at Bayern and now at Manchester City, Guardiola continued to develop his concept. He adapted it to the specific conditions of the respective leagues and arguably changed football like no manager before him had done. Even coaches playing very different styles were profoundly influenced by his tactics.

Jürgen Klopp, for example, is widely known as the man who made *Gegenpressing* fashionable. The Swabian will not deny, however, that his concept was strongly influenced by Guardiola's Barcelona. They were the first team who tried to win back the ball immediately after losing possession in such radical, systematic fashion.

I can still recall the effect of witnessing this awesome pressing machine for the first time in the flesh. Against Arsenal in the quarter-final of the Champions League in April 2010, Guardiola's team were positioned so far up the pitch that even their two centre-backs were deep inside the Gunners' half. I sat in the Camp Nou's press stand, right beneath the roof – the view's great from up there. My first thought was 'madness', followed by 'you can't play like that'. But you could. The game of Wenger's team was suffocated to the extent that one of the biggest club games of the year felt more like a cup game between a top division side and semi-pros from division four. Barça were 3–1 up at half-time and that flattered the visitors; the final score was 4–1. Today, defending this high up the pitch and *Gegenpressing* are well-established tactical ploys. But then, they felt breathtakingly new.

Barcelona and Guardiola are more readily identified with their possession game, which is also far more difficult to emulate. They became famous, some might say infamous, for endless passing combinations. People called it 'tiki-taka'. The label stuck, even though Guardiola hated it: he considered it derogatory, a description of sterile possession for its own sake. That's not what he wanted.

It is true that his high-passing style had defensive connotations. Barcelona would sometimes rest in possession. But more import-antly, the series of passes tired out the opposition. After a while, their physical and mental powers were exhausted from chasing after the ball. Guardiola's 'death by a thousand passes' was a ruthless way of grinding down the opponents until they collapsed. Unsurpris-ingly, his team scored many goals in the second half.

At the centre of this orgy of passes stood two players whose diminutive physiques amounted to a break with the rules as well.

Xavi and Andrés Iniesta were the opposite of the powerful, tall and intimidating midfielders who had come to dominate the game in the previous years. Everyone had agreed that it was crucial to have warrior-type figures such as Frenchman Patrick Vieira (Arsenal) or Manchester United's fighter-in-chief Roy Keane at the heart of every team, leaders of men who could wrest control of the game by virtue of brute force and their indomitable spirit. Barcelona, however, turned the logic of having hard men battle to win the decisive one-vs-ones in the middle of the park on its head. They passed the ball so well that their opponents couldn't get near enough to challenge them.

Barcelona had three playmakers in the centre, if you include Sergio Busquets. Guardiola's players often defied the usual labels, as their roles kept shifting from game to game, sometimes even within the game. His most spectacular re-imagining of a player's position occurred after the experiment of fielding a regular target man in Zlatan Ibrahimović had failed, for footballing and personal reasons. Lionel Messi, the 1.70m tall Argentinian, was moved centrally, not to lead the line in the classic sense, of course, but to play as a 'false 9', a striker who attacked the goal from deep. There had been forwards who withdrew into midfield before in the history of football, to become both playmakers and strikers at the same time. But in modern times, no one has ever played this hybrid role with such other-worldly brilliance. Messi scored 211 goals in all competitions in four years under Guardiola.

Messi wasn't the only Barça player with a new job title. In a way, Busquets played as a 'false 6', Iniesta as a 'false 8' and the Brazilian full-back Dani Alves as a 'false 2' – he was really more of a winger. In Munich, Guardiola sometimes pushed his wide defenders inside and forward, into midfield positions.

It's fair to say that Guardiola thought about the game in a unique way and that Barcelona were a test lab for the development of a new type of football. Did his teams play 4-4-2 or 4-3-3? Basic formations lost much of their relevance; in fact they seemed to dissolve altogether, into a fluid order, a series of situations and tasks blending into each other.

Thomas Tuchel saw things similarly. He has made no secret of his admiration for Guardiola, and the ideas he talked about with students at Universität Witten-Herdecke in 2016 would have chimed with those of his mentor. 'We are beginning to learn that the narrowness and rigidity of formations are no longer quite there,' Tuchel, then at BVB, said. 'Maybe they are no longer that important. It's more about principles of action that arise in certain situations.' He added that preparations for one game had him suddenly arrive at a 3-2-4-1 system. 'I didn't even know you could play like that. If you constantly try to find ways to switch flanks quicker or to change the distance for the passes, you at last get to the point where you can line up in a different basic formation.'

Managers such as Guardiola or Tuchel see football as a relentless struggle to create numerical superiority in proximity to the ball, in attack and in defence. Spaces on the pitch have to be taken up anew continuously, to create options for passing. Tuchel tells his players to 'respect space'. That sounds strange at first, but is meant to emphasise the idea of space as a dynamic concept.

'Spaces often only open up for a moment, and then you have to be sure that your team-mate will be exactly where you'd expect him. The ball has to get there, as quickly as possible, as precisely as possible. There is, without a question, a type of butterfly effect on the pitch: the control of the ball and the second touch or a pass from the right inside channel into the left inside channel can cause a storm – in a football sense – but only if the ball is played into the right foot, into the right space, with the right pace.'

This incredibly subtle, granular way of understanding the game has come to be shared by many football coaches around the world. They think less of systems and more about mastering hundreds of different situations that occur on the pitch. They go as far as worrying about the exact positioning of the feet and the distance between players. Even 40cm can make a difference.

There is a deep-seated aversion among fans (and some members of the media) to football that looks as if it has been devised on a blackboard, and associated fears that players are being moved around the pitch like pieces in a game of chess. In his university talk, Tuchel denied this was the case. 'The system is only the framework that enables individuality to function. It's not rigid, it's meant as guidance, to show where the opposition have problems, where they leave spaces for us, where they have players who don't do the right things tactically. It tells them where to attack and how. We provide those patterns and show them on video. We don't practise them much, really, we almost exclusively concentrate on our defensive movements in training. Our attacks arise from different patterns, at different times, against different opponents. It's important to be in those spaces, to give our players the opportunity to come to the fore as individuals, there and then. That's the reason why players have to be exactly where they can be their best as well.'

Tuchel can be considered a rule breaker, too, because he wants to continue to learn and innovate. During his sabbatical, he met with Matthew Benham in London, and they got on very well. For a while, Smartodds sent their statistical evaluations of Borussia Dortmund's performances to Tuchel. He was also one of the first coaches to show a keen interest in the Packing metric devised by Stefan Reinartz, having already taken on board the concept of Expected Goals and made it part of his coaching. He probably knows one or two other things about the game's machinations that most of his colleagues are yet to discover, which might explain why he's stopped doing interviews. He wants to guard his secrets in the same way that his teams tend to guard the ball at their feet.

MAKING DEAD BALLS DEADLIER

In a world of highly complex tactical schemes, there is also an ugly duckling that no one really cared about for a long time: set-pieces.

On average, a team takes five corners and ten free-kicks per game, eighteen throw-ins and eight goal-kicks. Between a fifth and a quarter of all goals in a season are scored from corners and free-kicks; in the 2017–18 Premier League season, dead balls accounted for 21 per cent of goals, penalties excluded. Taking account of stats from football played worldwide, teams score 0.3 goals per game on average from set-pieces.

Some sides who have specialised in corners, free-kicks and throw-ins do significantly better, however. The following table shows the teams in Europe who scored the most goals from dead balls as well as those who had the highest proportion of dead-ball goals in the 2017–18 season. In Portugal, one side managed to come out top in both criteria.

League	Team	Table	Set Piece Goals	Goals Total	% of Set Piece Goals
Bundesliga	Hertha BSC Berlin	10	14	43	33%
	FC Bayern	1	16	65	25%
Premier League	Bournemouth	12	16	45	36%
	WBA	20	12	31	39%
Serie A	Juventus	1	19	86	22%
	Benevento	20	12	33	36%
La Liga	Real Madrid	3	20	94	21%
	Girona	10	19	50	38%
Ligue 1	Monaco	2	16	85	19%
	Angers	14	12	42	29%
Portugal	Maritimo Funchal	6	17	34	50%

Source: whoscored.com

FC Bayern and Juventus were the two championship-winning teams who were also most proficient from set-pieces. As a basic rule, top teams tend to find the net more often from dead balls as they dominate games and are awarded significantly more corners and free-kicks in dangerous areas as a result of their pressure.

But there are also some more limited sides who eke out an advantage by focusing their efforts on set-pieces. French team Angers would probably have been relegated without their dead-ball expertise, and newly promoted La Liga club Girona might not have finished comfortably in mid-table either.

If goals conceded from non-open play are taken into account as well, the best overall set-piece team were Sporting Braga of Portugal. They scored sixteen times but only conceded three. Barcelona were no less impressive: their opponents managed one solitary goal from dead balls.

For underdogs deficient in technical quality in open play, set-pieces are one of the key weapons they can use to win points. Sole reliance on dead balls is unlikely to result in a sufficient number of matches won, however. Benevento (Italy) and West Bromwich Albion scored the highest proportion of their goals that way, but both still finished bottom of their respective leagues. In the previous campaign, West Brom had scored a remarkable 47 per cent of their goals from set-pieces. Their coach Tony Pulis and Sam Allardyce were among the first coaches in England to dedicate themselves to this discipline with a methodical approach. Pulis arguably went the furthest (and longest) when in charge of Stoke City from 2006 to 2013.

Everyone had considered the Potters a relegation certainty after their promotion in 2006. But Pulis confounded the doubters, not least by focusing on the plainer parts of the beautiful game. He not only turned corners and free-kicks into dangerous opportunities, but throw-ins, too. Few teams really spend too much time thinking about throw-ins, and some frequently suffer the consequences of their ignorance. But Stoke City created 53 shots on target after throw-ins in 2008–09 and found the net eight times.

The throw-ins were mostly launched by Irishman Rory Delap, a former javelin thrower blessed with tremendous upper body strength. He could catapult the ball 35 metres, right into the goal-mouth. Pulis made sure Delap's starting position was as close to the danger zone as possible – he had the pitch narrowed, down to the very minimum permissible under Premier League rules.

Since you can't be offside from throw-ins, they are harder to defend against; teams aren't able to simply keep a high line outside of their box, as has become customary with free-kicks. Pulis also made sure to overload the six-yard box to create as much chaos as possible right under the nose of the opposition keeper.

Away fans often trolled the home crowd with chants of 'You're only here for the throw-ins'. They had a point. 'Pulisball' was founded on the principle of playing as little football – in the sense of a passing game – as possible. Later engagements at other clubs showed that he deliberately put together squads to extract the most from dead-ball situations. He often let the grass in the Britannia Stadium grow a little longer than at other clubs, to slow down the passing game of technically superior clubs while his men usually played a long-ball game.

The ground's four open corners let in plenty of gusts. 'A wet and windy evening in Stoke' became shorthand for fancy dan top teams struggling to come to grips with gritty, old-fashioned English sides with a clear game plan. Arsenal, the Premier League's most aesthetically-minded side before the arrival of Pep Guardiola, suffered in particular.

Pulis' teams were never interested in pleasing the purists, but the sheer bloody-mindedness of his solution to the problem of not being the best in the business was quite ingenious. The stats from his time at West Bromwich Albion show that he stayed true to his brutalist vision and continued to be the league's number one dead-ball exponent.

Set-pieces have a bad reputation. Teams that focus on their perfect execution are seen as uncool, and there is a sense that corners and free-kicks are the domain of low-quality sides unable to score goals playing 'real football'. Even Sir Alex Ferguson, however, was well aware of the benefit of good dead balls in his last couple of seasons at Man Utd. In 2009–10 and 2010–11, his team had only scored 13 goals from corners and free-kicks per season. A year later, the success rate inched upwards to 18 and, in his final campaign before retirement, Sir Alex saw his men score 22 times from set-pieces. They were partly the reason why Ferguson departed as a league winner.

Midtjylland's title win as rank outsiders wouldn't have been possible without their specific expertise, and Atletico Madrid wouldn't have won the league in Spain in 2014 without their 18 dead-ball goals either. The goal that sealed the deal on the last day of the season and pipped the giants of the Spanish game, FC Barcelona and Real Madrid, to the number one spot in sensational fashion came from a corner.

The statistical importance of dead balls is such that football teams might be expected to devote a significant part of training to them. Curiously, they don't. Footballers hate practising set-pieces. They're bored by the amount of time spent standing around on the pitch, getting cold feet and becoming more injury-prone as a result. On top of that, a successful strategy for set-pieces needs a lot of careful preparation. You can see the odd choreographed run in the box, with players blocking defenders or impeding goalkeepers, but few teams take more than a passing interest.

However, at the 2018 World Cup in Russia, many national managers seemed to have put dead balls top of their agenda. Of the 169 goals scored at the tournament, 47 were from set-pieces. The rate of 28 per cent was the highest ever in the history of the competition. The success of some teams was largely down to their dead-ball strength. Uruguay and Colombia scored two thirds of their goals that way. Gareth Southgate's England only found the net three out of twelve times from open play. A further three goals came from penalties, the remaining six from corners and free-kicks.

A number of theories were put forward to explain this flood of dead-ball goals. Some suspected the newly introduced Video Assistant Referee (VAR) had clamped down on the pulling of shirts in the box in the run-up to free-kicks and corners. Increased supervision might have played a role but a bigger factor was probably the extra amount of time many coaches had spent on honing their set-pieces. Southgate and his staff, for example, had done thorough research and spoken to many club managers who were specialists in playing that way.

The previous World Cup in Brazil had already shown that there was much to be said for paying attention to the more static part of the game. For years, Germany's assistant coach Hansi Flick had tried and failed to convince Joachim Löw to practise set-pieces; the national manager's lack of interest had become a running joke. Things only changed in the pre-tournament training camp, with the introduction of a closed-session 'dead-ball competition'. The players were divided into two groups, given pen and paper and 15 minutes to come up with ideas. The procedure was regularly repeated in Brazil. Germany scored five times from set-pieces on their way to victory, more than any other side at the 2014 finals.

Iceland, too, found unprecedented success thanks to their dedication to football's basics. In the spring of 2017, I sat on the sofa of Heimir Hallgrímsson's living room on the island of Vestmannaeyjar. A violent storm loudly rattled the window frames as the Icelandic national manager told me that he had first started to look into dead balls when he worked as assistant to the Swedish national manager Lars Lagerbäck.

Set-pieces had to become even more of a priority for Hallgrímsson as manager of Iceland, one of world football's eternal minnows. There are only 300,000 inhabitants in the whole country, the equivalent of the population of Nottingham. Iceland has produced some top players, of which Everton's Gylfi Sigurdsson is currently the most gifted. But on the whole, the team's ability is not sufficient to dominate opponents with combination football. 'We know that we don't get many touches,' Hallgrímsson said. His side naturally specialised in counter-attacks and would only seldom attack the opposition goal in large numbers. With the help of dead balls, however, the playing field could be levelled, to an extent; Hallgrímsson understood that dead balls offered the greatest chance for inferior footballing sides to unnerve opposition defences.

'Players hate rehearsing set plays. Ours are no different. But they also know just how vital they are for us,' Hallgrímsson said. A large portion of his time with the team was spent on perfecting their execution. His dead balls became more sophisticated still after he had met Nicolas Jover at a football analytics conference in Barcelona. The Frenchman was giving a lecture on set-pieces in Ligue 1, having catalogued all variants and outcomes over the preceding years. 'We became friends. I was probably the only guy in the audience who enjoyed listening to the topic,' Hallgrímsson laughed. He had already worked on that aspect of the game for six years. But Jover opened his eyes: he found out why Midtjylland and Atletico were so successful from corners, free-kicks and throw-ins. 'They practised going for the second ball. I had never heard about that before in relation to set-pieces,' Hallgrímsson said. 'But after that, we started doing that, too.'

'Second balls' are ricochets or loose clearances that are there to be won. In the context of dead balls, teams rehearse different patterns of behaviour, depending on where the clearances are likely to fall, long or short, left or right. Second balls, by their very nature, are unpredictable. But the aim is to prepare the team to be ready for different eventualities.

Nicolas Jover had studied sports science and started out as an analyst at Montpellier HSC. He was part of the staff when the small club from the south of France upset the odds to win the league in 2012. At the time, Jover and his team of analysts looked at thousands of corners, free-kicks and throw-ins in Ligue 1. He loves talking about the subject in great detail and with much enthusiasm. Listening to him, you appreciate the fascinating hidden complexity of situations that appear rather banal to the untrained eye.

Fundamentally, he regards dead balls as a system of causal relationships that bears some structural similarity to chess. We might think a decent set-piece involves some form of choreographed run-up, followed by a cross and someone heading or shooting the ball into the net. You can add blocking a defender or cutting off a goalkeeper within the confines of the laws of the game, too. But Jover didn't simply want to do the equivalent work of American football, where running patterns and specific movements are part of a playbook and practised incessantly. Watching set-pieces with him, you discover a whole new world of possibilities.

Hallgrímsson introduced me to him at a conference in Germany. Jover asked me not to write about his ideas in too much detail. They were his trade secrets. He has since become – you guessed it – a full-time member of the Brentford staff. Before that, Benham's club had worked with Gianni Vio, the Italian who had increased the numbers of dead-ball goals at Catania and Fiorentina. Vio had moved on to Leeds United. Throw-in specialist Thomas Gronnemark, too, had worked for the Bees before moving on to teaching the players of Jürgen Klopp's Liverpool to throw the ball longer and better.

Jover was faced with an interesting dilemma at Griffin Park. He had to devise a set-piece strategy for a team that didn't play typical

Championship football. A squad built for a combination game lacked the tall, physical players needed for successful aerial combat. They could never get anywhere near the number of goals that Tony Pulis' giants were scoring.

Instead, Brentford players were supposed to read situations and draw the right conclusions. In order to achieve this aim, Jover was contractually entitled to work with the team for ten to fifteen minutes each day. For him, goal-kicks, throw-ins, free-kicks and corners were subject to the same principles as the modern football tactics we have described earlier: the challenge was to get players to appreciate the task at hand and provide them with possible answers. 'I dream of developing a recognisable style of set-pieces, just like a playing style,' Jover told me.

Jover loves bouncing ideas off Mads Buttgereit, who works in the same role at Brentford's partner club FC Midtjylland. With physically stronger players in their ranks, they nearly averaged one set-piece goal per game and probably wouldn't have won the league in 2015 and 2018 without that special capability. 'The more I think about what we're doing here, the clearer the advantages are to me,' captain Kristian Bach Bak told me during my visit in spring 2015. Getting the players fully on board was an important part of the process, he said, as corners and free-kicks weren't just about the right strategy but also about the right mentality: 'For us, every dead ball is a matter of life and death.' Sometimes, a game could turn on the determination of a man like Bak, who threw himself at every corner as if it was his last.

ADOPTING A
FRESH OUTLOOK

From snapshots to X-rays. The use of video footage revolutionised football in the past, while complex mathematical models help to analyse the game more profoundly today.

THE ART OF VIDEO ANALYSIS

That coaches are able to think about the set-pieces in such detail is only possible because of the modern ubiquity of video. As coach of Mainz 05, Thomas Tuchel studied videos of Pep Guardiola's Barcelona. The ability to watch other teams' games at will has helped managers to better appreciate their colleagues' ideas and develop their own. It's taken for granted now that every game is instantly available to watch online, but the history of scouting opposition teams was very different.

After Ottmar Hitzfeld became coach of Borussia Dortmund in 1991, he qualified three times for the UEFA Cup, twice competed in the newly founded Champions League and won the European Cup in 1997. The flurry of European fixtures posed a problem, however.

Hitzfeld and his assistant Michael Henke knew very little about their opponents. There was no internet at the time. German television only showed highlights of foreign leagues. They could go on scouting trips to watch those teams in person but the insight afforded by a random game or two was strictly limited. There was also no way to show members of the staff or the team any footage afterwards.

One Borussia Dortmund team had already found a solution to that specific problem, however. The club's women's handball team were among the best sides in Germany in the 1990s and successful in Europe, too. In preparation for international fixtures, their coach had instructed sports science students to edit video material that they had painstakingly acquired from abroad.

Michael Henke was thrilled. He asked BVB's handball analyst Markus Schulz to put together similar videos of the foreign football teams Dortmund came up against. Shortly after, the two of them founded a company called Sports Analytics, to become pioneers of video analysis in Germany.

Similar developments were taking place in other footballing nations. Many players still shudder at the thought of the never-ending, torturous video viewings in those years, when entire games would be shown, or the tape would be manually fast-forwarded to the important moments. Relief came in the shape of a second VCR: assistant coaches learned to edit and copy only the scenes relevant for the tactical briefing of their players, or for the analysis of the strengths and weaknesses of opposition teams.

At the turn of the century, Sports Analytics secured the right to film Bundesliga games with their own cameras. Most managers had realised that regular TV footage offered an incomplete view of the game. Sports Analytics set up additional cameras that captured the entire playing field and therefore gave a much better sense of the teams' tactics.

A Bundesliga coach sitting on the team bus on the way home from an away game was suddenly able to watch the match back on a CD-ROM on his laptop. A few years later, he would receive an email with a data code, making it even easier for him to zoom in on defining situations, to concentrate on corners or on his side's misplaced passes in their own half.

No other technological invention has influenced football as much as VCRs have over the last quarter of a century. Coaches found it much easier to learn from their best colleagues and analyse their own games. They could show players what they were doing right or wrong rather than simply talk about it. Visual learning engendered great improvement across the board. What's more, no one ever went into matches blindly any more, not knowing what to expect. Players could literally see what type of opponent and patterns of play they were up against in advance.

Michael Henke was appointed chief analyst at FC Bayern by Jürgen Klinsmann in 2008. Part of his work was done under the roof, on the sixth floor of the Allianz Arena, with a perfect view of the pitch. During games, he and a young analyst called Michael Niemeyer sat there, in a kind of gallery. With the use of digital editing equipment, they could cut up important moments and send them down to the dressing room in time for the manager's half-time talk. At the time, no other Bundesliga club had the same capability.

Niemeyer, born in Munich in 1976, had done plenty of other things before landing upon football analysis. He had studied sports science, art and photography. 'But it's not important what kind of degree you have or how high up you've played yourself,' he told me at a meeting in Berlin. 'What matters are the managers you get to work with.'

Today, Niemeyer is Head of Department Match Analysis at Bayern, with a staff of eight. He believes he got very lucky having had the best possible mentors. After starting out under Michael Henke and Bayern's long-term head scout Wolfgang Dremmler, he worked for Louis van Gaal, one of the trailblazers of game analysis. The Dutchman made it an integral part of his coaching as early as the mid 1990s. There are few coaches who have worked as systematically and structurally over the last two decades.

Videos were a crucial tool in the development of Van Gaal's teams. In Max Reckers, he employed a specialist for IT and visual analysis years before some of the biggest clubs in the world had even thought about doing so. On Van Gaal's orders, Bayern began recording all training sessions, plus game analysis with team and match preparations, in 2009. The club has become a visual library of football wisdom in the ensuing decade. Anyone working there could and can study the ways of Van Gaal, Jupp Heynckes, Pep Guardiola and Carlo Ancelotti. Four of the best managers in recent times, they have very different strengths and ideas of how they want the game to be played.

Niemeyer is full of compliments for each and every one of those greats. But working with Guardiola was the biggest thrill of all for him. 'Pep took meetings that lasted for hours. With us analysts and with the players. They were a footballing epiphany for me. He's all about finding a way to get into the box and to create superiority, with a position game. He would think things through for hours on end, sometimes throughout the night, discussing it with the analysis team. He would watch games himself as well, to come up with ideas for a strategy. Perhaps some work was done twice that way, but it was necessary.'

Guardiola is representative of a type of management that would be inconceivable without video technology. His habit of holing himself up with videos of games and going incommunicado for hours in search of tactical solutions, even against more mundane opponents, has become part of the mythology that surrounds him. Niemeyer feels that he has changed the job description of a football manager in the process. 'For me, a good coach is also an analyst. After working with the kind of brilliant teachers that we have had, you, as an analyst, start thinking like a coach, too. Not in the sense that I will direct players to do some exercises from the touchline or explain to them how they should cross the ball – but in the way you understand the game.' There's a clear trend towards roles converging: analysts have to think like coaches and increasingly work with coaches who work like analysts themselves.

Today's top managers and their staff have access to footage from all of their own games and those of their opponents. Yesterday's dearth of information has become a flood of noughts and zeros. The biographies of successful managers often detail periods of fanatical video study. Klopp was no different to Guardiola and Tuchel in that regard, and the Swabian was also the first man on German television to bring his tactical insights to the attention of millions of viewers during the 2006 World Cup, when he worked as a TV pundit. Other Premier League coaches – Mauricio Pochettino, Unai Emery and Sean Dyche – are advocates of extensive video sessions, too. Without the help of this technological tool, they would have become different kinds of coaches, reliant on their eyes and perception, or that of their assistants. Tuchel would probably not have emerged as a rule breaker. Or not in the same way, in any case.

Guardiola could certainly not have revolutionised football without having watched thousands of hours of games either. The ubiquity of video material hasn't just had a transformative impact on management but on football itself. 'You can see that coaches like Pep, Tuchel and many others who work in that vein have made the game more tactical,' Niemeyer said. The public's interest in the theoretical side of the game has grown as well.

In 2010, Michael Cox set up a website called zonalmarking. net. He sat at home in front of a television screen with a magnetic blackboard and tried to appreciate what was happening on the pitch on a tactical level. Afterwards, he wrote down his observations and analyses and found that people wanted to read them. Zonal Marking became a big success in a short space of time – the site's popularity showed that many supporters were keen to learn more about that side of the game. But there's a different way to look at it, too. Football teams were at last playing the kind of complex, multi-layered game interesting enough to warrant deciphering in 2,000-word pieces.

A year later, a bunch of German obsessives were inspired by Zonal Marking to start their own tactics website, spielverlagerung. de and there was a similar project in the Netherlands. The guys – for it is invariably guys – behind these sites are often derided as nerds and their work gets dismissed as niche or smart-arsed in some quarters. Perhaps that's to do with some blog entries suggesting that tactics were the only, or most important, decisive factor in a game. But the emergence of popular tactics analysis also proves that the perception of the game has changed and become much more intricate.

Some supporters still vent their anger at 'cowardly' players 'not wanting it enough' on the pitch, of course, but almost nobody would seriously insist any longer that tactics were unimportant or subordinate in football. As the coverage of the sport has become more varied and deep-layered thanks to self-publishing, the conversation has changed: it will, for example, now include criticism of a manager who has picked the wrong formation and let the opponent dominate the midfield at will with an extra man or two. That is not to say that mentality or a lack of commitment can or should always be ruled out as an explanation. But many followers of the game are increasingly prepared to look past the metaphysical and instead at positions, passing lanes and pressing patterns. 'Football is not about players, or at least not just about players; it is about shape and about space, about the intelligent deployment of players and their movement within that deployment,' Jonathan Wilson writes in *Inverting the Pyramid*, a book on the history of tactics.

But how can all of that be represented in numbers? How can data help to find answers to tactical questions and help to understand events on the pitch more precisely?

THE BIG DATA HANGOVER

March 2017. It's cold in Boston. Icy winds have blown in from Canada and rush past the houses. I put up my collar as I cross the street. It's a welcome relief to enter the John B. Hynes Veterans Memorial Convention Center, having scurried across from the sports bar opposite. Once inside, I collect my accreditation for the MIT Sloan Sports Conference.

The seats at the front are taken up by punters wearing Boston Bruins jerseys: the local ice hockey team's game is live on television. But there's a more convivial atmosphere at the back, where Howard Hamilton is welcoming his guests wearing the black and red colours of Atlanta United, the newly founded Major League Soccer team. The giant of a man, almost shy in his gentleness, hosts the annual global meeting of football analytics.

There's Zach Slaton, a former mechanical engineer who writes about football stats for ESPN and *Forbes*. He's next to Chris Anderson and his colleague, David Sally. Both are talking to Ted Knutson, co-founder of the influential statsbomb website. Knutson used to work for Matthew Benham in the analytics department of Smartodds but is now providing services to other clients. Daniel Stenz has travelled from Canada. The German was assistant coach at second division Union Berlin before working as Head of Scouting and Analysis for the Vancouver Whitecaps and in a similar role for the Hungarian Football Association. A few months later, he would be appointed Technical Director at one of China's biggest football clubs, the Super League side SD Luneng.

Raúl Peláez Blanco, Head of Sport Technology Innovation at FC Barcelona, pops in and soon leaves again. But Padraig Smith, Sporting Director of the Colorado Rapids, is engaged in a lengthy discussion with Hamilton, who holds a PhD in Aeronautics and Astronautics from Stanford University and used to work for the space and military industries. He was one of the first Americans interested in quantitative analysis of football and founded a company called Soccermetrics in 2009.

The mood is relaxed and the beers keep coming. But in truth, this is a crisis meeting in all but name. Many participants are worried that they might have taken up the wrong career. A decade ago, when giant data sets were available for the first time and football became quantifiable, the future seemed to belong to them. Every shot, every pass, every run could be recorded. Chris Anderson had not been the only one dreaming about revolutionising football through data analysis in this room, one suspects.

On this freezing cold evening, though, more pressing questions took priority. Will we be able to earn a living with football in the coming years? Will those in charge of football today ever let outsiders have a say – the mathematicians, physicists, economists and pollsters who know how to handle numbers but have never kicked a ball professionally?

The following two days in Boston can either be seen as greatly encouraging or deeply disheartening for the football analysts community. Almost 4,000 people cram into the hallways of the Convention Center to attend panel discussions on subjects like 'The Future of Basketball Analysis', 'Data-based Storytelling' or 'Quantifying Injury Risk'.

The MIT Sloan Sports Analytics Conference was first hosted in 2006. Only a few freaks descended onto the Sloan School of Management within the Massachusetts Institute of Technology campus at the time. Today, the event is a gigantic mix of a scientific congress, a sales fair, shows and TED Talk-style lectures. The genre's stars such as Billy Beane, Daryl Morey (Houston Rockets) or stats guru Nate Silver command audiences of up to 2,000 people. The crowd's excitement mirrors that at a rock concert.

Football is only one of the fringe acts, however: the most important panel on 'soccer' is scheduled at the same time as the conference's most popular event with Beane and Morey.

The cautiously titled 'Juggling Expectations: The Emergence of Soccer Analytics' talk isn't exactly oversubscribed. Only 250 people have turned up. With the exception of FC Barcelona, none of the big European clubs attend. On the stage, spirits are dampened. 'Football clubs are hyper-engaged when it comes to signing players and managers, but not analysts. That will change,' says Ted Knutson, one of the most important voices in the field. It's not quite clear whether that's a prediction or more of a prayer.

The whole community hasn't quite overcome the big data hangover that set in after the short-lived frenzy.

Football's transformation into a game of numbers started with the founding of Prozone in 1995 in Leeds. It has since become part of the American corporation STATS. Prozone was initially called Professional Zone. Its hardware consisted of 22 massage armchairs, lined up in a container on Derby County's training ground. Each morning at 10:30, the players would sit down to get their muscles loosened by the electrical impulses in the seats, while an assistant coach called Steve McClaren – yes, the future England national team manager – showed them a few clips from games.

From those humble beginnings, an idea was born: Prozone founder Ram Mylvaganam wanted to find ways of cracking the game's secrets that were not dependent on video. He bought a quarter of the shares of French company Video Sports, who had developed one of the earliest tracking programs. In order to capture the players' movements, eight heat-sensitive cameras were installed at Pride Park. They were supposed to convert actions into numbers. But the technology didn't work at first. The cameras lost the players or missed out on certain moments. Prozone had to rewrite the software.

'Nevertheless, it was groundbreaking. We statistically defined a football game,' Mylvaganam told a reporter of *Wired* magazine. Sports Universal Process, a French company that had brought its trading technology to market in 1996, can claim to have started the revolution, too. But irrespective of who digitally captured the first shot, football was about to change.

There had been no systematic collection of game data at all before. Obsessives like legendary Wing Commander Charles Reep wrote down tally charts in notebooks, and sports science students watched back videos and counted certain actions. There is no way of knowing today how many times Manchester United shot on goal at home to

Liverpool in the 1982–83 season. We don't know how many passes Diego Maradona played in his best-ever season at Napoli, and what kind of Expected Goals rating Pelé clocked up at Santos FC. Billy Bremner's win percentage for tackles is a mystery, as is the average number of kilometres run per game by Paul Gascoigne.

Tracking technology, for all its initial bugs, made that type of information available. In early 1999, Steve McClaren became assistant to Sir Alex Ferguson at Manchester United and was allowed to continue his work with Prozone. The company had their first client willing to pay for their data. The timing of that breakthrough couldn't have been more auspicious: United were having the best season in their history, winning the treble of Champions League, Premier League and FA Cup.

Within 18 months, six clubs from England's top flight employed Prozone's services. Sam Allardyce, then in charge of Bolton Wanderers, used the data to make football history.

'Big Sam' had played for Tampa Bay Rowdies at the end of his career in the 1980s. He had been fascinated about the wide-scale use of technology in the US at the time. Inspired by the Americans, he developed a data-based playing style that he hoped would help Wanderers survive in the Premier League following their re-promotion in 2001.

Allardyce and his analysts developed a model they called 'The Fantastic Four'. It was based on four pillars. They had calculated that they needed to keep at least 16 clean sheets in 38 matches. They knew that they had a 70 per cent chance of winning if they took the lead. They also knew that dead balls accounted for up to a third of all goals and were more dangerous if they were played towards the opposition goal, as so-called inswingers. Bolton practised free-kicks and corners extensively, and employed throw-ins, too, to create havoc in the box. Finally, the numbers had told them that there was an 80 per cent chance of at least drawing a game if your own team ran a greater combined distance during the match at a speed above 19.8 miles per hour. These four principles didn't translate into a wildly attractive playing style. But they made the unfashionable club from Greater Manchester fantastically successful in relative terms. Between 2003 and 2007 they regularly finished in the top eight of the table and twice qualified for the UEFA Cup.

Since 2005, comprehensive game data has been aggregated in all of the top divisions. Interest in the new information was at first bigger in England and Germany than in Italy and Spain.

In his book *The Mixer*, Michael Cox noted that passing accuracy in the Premier League rose from 70 per cent in 2003–04 to 81 per cent a decade later. In the first three campaigns of that period, the rate of successful passes only went up by 1 per cent, but in the final two, it improved by 6 per cent. Cox found that managers at the time were talking a lot about increasing the number of good passes, in an attempt to emulate Barcelona. In his autobiography, Manchester United's Rio Ferdinand derided David Moyes, Sir Alex's successor, for demanding a certain quantity of passes. 'He'd say: "Today I want us to have 600 passes in the game. Last week it was only 400." Who cares? I'd rather score five goals from ten passes.' Ferdinand's dismissive reaction somewhat belied his deep understanding of the game. But it showed what happened when freshly acquired knowledge suddenly became prescriptive for behaviour.

Data changed the game by making its main components countable, comparable and factually debatable. The new numbers influenced the playing as well as the perception of the game. But at the same time, there was scepticism, especially when managers and technical directors found that data wasn't necessarily accurate nor objective. Data has the potential to intimidate because its figures seem unassailable. There's a real danger that their relevance is over-estimated; not just in football. But knowledge of the numbers' weaknesses shouldn't have us discount them too quickly, either.

One of the problems of football data that hasn't quite been solved yet is its non-uniformity. The numbers are accumulated in different ways and aren't always wholly reliable. Automatic tracking, for example, at times needed human follow-up work because the heat-sensitive cameras couldn't distinguish players in a cluster. Data input by spotters making digital notes of events in stadiums or in front of TV screens was very faulty in the beginning and probably still is. At the 2018 World Cup in Russia, FIFA were surprised to find different data providers delivering wholly different numbers for the same match. At Brazil vs Mexico, bizarrely, three divergent figures were recorded for the Mexicans' running stats: 93.01km, 97.01km and 104.7km.

Different providers also employ different definitions for their data. The consequences of these discrepancies are considerable. A symposium of analysts could spend days debating what constitutes a won tackle, to name but one contentious issue.

Further to these technical problems there's a more fundamental one, as the data set below shows. These numbers originate from a momentous game everyone remembers. Have a friend look at them and make them guess at the result. You're likely to win a bet that they will get it badly wrong.

	Team A	Team B
Possession	52%	48%
Passes into the 18-Yard Box	19	11
Crosses	22	10
Corners	7	5
Dangerous Attacks	55	34
Tackles Won	5	1
Lost Balls	69	76
Shots	18	14
Shots on Target	13	12
Goals	?	?

Instinctively, one would suspect Team A to have emerged as clear winners. They were on top in all parameters, and in some of them, by quite a margin. Knowing of the importance of randomness in football, you might arrive at a more cautious reading. Might it have been a draw or a narrow victory for Team B?

No, that's wide of the mark, too. The data in question is from one of the most sensational results in football's history: the semi-final between hosts Brazil and eventual World Cup winners Germany in 2014. Joachim Löw's side won 7–1 in Belo Horizonte. Never before had the hosts of a World Cup been beaten this badly. A semi-final had never seen such a one-sided result before. Triumphant Germany, incidentally, were Team B though – statistically inferior in all the so-called 'Key Performance Indicators'. The upshot was both obvious and unsettling: those numbers weren't key at all when it came to predicting success. At least not in their present form.

Even professional analysts arrived at the same conclusion. After the 2014 World Cup, I spoke to Christofer Clemens, Head Analyst of the German national team, about the role data analysis had played in lifting the cup. His answer was remarkably blunt. 'We, as analysts, disregarded almost everything that we had looked at in previous years, from time spent on the ball to the number of vertical passes and so on,' he said. 'We're increasingly convinced that there's a lack of data that provides real information about the things that make you successful in football.'

Clemens' admission is surprising. He's in no way a data sceptic; on the contrary, he's among the best analysts in Germany and has as much experience in the use of video and data analysis as anyone in the world. After graduating in sports science in Oslo, Clemens had worked with Norwegian national team manager Egil Olsen, a man with an affinity to sports technology. He returned to Germany in 2001 to take a job at the German branch of French company Sports Universal Process, who were the first to offer a functioning tracking system for the German market, along with Amisco.

Soon, it was easy to see how many accurate passes were played in the final third, how much average time players spent between two intensive runs or how many passes a team needed, on average, to score a goal. Fitness coaches in particular benefited from data that enabled them to scrutinise a player's physical condition.

The use of numbers for that side of the game has become widely accepted practice. The fact that someone suddenly runs less or sprints less frequently is a strong indicator of a problem. Being able to quantify physical exploits in training and during games has markedly improved a coach's ability to determine the right workload in practice sessions and to strike a balance between keeping fitness levels high and the risk of injury at a minimum.

Perhaps the application of data in this specific field found quick acceptance because the people in charge were sports scientists well versed in working with numbers. Head coaches probably appreciated the advantage of having fit players at their disposal as well.

The data's usability for devising successful strategies with the ball and tactics was less clear-cut, however.

Clemens, along with Stefan Reinartz and Jens Hegeler, the two pros we met at the start of this book, weren't the only ones who had noticed an obvious disconnection between the numbers and success.

In the 2016–17 Bundesliga season, teams coming out on top in the categories on the left won the following percentage of games that didn't end in a draw:

More possession	in 54 per cent
More duels won	in 56 per cent
Longer distance run	in 60 per cent
More shots	in 61 per cent
More chances	in 75 per cent

Source: Impect

Two years after the World Cup in Brazil, I met Clemens once more at a workshop for national team coaches. His view of football data had only become more negative in the meantime. 'All usable data only illustrates the game retrospectively,' he said. 'It describes what happened and is basically so superficial that we cannot make any predictions based on it. We cannot use it to draw up an idea for developing players in a specific way or to come up with concrete instructions. It tells us nothing of relevance about a player, about success or the impact of a strategy.'

Clemens' honesty was all the more striking considering that Löw himself had partially explained the national team's success story in terms of data. In the winter of 2010, for example, he had offered a statistical recap of his side's performances that year: 'We have committed the fewest fouls of all national teams. We won the most balls in direct duels and took the quickest shots. Contact times on the ball were of the highest level. In 2005, it took 2.8 seconds on average between controlling the ball and playing it. Our game had been slow and was going wide a lot, losing a lot of time. In 2008 at the Euros, we were down to 1.8 seconds, in 2010 we went to 1.1 seconds. Against England and Argentina, we were below one second. Only Spain were slightly better...'

Löw didn't mention any results in his annual report, even though he easily could have: Germany had come third in the World Cup in South Africa, playing spectacular stuff at times. Instead, he mentioned performance indicators such as the number of fouls or contact times. *My work has been measurably good, independent of wins or defeats*, Löw was really saying. He was able to do that because the general view of the game had evolved.

And yet, Clemens was right of course. Löw's data summary was merely retrospective, too. Germany's chief analyst seemed to suggest that much of his own work had been in vain: the data did not produce a guide to becoming successful. Had everybody been caught up in the digital hype; had the data bubble burst? Clemens shook his head. 'No. But what matters is generating data that is not obvious.' To put it differently: things were about to get more complicated still.

FROM TALLY SHEETS TO ALGORITHMS

Colin Trainor hadn't just been interested in the amount of bad luck Jürgen Klopp's Dortmund had suffered in their poor first half of the 2014–15 season. He wanted to discover why one of Europe's top sides had become embroiled in a relegation struggle. A deep dive into the numbers was to provide answers.

As we have seen, the definition of 'data' in football is inexact and therefore potentially misleading. There are simple statistics – goals, shots, passes – that can easily be tallied up with pen and paper, or by logging them electronically. Other numbers already need precise definitions to be comparable; not everybody agrees on what constitutes a tackle or dribbling, for example. At the most complex end of the spectrum, we find values derived from calculations and mathematical models, like Expected Goals. Data analysis in football becomes more layered as the data itself appears more extensive and the metrics for the calculations get more complex.

For his analysis of BVB's horrific run of results, Trainor developed a new category, looking at a shot's trajectory. He called it 'After Shot Expected Goals'. If shots were blocked or went wide of the target, they were rated as zero – they had in fact been worthless. If they went towards sections of the goal that made it difficult for the keeper, on the other hand, they were garnered a high rating. Looking at all the finishes through that specific prism reduced the initial Expected Goals figure of 25. But Borussia should have still scored 21 goals rather than the 18 that they had in fact mustered.

Since Dortmund had been wasteful with their shooting opportunities, Trainor examined the quality of the finishing by players who had shot at goal more than 12 times. The results were a little depressing. Trainor had come up with a formula that ranked players according to their inability to score goals.

Henrikh Mkhitaryan was the unfortunate league leader in that respect. The Armenian had attempted 33 shots in the first half of the 2014–15 season and not found the net once. He was the only player in the Bundesliga with more than 21 shots who had failed to score. Trainor's calculations also showed that the attacking midfielder's shots were below average in quality. They should have resulted in 2.24 goals in terms of position, but since many had been blocked or missed the target by a huge margin, that number was reduced by two thirds. Ciro Immobile, signed for a lot of money as the main goalscorer, was almost as bad as everyone else, finishing-wise. Only the shots of Marco Reus and those of Pierre-Emerick Aubameyang were more dangerous in practice than statistically expected.

Player	Shots	Goals	xG	After Shot xG	Deviation
Aubameyang	50	5	5.04	6.37	1.33
Mkhitaryan	34	0	2.24	0.76	–1.48
Immobile	31	3	4.10	3.63	–0.47
Reus	29	3	2.46	3.25	0.79
Ramos	18	2	2.90	1.73	–1.17
Kagawa	16	1	1.40	0.81	–0.59
Schmelzer	14	0	0.42	0.11	–0.31
Gündogan	14	1	0.93	0.90	–0.03
Jojic	14	0	0.67	0.52	–0.15
Großkreutz	13	0	1.05	0.51	–0.54

Source: Colin Trainor

The reduction of BVB's shot quality was evident in their lower goal ratio. It had gone down by 2 per cent in relation to the previous campaign. Yet only Bayern Munich and Bayer Leverkusen had shot at goal more often. Dortmund's tally was even higher than it had been when they won the double two seasons before. But their shots had rarely gone in. Across the Bundesliga, only 1. FC Köln and Paderborn, who ended up getting relegated, had achieved a lower success ratio.

Season	Shots per game	Goal ratio
2012–13	15.9	10.6%
2013–14	17.8	10.3%
first half of season 2014–15	16.9	8.3%

* without penalties

Source: Opta

Trainor found a preliminary explanation for the lower rate of success in the average distance of the shots from goal: it had gone up by almost a metre in comparison to the previous campaign.

To be sure, there is no direct link between average shooting distance and sporting success, Bayern's dominance in all three seasons notwithstanding. At Leverkusen, the drastic change reflected the playing philosophy of new coach Roger Schmidt, who wanted his team to finish quickly rather than move into better positions with a patient passing game. In principle, however, the probability of scoring goes up as shots gets closer to goal. Dortmund, though, were taking their shots from further and further away.

Club	2012–13	2013–14	first half of season 2014–15
FC Bayern	16.21 m	16.36 m	16.31 m
Eintracht Frankfurt	19.33 m	17.40 m	16.37 m
Mainz 05	19.43 m	17.77 m	16.92 m
Hannover 96	17.60 m	18.30 m	16.97 m
Schalke 04	17.01 m	17.64 m	17.44 m
VfB Stuttgart	18.44 m	19.16 m	17.57 m
Hamburger SV	19.32 m	20.46 m	17.71 m
Hertha BSC	2. Liga	17.89 m	17.86 m
SC Freiburg	18.19 m	18.71 m	18.29 m
Borussia Dortmund	17.42 m	17.88 m	18.86 m
Werder Bremen	18.93 m	17.65 m	19.12 m
SC Paderborn	2. Liga	2. Liga	19.16 m
VfL Wolfsburg	18.20 m	19.54 m	19.30 m
Borussia M'gladbach	20.28 m	19.06 m	19.50 m
FC Augsburg	20.36 m	19.84 m	19.83 m
TSG Hoffenheim	22.96 m	21.98 m	19.97 m
Bayer 04 Leverkusen	17.26 m	18.27 m	21.56 m
1. FC Köln	2. Liga	2. Liga	22.43 m

Source: Opta

To get to the bottom of the Black and Yellows' problem with reduced shot quality, Trainor compared individual stats from the bad first half of 2014–15 with the distinctly better previous year. His findings indicated what every football supporter would have known without recourse to the complicated shooting metrics: the departure of Robert Lewandowski to Bayern had left a whole the size of a crater. And none of the new arrivals had been able to fill it.

According to Trainor, Lewandowski had combined 'a fairly good shot volume with terrific shot quality', and his Expected Goals per shot rarely changed from season to season. It had been no different for Ciro Immobile in Italy, albeit from a lower starting point. 'Players have individual tendencies,' he wrote, 'the positions they take up, the runs they make and the awareness to be in the right place at the right time.' His view corresponded with Omar Chaudhuri's analysis of Cristiano Ronaldo's finishing.

If the stats are anything to go by, Dortmund had been right to sign Adrian Ramos from Hertha Berlin. Unfortunately, the Colombian played very little, while Immobile's shot quality was almost a third worse than Lewandowski's.

When I met Peter Krawietz in the summer of 2017 to talk about Dortmund's travails that season, Klopp's assistant was still coming to terms with that awful series of results. He was very animated and extremely self-critical. Krawietz refused to point the finger at Lewandowski's move to Munich and Immobile's poor performances. 'Losing Lewandowski was massive, of course. Our game had been very much tailor-made for him, and we had developed automatisms. You could rely on him scoring. When you have such an ideal type of

first half of season 2014-15					2013-14			
Shots*	Player	xG per shot	xG per 90 minutes		Shots*	Player	xG per shot	xG per 90 minutes
50	Aubameyang	0.101	0.319		112	Lewandowski	0.162	0.565
34	Mkhitaryan	0.066	0.207		104	Reus	0.081	0.333
30	Immobile	0.111	0.427		71	Mkhitaryan	0.092	0.234
29	Reus	0.085	0.369		64	Aubameyang	0.112	0.317
18	Ramos	0.161	0.383		54	Sahin	0.065	0.111
16	Kagawa	0.088	0.157		30	Großkreutz	0.059	0.055
14	Gündogan	0.067	0.136		21	Hummels	0.160	0.150
14	Schmelzer	0.030	0.068		21	Sokratis	0.087	0.070

* without penalties

Source: Colin Trainor, Statsbomb

striker, you try to replace him with a similar type. But the coaching staff also have to be ready to change certain things and to react in various ways to the situation at hand.' In other words: Dortmund had signed a very different type of centre-forward in Immobile, but the team had continued to play the same football as they had done with Lewandowski up front.

Krawietz's point was not that BVB would have been better off leaving their old ways behind. On the contrary. 'We, as coaches, have our idea of football and of playing the game. The aim is to defend actively. We want to win, we have to score goals, we need to have the ball. And scoring goals gets easier the earlier you win back the ball – that's not up for debate.'

But Dortmund weren't winning back the ball early any more. At least not as early and as often as before. Trainor was able to demonstrate the size of their regression with a new metric he called PPDA: passes per defensive action.

'My day job has taught me to approach things in a systematic and logical manner,' he told me. 'When I hear someone say: "That team plays a good pressing game," I wonder how that can be measured and be made comparable.' That's how he arrived at PPDA, adopting Opta's definitions for types of defensive actions – tackles, challenges (failed tackles), interceptions and fouls – for his model.

The PPDA value offered a sense of the degree of aggression with which a team without possession was attacking the ball in the first 60 metres of the pitch starting from the opponent's goal. A smaller PPDA number signified greater defensive intensity, as the attacking team were unable to play many uncontested passes.

This is where it gets interesting as far as Dortmund were concerned. Pressing was one of the central tenets of Klopp's tactical dogma at Signal Iduna Park. After defeat in the 2013 Champions League final against Bayern, the Swabian had promised that he would build 'a new team, a new pressing machine'.

The figures from the first half of 2014–15 told a different story. The intensity of Dortmund's pressing had dropped in comparison to the season before. On average, opponents were allowed to play one more pass before Dortmund's strikers or midfielders put pressure on the ball.

Dortmund's decreasing intensity 'against the ball' was made all the more crucial by the fact that they would have needed the ball more often than before. They were leading for far less time in games and thus could have done with more possession.

	PPDA	% of Time leading
2012–13	8.76	51%
2013–14	8.72	40%
2014–15	9.59	25%

Source: Colin Trainor, Statsbomb

Krawietz told me he wasn't overly interested in game data. 'In the last few years I did look at our number of passes, however, to check on our playing style.' In a really good game, a dominant Klopp team (Dortmund then, Liverpool now) play up to 600 passes. More passes, he added, didn't mean a better performance but probably a lack of solutions and sterile possession. 'And if you put in 15 crosses from the right and two from the left, there's a problem – probably on the left,' Krawietz laughed.

He had never heard of PPDA. The concept made sense to him immediately, but he cautioned that the value would be affected by individual match tactics. 'Sometimes you say: "Today we're going for it, really high up the pitch." But there are also games where the scouting of the opposition and the match preparation determine that you let the other side play three passes before you press them, in areas where they aren't comfortable on the ball or don't cover the spaces sufficiently.'

Krawietz believes Dortmund's 2014 malaise was more accurately reflected in the many early goals they conceded. As mentioned before, they had suffered the earliest goal in Bundesliga history, going behind after a mere nine seconds against Bayer Leverkusen.

'It can happen, but that should really be it for the rest of the season. For us, it became a kind of pattern. We're talking about attitude, about being awake, about what happens before kick-off and the kind of energy levels you go into a game with.' He felt that Germany winning the World Cup in 2014 was an important factor in that respect. Five Dortmund players had been part of Löw's squad in Brazil, but only Mats Hummels had played regularly. Erik Durm, Kevin Großkreutz, Matthias Ginter and keeper Roman Weidenfeller didn't feature a single minute between them at the competition.

'What happened in their heads, how did they feel? They had achieved a fantastic feat, the greatest possible. But our boys had mostly been in Brazil to make up the numbers in training and ensure the mood was good in the dressing room. What kind of pressure did they feel under as a result? How are things back in the Bundesliga, when opponents go into the game saying, "World Cup winners? We'll show you what's what." No one ever talked about that. But it was there.'

To examine who was pressing less than in the previous season, Trainor compared the amount of times BVB started defensive action in the opposition half. Players had to have played at least 40 per cent of all games and to be positioned at least 45 metres away from their own goal – keepers and defenders were excluded from the analysis. The table opposite lists players who were furthest forward in descending order.

One thing that's obvious: Robert Lewandowski wasn't just a huge loss as a goalscorer. The Pole was also badly missed for his high amount of defensive work. His successor Ciro Immobile was barely half as active, while the other new signing in attack, Adrian Ramos, was a much better fit but didn't get enough game time. Shinji Kagawa, the returnee from Manchester United, wasn't doing much pressing. Henrikh Mkhitaryan's number of defensive actions collapsed in relation to his previous season, and Nuri Sahin, who had done really well in the pressing stakes in 2013–14, only played seven minutes due to injury. Marco Reus, too, wasn't available to hassle opposition defenders on the ball. He was kept out by injury.

But could the collective drop in pressing activity perhaps be explained by opposition teams adapting to Dortmund's style and keeping the ball for less time in their own half? No, it couldn't. The variance was a mere 1 per cent compared to the previous season.

first half of season 2014-15					2013-14			
Player	Defensive actions opposition half	Minutes played	Defensive actions opposition half per 90 minutes		Player	Defensive actions opposition half	Minutes played	Defensive actions opposition half per 90 minutes
Immobile	13	703	1.66		Lewandowski	103	2,898	3.20
Ramos	28	682	3.70		Reus	58	2,281	2.29
Aubameyang	34	1,424	2.15		Aubameyang	58	2,029	2.57
Kagawa	15	807	1.67		Mkhitaryan	119	2,511	4.27
Mkhitaryan	26	975	2.40		Großkreutz	57	2,898	1.77
Großkreutz	22	954	2.05		Sahin	124	2,865	3.90
Piszczek	21	1,365	1.38		Schmelzer	33	1,640	1.81
Durm	17	1,085	1.41		Piszczek	21	1,454	1.30
Kehl	29	1,109	2.35		Durm	24	1,440	1.50
Bender	29	986	2.65		Bender	57	1,411	3.64

Source: Opta/Trainor

'We work hard for nothing and the opponent doesn't have to do much to score against us, that's the situation,' Klopp lamented at the time. More precisely, his team were less effective than in the season before but got a lot less fortunate still, while Dortmund's opponents got luckier. They scored with 15 per cent of their shots – no team in the league conceded a higher percentage; and 6.3 per cent of shots from outside the box found BVB's net, almost double the league average of 3.6 per cent.

Unsurprisingly, Klopp's men ended up with 26 in the 'against' column at Christmas, instead of the 17 goals they would have expected to concede according to Trainor's calculations.

Goalkeepers playing poorly were a significant part of the problem. Dortmund's No.1 Roman Weidenfeller was beaten 18 times; Trainor's 'After Shot Expected Goals' model only predicted 13.2 goals. Weidenfeller's weakness had Klopp swap the veteran for Mitch Langerak in November. The Australian failed to stem the tide, however. Statistically, he played even worse than his team-mate. Langerak conceded seven goals whereas Trainor expected 4.2.

Krawietz understandably refused to discuss individual performances. For him, a combination of separate issues had come together to make for one awful, frustrating experience. While the conversation with him provided background information on the reasons for Dortmund's game malfunctioning, Trainor's metrics showed up the shortcomings in cold, hard numbers.

It would have been interesting to see what would have happened if Trainor hadn't just delved into the mystery to quench his thirst for knowledge and to delight the readers of a niche website. Would Adrian

Ramos have played more games or Pierre-Emerick Aubameyang been moved to centre-forward to get the most dangerous players into a position to shoot more often, if the Ulsterman had been part of Klopp's coaching staff and offered up the statistical reading of the situation? His results have to be seen in context, of course. They amount to suggestions, not indisputable answers.

But neither does video analysis. Watching back a few scenes is not the same as analysing the game; context is crucial, always. Pep Guardiola didn't further the development of football because he had access to a laptop with unlimited game footage. He looked at those videos with a sharp eye, a deep understanding and a firm idea of what kind of football he wanted to play. And he saw what others didn't. Technology helped him to achieve brilliance more quickly, maybe. But videos and computers were merely tools, not the origin of his genius.

Trainor's in-depth analysis of Dortmund's game is symbolic of a paradigm change. The misleading numbers from Germany's 7–1 win over Brazil were simplistic to the point of irrelevance, a tally sheet: one shot, one mark; one pass, one mark. You can paint a picture of the game in numbers that way, obviously, but it won't be particularly reliable or informative. The fact that an action has happened on the pitch isn't nearly as interesting as knowing where on the pitch it happened.

Bayern analyst Michael Niemeyer told me that Pep Guardiola was not interested in data; he drew all the information he needed from videos. The Catalan is not a numbers man but a visionary, in the literal sense: his fanatical search for paths towards the opposition goal, for spaces and numerical superiority is more readily facilitated with the help of pictures.

Guardiola and his generation honed their expertise by watching countless hours of videos. The near-future is likely to see the emergence of data analysis geniuses but they will almost certainly be outsiders. For them to get anywhere in football, a few more rules might need breaking first.

'EXPECTED ASSISTS' AND 'EXPECTED GOAL CHAIN'

Trainor's analysis of Dortmund's failings in 2014 produced a series of new metrics that attempt to provide clues about the game's inner machinations. The quantification of certain situations – such as PPDA, a measure of pressing intensity – has become one of the key analysis trends in recent years, more often than not derived from work done by obsessive members of the global data underground.

New metrics frequently look at attacking play. Scoring goals, the game's aim, has traditionally taken centre stage, but assists have become increasingly of interest, too. As early as 2012, Devin Pleuler – who now works as an analyst at Toronto FC – developed the concept of 'Expected Assists' (xA). They measure the probability of a pass being an assist. Calculations are based on the destination of the pass, on the type of pass and other factors. This model is not reliant on whether a shot comes off. All passes are taken into account. Expected Assists have since become an established metric; data providers collate its numbers.

The following table shows the ten best players for assists in the Premier League in 2017–18. 'Chances created' is a metric exclusively calculated by OptaPro.

Player	Team	xA	Assists	Chances created
Kevin De Bruyne	Manchester City	11.67	16	106
Christian Eriksen	Tottenham	10.69	10	95
Alexis Sánchez	Arsenal/ Manchester United	9.91	6	71
David Silva	Manchester City	8.11	11	61
Mesut Özil	Arsenal	7.71	8	84
Cesc Fabregas	Chelsea	7.59	4	90
Xherdan Shaqiri	Stoke City	7.38	7	77
Eden Hazard	Chelsea	7.36	4	84
Leroy Sané	Manchester City	7.21	15	58
Riyad Mahrez	Leicester City	7	10	58

Source: OptaPro

Comparing Expected Assists, a measure of passing quality, with actual assists, makes for a clearer picture. Kevin De Bruyne, the best assist-giver in the league, benefited a lot from the finishing prowess of his team-mates in attack, as did Leroy Sané. The opposite was true of Eden Hazard and Cesc Fabregas at Chelsea. Xherdan Shaqiri's numbers, meanwhile, would have been one of the reasons why Liverpool bought him from Stoke City.

You can go one step beyond Expected Assists and have a look at the players involved in the passing chain leading up to a shot at goal.

League	Team	Player	xGC/90
La Liga	FC Barcelona	Lionel Messi	1.73
Serie A	AS Roma	Mohamed Salah	1.50
Bundesliga	FC Bayern	Arjen Robben	1.47
La Liga	Real Madrid	Álvaro Morata	1.41
Bundesliga	FC Bayern	Thiago Alcántara	1.39
La Liga	FC Barcelona	Luis Suárez	1.38
Bundesliga	FC Bayern	Philipp Lahm	1.38
Bundesliga	FC Bayern	Robert Lewandowski	1.35
La Liga	Real Madrid	Cristiano Ronaldo	1.34
Serie A	SSC Neapel	Dries Mertens	1.31
La Liga	FC Barcelona	Arda Turan	1.31
Bundesliga	FC Bayern	Arturo Vidal	1.28
Bundesliga	FC Bayern	Douglas Costa	1.26
Bundesliga	FC Bayern	Franck Ribéry	1.25
Bundesliga	FC Bayern	Joshua Kimmich	1.25
Bundesliga	FC Bayern	Thomas Müller	1.24
Premier League	Manchester City	Nolito	1.24
Serie A	AS Roma	Edin Džeko	1.22
La Liga	Real Madrid	Gareth Bale	1.21
Premier League	Liverpool	Philippe Coutinho	1.21

Source: Opta

It sounds complicated but isn't really: whoever was involved in an unbroken spell of possession is assigned the resulting shot's Expected Goals value. That includes goalkeepers setting up an attack with a throw or a defender playing the first of 11 subsequent passes before a shot is taken. The metric is called 'Expected Goals Chain' (xGC).

The xGC top 20 of players who played at least 600 minutes in one of Europe's big five leagues is mostly made up of attacking players, as one would suspect. But there are also defenders, like Philipp Lahm and Joshua Kimmich.

In an effort to identify creative players that might otherwise get overlooked, Pleuler excluded shots and assists in his next calculation. His not-so-catchily-titled 'Pre-Expected Goals Chain' (pre-xGC) revealed interesting forces at work in teams' engine rooms, including a remarkable number of Bayern Munich players. The results underline the keen loss felt by the retirement of both Philipp Lahm and Xabi Alonso in Bavaria as well as the fact that the creative side of Real Madrid's hard-man Pepe had perhaps been somewhat underrated. Curiously, very few players feature from the Premier League, as was the case in the previous table.

League	Team	Player	pre-xGC/90
Bundesliga	FC Bayern	Thiago Alcántara	1.36
La Liga	FC Barcelona	Lionel Messi	1.29
Bundesliga	FC Bayern	Philipp Lahm	1.24
Bundesliga	FC Bayern	Arturo Vidal	1.19
La Liga	Real Madrid	Pepe	1.10
Bundesliga	FC Bayern	Xabi Alonso	1.05
Bundesliga	FC Bayern	Franck Ribéry	1.02
La Liga	Real Madrid	Toni Kroos	1.01
La Liga	FC Barcelona	Samuel Umtiti	1.01
Bundesliga	FC Bayern	David Alaba	1.01
Bundesliga	FC Bayern	Arjen Robben	1.00
La Liga	FC Barcelona	Ivan Rakitic	1.00
Serie A	SSC Napoli	Jorginho	0.99
Serie A	Juventus	Paulo Dybala	0.99
Bundesliga	FC Bayern	Mats Hummels	0.98
Premier League	Arsenal	Alex Iwobi	0.98
La Liga	FC Barcelona	Sergio Busquets	0.96
Ligue 1	Paris Saint-Germain	Marco Verratti	0.95
Bundesliga	FC Bayern	Douglas Costa	0.95
Bundesliga	Borussia Dortmund	Julian Weigl	0.94

Source: OptaPro

There's an element of frivolousness to such metrics, to be sure, and their practical use seems limited. Does it really matter that Ivan Rakitic is a better player than Mats Hummels – by a margin of 0.02 pre-xGC?

But it would be wrong to adopt an excessively narrow view. The results of these calculations should be digested casually, with a degree of open-mindedness. Instead of worrying too much about small statistical differences, it would be much more interesting to ask bigger questions. Why is it that Paulo Dybala shows up in the ranking but Robert Lewandowski doesn't? What does that tell us about their respective games? What role does Samuel Umtiti play in Barcelona's build-up play considering his high value? And how come there are so few players who are at Premier League clubs?

Ultimately, the aim is to quantify the performances of players whose very position makes that more difficult. Goalkeepers are a case in point. It's often hard to distinguish between signal and noise with them. The odd big blunder sticks much more in the memory than a keeper muddling through for lengthy periods of time without ever saving difficult shots. How do you evaluate a keeper conceding tons of goals at a team battling relegation? And do the most clean sheets kept really make you the best keeper or rather show that you have the best defence ahead of you?

The rationale of Expected Goals and Expected Assists seamlessly extends to a special metric for keepers. How many shots did he have to parry and how good were they in terms of location and situation for the shooter? A keeper catching a shot from 30 yards is assigned a lower rating than somebody keeping out a shot from close

Player	Team	Expected goals on target	Goals	Keeping goals prevented
David de Gea	Manchester United	42.64	37	5.64
Martin Dúbravka	Newcastle	17.77	13	4.77
Nick Pope	Burnley	43.18	40	3.18
Karl Darlow	Newcastle	48.35	47	1.35
Lukasz Fabianski	Swansea	29.78	29	0.78
Jack Butland	Stoke	24.70	24	0.70
Adrián	West Ham	49.73	50	−0.27
Jordan Pickford	Everton	15.64	16	−0.36
Simon Mignolet	Liverpool	16.90	18	−1.10
Wayne Hennesey	Crystal Palace	17.76	19	−1.24
Hugo Lloris	Tottenham	47.56	49	−1.44
Julian Speroni	Crystal Palace	10.73	13	−2.27
Petr Cech	Arsenal	39.22	43	−3.78
Thibaut Courtois	Chelsea	46.21	50	−3.79
Mat Ryan	Brighton	18.06	22	−3.94
Loris Karius	Liverpool	34.86	39	−4.14
Ederson	Manchester City	33.67	38	−4.33
Robert Elliot	Newcastle	50.17	55	−4.83
Asmir Begovic	Bournemouth	18.13	23	−4.87
Heurelho Gomes	Watford	36.93	40	−3.07

Source: OptaPro

range thanks to his amazing agility and courage. 'Expected Goals Against' (xGA) are compared to actual goals conceded. Opta calls the difference 'Keeping Goals Prevented', and they're a good indicator of the man between the sticks doing his job well – or badly, if the difference is a negative one. In the 2017–18 Premier League season, the Keeping Goals Prevented table looked as shown opposite.

These new metrics shed a light on individual player performances. And they also reveal idiosyncrasies of managers.

THE FAVRE ENIGMA

Borussia Dortmund's Swiss coach Lucien Favre is one of the nicest and most erratic managers I've ever met. He can be the most charming and genial conversationalist or appear sulky, resistant to all questions, as if they were insults. You always get the sense that he lives in his own particular world, however. He probably does. And it's probably an ascetic world of watching football videos behind closed curtains.

During his time as Mönchengladbach manager, club staff tell you, he was watching videos whenever he didn't directly work with the team; at home and on weekends, too. He had even perfected a technique to navigate the footage quicker: he would press the fast forward button whenever the game was interrupted.

Favre is also infamous for his inability to decide on player transfers, as every club boss or sporting director who has ever worked with him can testify. Every once in a while, he was overcome by a sudden sense of dread and tendered his resignation, convinced that the relationship between him and his team had run its course, only to return a few hours later after his superiors had changed his mind. But after losing the first five games of the season in 2015–16 even the Gladbach bosses couldn't get to him to reconsider his decision to walk out.

You might think that most clubs were in the end happy to get rid of such a highly strung and volatile coach. But the opposite is true. Favre isn't just a lovely man but an exceptionally successful coach. He exceeded expectations almost everywhere he went.

Favre got promoted to the Swiss second division with tiny club Echallens. He led Yverdon to the top flight, lifted the Swiss Cup with Servette FC and won two championships and two cups with FC Zürich. At Hertha Berlin in Germany, he nearly reached the Champions League. He first saved Borussia Mönchengladbach from near-certain relegation and then twice made the Europa League before getting into the Champions League. In France, he took OGC Nice to third place at the first attempt.

It's all pretty spectacular in relation to the resources of those clubs. But the underlying statistical figures for his teams are both sensational and confusing. At Mönchengladbach and at Nice, Favre's team dramatically overshot Expected Goals, both in goals scored (xG) and goals conceded (xGA). This is how the 2016–17 Ligue 1 season shaped up in those terms.

Team	xG	Goals	Attacking efficency	xGA	Goals against	Defensive efficency	Efficiency
Nice	50.88	63	12.12	61.09	36	25.09	37.21
Monaco	78.73	107	28.27	39.68	31	8.68	36.95
Marseille	56.92	57	0.08	53.66	41	12.66	12.74
Bordeaux	50.30	53	2.70	49.04	43	6.04	8.74
St. Etienne	49.01	41	-8.01	55.43	42	13.43	5.42

Source: Opta

Favre's team should have had a goal difference of minus ten according to Expected Goals. But they had plus 27, a swing of 37 goals. Favre might simply have been the luckiest manager in Europe that year. But this wasn't a one off. In 2011–12 and each of the two subsequent seasons, he beat the Expected Goals model three times, and on two of those occasions, his team over-performed by the highest margin in the league. It was the same story with Expected Goals Against and actual goals conceded. Twice, Gladbach conceded fewer goals than anyone, relative to the model's prediction.

Over the course of his three years at Borussia-Park, the 'Foals' registered 1.2 actual goals for every Expected Goal. Put differently, Favre consistently achieved a 20 per cent higher return than the model anticipated. That's a lot. But the numbers become truly astonishing in a wider context. Three teams in the top five leagues registered surpluses of similar sizes in the same space of time but they each only did it for one single season. Sunderland in 2012–13, 1.23; Man City in 2010–11, 1.21; and Levante in 2013–14, 1.30. The chance that

Gladbach should over-perform three times to that extent was about 1 per cent. It could not just have been luck. But what was it?

Expected Goals provide pointers for the gap between performance and yield, as already shown. But if Favre's teams were consistently more successful than anticipated, he must have found the model's blind spot. No wonder the football analytics community were fascinated by his sides and eager to unravel the mystery. The most extensive attempts were made by American Michael Caley in 2014 and Ashwin Raman from Bangalore three years later. Both tried to describe Favre's playing style in quantitative terms, in order to find an explanation for his serial over-performance.

Caley had noted that Borussia Mönchengladbach were largely happy to let their opponents circulate the ball unimpeded. They allowed them to play more passes in all thirds of the pitch than any other Bundesliga team. But things were very different at the sharp end. Borussia slammed the brake once the ball got into the box. Opposition passes of 12 metres or less in front of Gladbach's goal were cut down to 70 per cent of the league average, and they allowed the fewest passes inside their box of all Bundesliga sides. Favre's team was fine with letting the other team play. But when things got serious, they stepped in forcefully.

Kai Peter Schmitz was a game analyst for Favre at Mönchengladbach. He recalls the coach telling even international players how they had to tackle in great detail: 'For him, the one-vs-one is the nucleus. He went up to seasoned pros and showed them which foot to use for blocking a shot, explaining that they'd have an extra few centimetres that way, to help them defend.'

In attack, there was a comparable pattern. At a time when most Bundesliga teams were focusing on moments of transition and fast counter-attacks, Gladbach were almost languid in possession and rarely counter-attacked. No other team in the league had such a low ratio between completed passes in the final third to completed passes in the defensive third. Lowly sides who are unable to get in front of the opposition goal and aimlessly pass it around at the back have a similar profile. But Gladbach were anything but.

Favre, an elegant playmaker in his playing days, is strongly influenced by Johan Cruyff's vision of football. He visited the Dutchman at Barcelona and studied his work close up. Favre was also deeply impressed with some of the ideas espoused by Cruyff's successors at the club. Favre understood that possession could be a defensive measure, but not just that. He wants his team to keep the ball until specific opportunities arise. Gladbach moved the ball slowly and cautiously at first, into areas that aren't really dangerous – to the flanks. The probability of creating a chance with a pass through the centre is three times higher than from the sides. Most sides attempt to cross from wide areas, but crosses are relatively easy to defend. Gladbach hardly crossed the ball. In fact, no other Bundesliga club played fewer crosses. They didn't have a target man up front who needed that kind of service, even if they had tried and failed to play that way with the Dutchman Luuk de Jong leading the line.

From those wide positions, Gladbach moved the ball back into central areas more often than anyone in their division. Twenty of their assists came from passes from 14 metres or more, which was another statistical outlier. The league average was 8 metres.

Kai Peter Schmitz explains that Favre's game did not follow a fixed blueprint but was the result of multiple game plans that were adapted to their opponents: 'Favre always knows how every player and the opposition team react in any given situation.' Schmitz adds that the manager had a phenomenal sense of predicting the line-up and tactics of the opposing team. During the week in training, he prepared his men for four or five situations they should wait for, or provoke, in the match. One of them was a ball played back to Granit Xhaka (now at Arsenal) for him to switch flanks in attack. The pass had to be crisp enough to let the midfielder move the ball on first time to the flank, where an attacking player was already making a run into a promising position. Such combinations were practised in XI vs 0 final training sessions before matches, with no opposing players on the pitch. 'That was relatively straightforward, very structured. Over the course of the season, the team picked up many well-rehearsed patterns like that,' Schmitz says.

Favre's stats at OGC Nice suggest the same things happened in the south of France. In his first season (2016–17), his team had the second-highest possession percentage behind Paris Saint-Germain, and they played the second-highest number of passes after the French champions, too. But Nice made it into the danger zone in front of the opposition goal a mere 653 times over the course of the season. Only Bastia, the relegated side from Corsica, did worse. In spite of that, Nice registered the second-highest number of shots from the danger zone. Conversely, they took the third-fewest shots from outside the box, where the probability of scoring is much lower.

The value Expected Goals calculates for a shot is a mathematical approximation. The model does have a blind spot, or maybe a semi-blind spot, however: it doesn't fully take into account the opposition. It makes for a huge difference, of course, if a striker is through on goal with all the time in the world or if he's being challenged by a tough centre-back who's been instructed to use his stronger left foot to tackle by his coach Lucien Favre. It also helps your chances of finding the net if there's only one defender, not three or four, throwing themselves at the shot. Most xG models use so-called proxies to estimate the presence of defenders. The pressure on the striker tends to be lower on counter-attacks compared with attempts to break down a deep block.

In his analysis of Nice for chanceanalytics.com, however, Ashwin Raman was able to use the data of a betting company that rated opposition pressure on a scale from 1 to 5 according to the players' positions on the pitch. The results were once more startling: Nice's attackers took shots under more pressure than any other team in the league.

All. Very. Strange. How could a team that played slow football, that rarely got into good shooting positions and that faced the highest amount of pressure have been this successful?

Raman picked up on an interesting detail. Nice did shoot from pressurised positions but only when there weren't too many outfield players between the ball and the goal; 2.27 on average. That was the lowest number in the league. But more interesting still was the fact that Favre's men took nearly 60 per cent of their shots when only two or fewer opposition players – goalkeeper excluded – were blocking their path to goal.

There was a mirror image in defence. Opponents could pass the ball just as much as they had done against Favre's Borussia Mönchengladbach but they were forced into shots with high defensive pressures and a high number of players between shooter and goal. Because of that, opponents didn't really benefit from taking shots from high probability positions.

Favre's game adhered to a simple idea: it ensured that his team took good shots and his opponents bad ones. Football is always about catching your opponents off balance. That explains the popularity of tactics focused on transition and counter-attacks: they are short-cuts, workable without much quality on the ball. Favre's approach is the antithesis. The former playmaker, whose career was cut short by a brutal foul, cuts opponents open with slow, surgical precision.

This example shows how a playing style can be analysed by deep drilling into several data layers. It also shows that Favre is a manager with unique abilities that make teams simply better. In a way it's surprising that he had never coached a top international team before taking over at Borussia Dortmund in the summer of 2018. In the first half of the season, he over-performed massively once more in relation to Expected Goals and Expected Goals Against, by a total of 13 goals.

The Favre case illustrates that the development of the Expected Goals model is ongoing. Data provider Statsbomb has been offering its clients an advanced model that factors in opponents more strongly. Opta, too, has prepared the model's optimisation by taking 'Shot Clarity' (the number of defenders between shooter and keeper) and 'Shot Pressure' into account; the two loopholes Favre's teams had exploited to beat the model's calculations.

Perhaps we just don't need more finely tuned metrics but new types of data altogether, to arrive at a better understanding of the events on the pitch. So-called advanced data has now started to offer a view into football's deeper layers, an X-ray image of the game. But maybe it takes the equivalent of ultrasound or, ideally, an MRI scan to help us figure out what's truly going on.

PACKING: THE SWISS ARMY KNIFE

On 15 June 2016, the fifth day of the European Championship in France, 'Packing' had come of age in Germany. Popular satirical website Der Postillon wrote: 'ARD's analysis tool Packing is causing a stir. But ZDF has now followed suit and presented a novel measurement destined to revolutionise football. The so-called Goaling counts how often a team manages to put the ball into the opposition net. Amazingly, teams with a higher Goaling rate than their opponents have a winning probability of 100 per cent. "The game has been waiting for such a reliable statistic for a long time," swoons former footballer Reinard Stefantz, who has developed Goaling over the course of two years in his garage in Fulda.'

At the time, many football supporters in Germany were talking about Packing; ARD pundit Mehmet Scholl had tried to explain the outcome of the matches to the audience by showing them the number of bypassed players taken out of the game by their opponents. They had been 'packed', as he told them. But Scholl's rather clumsy submissions left many viewers quickly annoyed by Packing. As Der Postillon's story underlined, the whole thing had become a bit of a laughing stock.

To be sure, Reinartz and Hegeler hadn't come up with the concept in Fulda, but in Cologne. The two Bundesliga pros hadn't sat in a garage either, but spent countless hours talking in Bayer Leverkusen's team hotel. The question they asked themselves was always the same. What kind of data could be a more reliable indicator of success than the one that was available now? 'Managers blaming your passing rate for a defeat only spurred us on further,' Reinartz told me in his Cologne office.

When they had first told me about their ideas in Berlin, I had jokingly asked whether they wanted to take part in 'Jugend forscht' [youth research], a very popular contest for youngsters interested in science and technology in Germany. But their data exploration did indeed involve a lot of research. They first thought about counting the number of bypassed lines of players but soon dismissed that plan. The game didn't work like table football, where different parts of the team were neatly lined up in rows. 'The conversation quickly moved on to "bypassed opponents",' Reinartz recalled. It seemed logical. You score goals by getting past opponents.

In a first experiment, Reinartz and Hegeler sat down in front of a television with pen and paper and watched ten games featuring Borussia Dortmund. They concentrated on the defensive duo of Mats Hummels and Neven Subotic.

But some practical problems arose. How did you evaluate a long ball forward from a centre-back that bounced off a striker's head into touch? The pass had bypassed a lot of opponents, but it was gone. They defined it as an ineffective event.

How important was the intended recipient of a pass in that context? And was all of this going anywhere? At first, they kept tally charts. Then, they loaded Excel sheets with data and, at last, they employed statistics software. Slowly, their task crystallised in their minds: they had to develop a theory of the game based on events on the field and extrapolate new parameters.

They examined the anatomy of the game, to find out how teams could get into dangerous areas. 'You need a pass giver and a pass recipient, to get into reasonably interesting spaces,' Reinartz said. 'You need someone drawing the ball and someone who plays the killer pass.' That's hardly a revolutionary insight. But up until then, there was no metric that told you how many players were no longer to defend an attack because a striker had collected the ball behind them. There was no corresponding metric for the pass giver, either. Breaking down the game and quantifying it in such a way was no less than a global first.

In 2015, their work had progressed to the point where they founded a company called Impect. A year later, Reinartz called time on his career at the age of 27, having struggled with chronic injury problems. It was a painful moment. But his retirement also made him dedicate himself fully to the advancement of the company.

* * *

A look at the Packing ratings of players helps to understand why the data collected can be interesting for coaches and club administrators.

Take Mesut Özil. He has a high number of fans all over the world: 13m followers on Instagram, 16m on Twitter, 30m on Facebook. Just as many people watching football suspect the 2014 World Cup winner of regularly failing to hit the heights when it really matters. His body language has long been a bone of contention at Arsenal and in the German national team before his retirement in 2018. There's a deep-seated presumption that he doesn't work hard enough, too.

Özil's effortless, floaty style will always rile those who like their footballers sweaty and bleeding. But he's also been unlucky that a significant part of his artistry is hard to recognise and generally impossible to quantify: the ability to 'draw passes', as Reinartz calls it. Without players mobile and smart enough to show in the right areas, led there by their own intuition or on orders of their managers, teams couldn't play dangerous passes in the first place.

On Özil's 30th birthday, in October 2018, Opta revealed that no player in the top five leagues had created as many chances as he had done since data was first collected in 2006. Packing also shows a different part to his game, however. He's a genius in collecting passes between the lines, the area behind midfield and in front of the defence. He bypassed 66 players on average per game at Euro 2016 as a pass recipient, marking him out as the best offensive midfield player.

It's a blessing for every team to have such a player in their ranks. In modern football, central areas are usually so congested that it's very hard getting into the spaces that Mesut Özil routinely occupies. At the same time, pass recipients are not nearly credited as much as pass-givers. Unfortunately, Özil's knack of being able to take the ball in dangerous areas has been less eye-catching than facial expressions denoting a supposed lack of effort.

In the disastrous World Cup in Russia, Özil bypassed 68 players on average per game as a target man. Only one player was better in the German team: Thomas Müller, with 72. What that shows you is that this metric, too, needs context for its interpretation. Neither

Özil nor Müller were top players that had somehow been overlooked in a desolate German team at this tournament. But at the very least, they had not lost their extraordinary ability to function as target men in Russia.

In any case, Packing helps us distinguish between a player simply playing a lot of passes and one making a real difference with his passing. In his last season at Borussia Dortmund, Mats Hummels had a passing accuracy of 84.6 per cent while the largely unknown Albanian international Mergim Mavraj completed 89.5 per cent of his passes at 1. FC Köln. So why did Hummels move to Bayern whereas Mavraj first went to Hamburger SV and then to Aris Saloniki in Greece? One answer can be found in the Packing stats. Hummels' 72 bypassed players per game set the benchmark in the league that season, while Mavraj was at the low end of the scale with 23.

Packing also breaks down events on the pitch into different categories that make it easier to quantify the quality of defenders. These days, players such as Hummels are evaluated in terms of their passing, too, but their main duty remains defending. Packing produces two different values for intercepted balls, which at first might be confusing. One signifies the number of opponents who are no longer able to defend after an interception. The second one shows how many teammates were out of the game before a successful turnover in possession.

Let's look at the first case. A player wins the ball in midfield, putting four opposing attackers behind the ball all of a sudden. They've been taken out of the game; they have been 'packed'. Teams playing *Gegenpressing* often register higher numbers in that regard. They attack the ball early, when opponents are fanning out.

The second metric quantifies defensive performance by looking at the number of team-mates that were no longer able to impact the game before the ball was won back. The classic example is a heroic last-ditch tackle from a defender who hunts down an attacker through on goal. The interception takes place without the help of nine of his team-mates, which makes this a spectacular saving effort.

One could also look at it from the point of view of the packed players. A ball lost in the build-up, with many team-mates ahead of play, spells immediate danger. Those who can't hold up the ball in attack or don't get to finish a move are detrimental to their team's offensive prowess. These versatile readings make Packing a kind of Swiss army knife for football analysis. It helps with quantifying performances in many new, small ways.

But how strong is the correlation between Packing rates and success on the pitch? That, after all, had been the starting point for Reinartz and Hegeler.

At the Euros in France (2016), 34 of 51 games were won by teams who had bypassed more players than their opponents. Only three suffered defeats. The relationship between winning and Packing was much stronger than between winning and passing or possession stats.

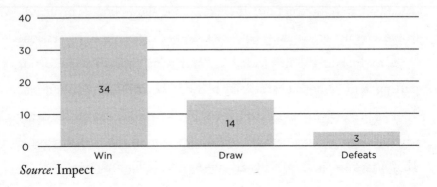

Source: Impact

168

In Russia two years later, the same dynamic was prominent in the group stage. Three games per team are a small sample size, admittedly, but seven out of the eight teams with the highest net number of bypassed defenders made it into the knock-out stages. Only Iran were somewhat unlucky to get eliminated early on.

Team	Bypassed defenders	Suffered bypassed defenders	Net
Belgium (3)	55	30	25
Russia (QF)	42	21	21
Sweden (QF)	39	21	18
Brazil (QF)	48	32	16
England (4)	36	21	15
France (1)	32	19	13
Croatia (2)	39	27	12
Iran (1st round)	28	20	8

Source: Impect

The figures become more meaningful over the course of a whole season. In 2016–17, the two Bundesliga teams placed first and second in the final table also boasted the most numbers of bypassed players. 1. FC Köln's good season, which finished with them in the Europa League places, was also mirrored in the Packing stats. Other teams could compensate for their low numbers of bypassed players by making it difficult for opponents to bypass them. Hertha Berlin, Eintracht Frankfurt and Mainz 05 were such sides. But Gladbach's lack of defensive stability cost them a better position. When

Team	Bypassed defenders per game	Suffered bypassed defenders per game	Net
FC Bayern	50	35	15
RB Leipzig	48	40	8
Borussia Dortmund	46	36	10
Hoffenheim	43	38	5
Mönchengladbach	42	42	0
1. FC Köln	42	36	6
Werder Bremen	41	40	1
Bayer 04 Leverkusen	40	46	-6
FC Ingolstadt	40	39	1
VfL Wolfsburg	38	40	-2
FC Augsburg	37	42	-5
Schalke 04	37	41	-4
SC Freiburg	36	38	-2
Hamburger SV	35	43	-8
Hertha BSC	34	37	-3
Eintracht Frankfurt	34	35	-1
Mainz 05	34	38	-4
Darmstadt 98	30	41	-11

Source: Impect

Darmstadt were promoted to the top flight in 2015, opponents were hardly able to bypass their defenders. But when they couldn't be as solid at the back and their problems in attack didn't abate, they went down to Bundesliga 2 again in the following season.

A team's defensive organisation is also reflected in the degree of danger that arises when they lose the ball with many of their players out of the game and unable to intervene. SC Freiburg had the fewest number of players 'packed' following a loss of possession whereas many of Hamburger SV's problems were evident here (see chart on next page).

The proliferation of new data creates a new reality. As Michael Cox explained, part of the reason passing rates in the Premier League improved was the fact that managers had started taking note of them.

Spending time getting to grips with Packing has changed my view of football games. The metric has sharpened the focus on 'killer passes' and 'suicidal' losses of possession; I pay more attention to passing recipients and less to the passer. It's not an entirely new way of looking at the sport, but we are now able to quantify something that was not possible to gauge accurately before.

There are real-life consequences, too. Julian Weigl was called up to Euro 2016 as one of the Bundesliga's shooting stars, having moved from second division 1860 Munich to Borussia Dortmund the summer before. During the championship in France he revealed in an interview that he was looking up to Toni Kroos, due to his ability to bypass players. His club coach Thomas Tuchel, Weigl added, had explicitly told him that he had to improve in that part

Team	Removed teammates per game
SC Freiburg	97
Hertha BSC	103
FC Augsburg	104
FC Bayern	106
1. FC Köln	106
Mainz 05	109
VfL Wolfsburg	111
FC Ingolstadt	112
Mönchengladbach	113
Hoffenheim	114
Darmstadt 98	114
Eintracht Frankfurt	114
RB Leipzig	116
Borussia Dortmund	118
Schalke 04	120
Werder Bremen	120
Bayer 04 Leverkusen	124
Hamburger SV	129

Source: Impect

of the game. Weigl bypassed 42 players per game on average at the time, whereas Kroos' passes took out 82 players per game.

Packing is still a novel concept and we're still at the stage of sounding out its possibilities. But with each year and each new league adding to the data, the potential treasure trove of knowledge becomes greater.

The model also offers a clearer view of team performances. When Bayer Leverkusen played well below the potential of their squad in 2016–17 and were sucked into a relegation battle, Reinartz consulted the data in search of an explanation. Most supporters were upset with a Bayer defence that conceded lots of goals at the time but Reinartz's analysis unearthed different problems. 'We would say: this is really good defence but everything else doesn't work.'

Leverkusen lost many balls in dangerous areas, leaving four or five players the wrong side of the ball, unable to support their back line. 'You have to think of it as waves. If you compare the defence of Bayern Munich with that of a team from the lower third of the table, Bayern's back four will only be faced with a third of attacks. That's why you need to look at the relation between the total number of waves and the number of waves that a defence manages to break.' Leverkusen's men at the back, as it turned out, stopped a high number of attacks, but their team-mates had allowed opponents to attack too often in the first place. Reinartz came to a similar conclusion analysing Germany's poor performance at the World Cup in Russia. There, too, defenders had been left to their own devices far too often.

Gathering Packing figures is laborious and expensive. In Germany, Impect uses the tracking data collected for the clubs by the Bundesliga. But automatic addition is only possible up to 75 per cent; the missing quarter needs to be logged manually. To key in numbers for games without any use of tracking data takes about seven hours per game. Forty sports science students from the University of Cologne make some money on the side working on the project.

The high cost of the data at first restricted its use for games in the Bundesliga, Ligue 1 and the UEFA Youth League, as well as matches at World Cups and Euros. But in spring 2018, Impect opened up a branch in Bonifacio Global City, the Philippine capital Manila's modern business district. 'The office rental is more expensive in Cologne than in Manila,' Reinartz said, but that cost is offset by the lower wages of the 21 full-time employees. The company is expanding. But more on that later.

SPACE CONTROL

Packing is but one attempt to procure a more rounded view of the game by linking and quantifying singular events.

American firm STATS offer a product called 'Playing Styles' that connects different Key Performance Indicators to make a team's style comparable to others. Since 2017, OptaPro has been working on so-called sequences, whose definition is easily understood. 'Sequences are defined as passages of play which belong to one team and are ended by defensive actions, stoppages in play or a shot,' they explain.

A sequence can be interrupted. But if the team retains possession, thanks to winning a throw-in or recycling a deflected shot, the sequence continues. The point of the exercise is to identify the passages of play in which one team dominates. There are about 200 such sequences in an average game, with each team being in possession between 90 and 100 times, switching from one side to the other.

The amount of time spent on the ball differs vastly, however. In the 2017–18 season in the Premier League, teams averaged between 5.5 (Manchester City) and 2.5 (Stoke City, West Bromwich Albion) passes per sequence. There's a clear difference between sides willing and able to control the ball for longer periods and those who set up to go forward more quickly, with fewer passes. There's a corresponding value for sequences without possession, delineating the amount of passes by opponents, but the gap between teams isn't that pronounced there. Guardiola's high-pressing Man City let opponents pass the ball only 2.4 per sequence on average, while Swansea were the most passive side, affording the opposing team 3.9 passes per sequence (see chart on next page).

Modern tracking technology can measure the pace of the sequences. This example from Liverpool vs Watford (2016–17) shows how. Jürgen Klopp's team won the ball thanks to a header from Joel Matip, who is represented by a triangle here. The ball's subsequent movement follows straight lines (for passes) and dotted lines (for players carrying the ball forward). In 14.5 seconds between Matip's header and the shot off target, the ball travelled 126.44 metres, making up a net distance of 55.96 metres. Dividing the space progressed up the field by the time span of the sequence produces a value OptaPro calls 'Direct Speed'. For this attack, it was 3.85 metres per second.

	Team	Passes per sequence	Passes per sequence (against)
1.	Manchester City	5.5	2.4
2.	Manchester United	3.9	3.3
3.	Tottenham	4.1	2.6
4.	Liverpool	4.1	2.8
5.	Chelsea	4	3.5
6.	Arsenal	4.4	2.8
7.	Burnley	2.7	3.3
8.	Everton	2.8	3.2
9.	Leicester	2.8	3.1
10.	Newcastle	2.7	3.6
11.	Crystal Palace	2.70	3.4
12.	Bournemouth	3	3.3
13.	West Ham	2.8	3.5
14.	Watford	2.8	3.1
15.	Brighton	2.9	3.8
16.	Huddersfield	2.7	3.4
17.	Southampton	3.3	3.1
18.	Swansea	3.2	3.9
19.	Stoke	2.5	3.4
20.	West Bromwich	2.5	3.8

Source: OptaPro

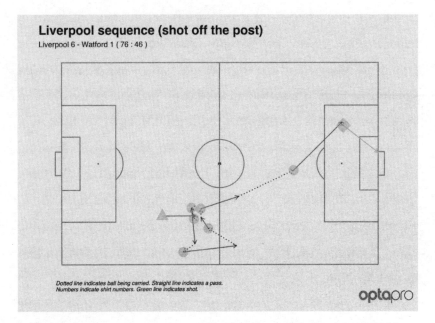

Liverpool sequence (shot off the post)
Liverpool 6 - Watford 1 (76 : 46)

Dotted line indicates ball being carried. Straight line indicates a pass.
Numbers indicate shirt numbers. Green line indicates shot.

optapro

Source: OptaPro

Game analysts can take such numbers as a starting point for further examination. They can categorise passing sequences resulting in shots according to their starting points. Does the opponent attack mostly from wide areas or through the middle? What other patterns can be identified? What player is part of successful passing sequences and who tends to break them up?

These kinds of numbers can expose further layers of the game. But one fundamental problem remains. An average player spends about 150 seconds touching the ball in the course of 90 minutes. In those two and a half minutes, he shoots, crosses, dribbles or does any of the other things with the ball that event statistics pick up on. But what happens in the other 87 and a half minutes? And is it even objectively good to be in action on the pitch? Paolo Maldini, one of the best defenders of all time, once famously said: 'If I have to make a tackle, I have already made a mistake.' Xabi Alonso (Liverpool, Real Madrid and Bayern Munich) was no less dismissive. 'At Liverpool I used to read the match day programme and you'd read an interview with a lad from the youth team,' he told *The Guardian*. 'They'd ask: age, heroes, strong points, etc. He'd reply: "Shooting and tackling". I can't get into my head that football development would educate tackling as a quality, something to learn, to teach, a characteristic of your play. How can that be a way of seeing the game? Tackling is a [last] resort, and you will need it, but it isn't a quality to aspire to.'

Alonso and Maldini avoided the need to tackle thanks to their game intelligence and excellent positional play. But how can you measure players who do nothing brilliantly?

The same question occupied the minds of the German national team's coaching staff. In 2013, they had entered a cooperation agreement with software firm SAP. Oliver Bierhoff, the business manager, Hansi Flick (German FA Sporting Director at the time) and head analyst Christofer Clemens had travelled to the company's office in Palo Alto to speak to the American experts. They wanted to learn about data sets, come up with practical apps for internal use with the team but also conduct some fundamental football research. SAP gave them eight people to work with, among them system designers, mathematicians and IT specialists. Their job was to help uncover new insight from data or generate new metrics altogether.

Brainstorming sessions about the nature of information most valuable to the German FA delegation turned up the subject of 'controlling space'. 'It's a term the coaching staff uses a lot,' Clemens told me. 'Modern football turns on the control of space. The team controlling the right space at the right time is likely to win the game.'

It's possible to evaluate individual performances in that context. Clemens is full of praise for Barcelona's Luis Suárez and he regards the Uruguayan as the master of the art. 'Controlling space in the opposition box is the ultimate skill. He doesn't score many screamers into the top corner but he's often completely by himself in the box. By making the right movements in the decisive moments, he's able to control space like no one else.' Suárez, in other words, is able to find the scarcest commodity in today's highly congested game: a bit of room to score.

'At the highest level of international football, the difference between scoring and not scoring is often a mere metre. One metre is the difference between controlling space and not controlling space,' Clemens said. The best players, like Lionel Messi or Cristiano Ronaldo, dominate space. It is that ability that lies at the heart of their brilliance. They don't specialise in winning one-vs-one duels but in evading them altogether. 'When the ball gets to them, they're never forced to fight for it,' Clemens said. Knowing as much produces many questions. What can be done against those space-finding capabilities? Can you learn to move that way? And can you teach players to do that?

The term 'controlling space', *Raumkontrolle* in German, was coined by Daniel Memmert, professor and Managing Head of the Institute of Exercise Training and Sport Informatics at the German Sport University in Cologne. He has been studying game data for many years and worked with Bundesliga club TSG Hoffenheim as well as the German FA on practical applications. The Bundesliga funded a study of 50 games from the 2014–15 campaign. He found that 'winning teams had a significantly better positional game relating to passes in the defensive zone and midfield as well as a significantly better vertical passing game in the attacking area. On average, they are faced with fewer opponents. The winning teams also bypass more players with passes from defence into midfield.' The concept was similar to Packing. But Memmert and his staff had taken a very different path to get there.

He worked with Voronoi diagrams, named after Russian mathematician Georgy Fedosievych Voronoy. They were invented in the early 20th century and are today being used to model the growth of crystals or cells, but they also work in relation to football.

Voronoi diagrams partition a plane – in our case a football pitch – into regions based on distance to points – the players. 'The border of two neighbouring regions marks the spot that both players can reach at the same time,' Memmert wrote. The pitch, to put it differently, is divided into sections that each contain one player closest to the ball. The frame below captures a moment from Werder Bremen against 1. FC Köln in a Voronoi diagram.

Bremen attack from left to right, Köln control the grey space. At this point, Werder already control 31.5 per cent of their attacking zone and 1.6 per cent of Köln's box, the tiny square on the left side of attack.

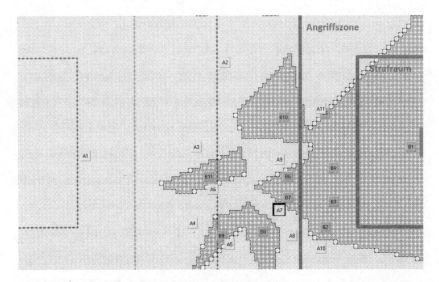

Source: Memmert/Perl, *Revolution im Profifußball*

This is necessarily just a snapshot, a fraction of an incredibly dynamic system. Control of space is constantly changing. 'Generally speaking, top teams are more successful in winning and keeping control of space in critical areas of the pitch,' Memmert concluded.

These are only the basic parameters of the concept, however. In theory, the regions' sizes are at least partially determined by the pace of the player. Pierre-Emerick Aubameyang can impact a bigger space than a Sunday league player. Other player characteristics would have to be factored in to produce a more complete measure of space control.

One way of achieving that was suggested by a 2016 essay in PLOS ONE, the online journal of the US-based Public Library of Science, cumbersomely titled 'Real Time Quantification of Danger-ousity in Football Using Spatiotemporal Tracking Data'.

The study was commissioned and financed by the Bundesliga's corporate body, Deutsche Fußball Liga (DFL) and its former Head of Technology and Innovation, Hendrik Weber. Without much fanfare, the German top flight have become the most progressive of the big leagues in their dealings with data. They were the first in Europe to collect tracking data for all games in the first and second division, starting in the 2013–14 season. All numbers were made available to the 36 professional clubs. In England, clubs only have access to the official positional data of their own games, which hampers research and complicates things unnecessarily.

Weber, an academic with multiple MBAs and a PhD in Mergers & Acquisitions, founded the DFL's subsidiary company Sportec Solutions in 2017 to take over 'operational responsibility for the collection, storage and distribution of official match data'. Apart from commissioning academic studies, the league's technology arm also invested in an Israeli start-up working on new forms of tracking in 2018.

The study detailed in PLOS ONE was led by Daniel Link, Chair of Training Science and Computer Science in Sports at the Technical University in Munich (TUM). Link and his colleagues Steffen Lang and Philipp Seidenkranz achieved a remarkable feat: they were able to measure attacking performance conclusively. The trio didn't work with the term *Raumkontrolle* but came up with a neologism instead: 'Dangerousity'. It described 'the quantitative representation of the probability of a goal for every moment during which a player is on the ball'.

'We want Dangerousity to have a recall value. A word that's a brand,' Link told me in his office in Munich.

A former competitive beach volleyball player, he studied information technology and attained a PhD in Sports Technology at TUM, where he developed a highly successful piece of software used by the German beach volleyball players at the Olympics in London (2012) and Rio de Janeiro (2016). It helped the gold medal-winning teams of Julius Brink and Jonas Reckermann, and Laura Ludwig and Kira Walkenhorst to prepare for their opponents. 'People tend to have certain patterns of behaviour, and when the pressure is on in big Olympic games, with 20,000 people screaming all around you, you go back to what you know best,' Link explained. 'You might not be aware yourself of such stereotypical behaviour but the software can help you find it.' Thanks to this type of game analysis, the German athletes had an idea how their opponents would react under pressure.

Link's interest in sport is numbers-driven but his own background as a competitor has given him a deep understanding of the psychology of sport as well. In 2010, he codified the data collected by the Bundesliga. As mentioned before, there are very divergent definitions of events like a pass or even a completed pass. His Dangerousity came with a plethora of intimidating formulas but it was based on practical realities. His starting point was the core aims of football: to create maximum danger for the opposition goal and at the same time minimise the threat at the back. 'Everything else is subservient to that need,' he said.

His calculation was based on four components. The first one, 'Zone', was concerned with the position of the player on the ball, not unlike Expected Goals. Link divided the final 34 metres of the pitch – the most probable area for scoring – into a grid with 2m x 2m sized squares and assigned each a probability value dependent on their distance and angle towards goal. The second part was called

'Control', a value informed by the average relative speed of the ball and that of the player in possession. High relative speeds occur when a player hits the ball first time after a pass, for example, whereas lower relative speeds indicate a player spending more time on the ball. The higher the relative speed of the ball, the more difficult it becomes for the player to control it. 'Pressure', the third component, describes a defending team's ability to prevent a player from completing an action on the ball, and the fourth factor is 'Density': it measures how many opposition players are in a position to defend between the player and their goal.

To calculate all those numbers from game data is a sophisticated and highly complex process but the results are convincing. Link determined the trend of Dangerousity values in 64 Bundesliga games of the 2014–15 season and showed the corresponding game footage to coaches and players. They were asked to rate the events in terms of danger, with 1 denoting the highest danger and 5 the lowest. Comparing the experts' view with his findings proved that he had developed an algorithm that could detail a game's fever chart, second by second.

Here is an example of a seven-second sequence from a game between Bayern Munich and TSG Hoffenheim. It's important to note that the 'Maximum value of Dangerousity' (DA) is 1: it would describe the moment the ball was stationary on the goal line, with no keeper and defender in sight, waiting for the attacker to pounce unimpaired.

As we can see, danger arises the moment Arjen Robben dribbles past his opponent, passes to Lewandowski and receives

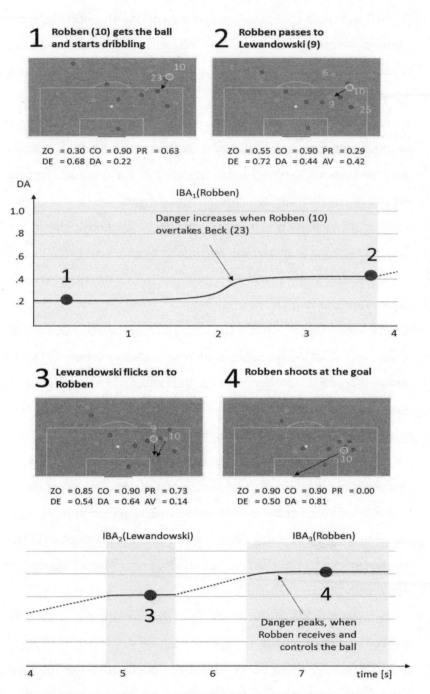

1 Robben (10) gets the ball and starts dribbling

ZO = 0.30 CO = 0.90 PR = 0.63
DE = 0.68 DA = 0.22

2 Robben passes to Lewandowski (9)

ZO = 0.55 CO = 0.90 PR = 0.29
DE = 0.72 DA = 0.44 AV = 0.42

DA

IBA₁(Robben)

Danger increases when Robben (10) overtakes Beck (23)

3 Lewandowski flicks on to Robben

ZO = 0.85 CO = 0.90 PR = 0.73
DE = 0.54 DA = 0.64 AV = 0.14

4 Robben shoots at the goal

ZO = 0.90 CO = 0.90 PR = 0.00
DE = 0.50 DA = 0.81

IBA₂(Lewandowski)

IBA₃(Robben)

Danger peaks, when Robben receives and controls the ball

time [s]

Source: Link, *Real Time Quantification of Dangerousity in Football*

the ball in return in a good shooting position. The DFL believes the fever chart could be interesting for media companies, especially broadcasters. The technology will supposedly be ready for use later this year.

Analysts and coaches could be helped in their evaluation of players and performances, too. The model could act as a filter, showing a player only the moments in which he wasn't able to increase Dangerousity and instruct him to produce more danger.

'But of course it's down to the manager to decide whether those clips are right for him. You can only make a judgement based on the video material and on your own philosophy. No algorithm will be able to supplant that,' Link admitted.

The model also computes an 'Action Value', the statistical worth of an event: did a pass, dribble or other action increase Dangerousity? 'We check how dangerous a situation is when the player gets on the ball and compare it to the danger after his action. The difference is the danger he personally contributed,' Link said.

His program has the makings of a useful tool to judge a player's performance more fairly. It could help scout players with consistently high Action Values that are decisive in games. Link: 'Football games are often locked in a state of equilibrium. At the end it comes down to creating the crucial moment of perturbation. Players who can do that command the highest fees.'

Perturbation is a mathematical term for disruption. A dribble by Robben or a through-ball from Kroos can be so incisive as to upset the opposition's balance. Tactical changes or the effects of substitutions could be measured in that way, too.

Dangerousity can put a number on a team's match performance. How much danger did they produce, and how much danger were they exposed to by the opposition?

The four examples below show once more that good performances are not inevitably rewarded with wins. In three of them, teams won points in spite of the statistics. But that's more to do with football's eternal predisposition to random events, less with the concept of Dangerousity itself.

	BVB – Hoffenheim	Schalke – Köln	Mainz – Wolfsburg	Gladbach – Hoffenheim
Result	1–0	1–2	1–1	1–4
Shots	19–6	15–6	22–8	22–12
Passing accuracy	71% – 70%	86% – 77%	65% – 76%	80% – 85%
Possession	50 – 50	58 – 42	46 – 54	44 – 56
Match performance	466 – 138	569 – 198	446 – 160	278 – 282
Difference Match performance	328	371	286	–4

Source: Link, *Real Time Quantification of Dangerousity in Football*

Link realised that his study of Dangerousity could be considered a breakthrough when Barcelona got in touch. The Catalan giants had already started using his algorithm and wanted to know a few more details. Link was understandably proud that one of the biggest clubs in the world had taken notice of his calculations. At the end of our meeting, I asked him how the idea for the system had occurred to him. His answer was simple and beautiful. 'I thought about it,' he said.

The big data hangover has passed. Data obsessives develop new metrics and complex models such as Packing or Dangerousity at breathtaking pace. Right now, advanced game data might only be a sideshow when it comes to analysing team play; the calculations are not quite eye-catching enough to fundamentally alter game analytics. But the latter will happen once models such as Link's become suitable for daily use, and when every action on the pitch will have a specific mathematical value. At that point in the not too distant future everything we thought we knew about football will be called into question again.

Data plays a crucial role in the automation of visual game analysis. A situation on the pitch is codified, data gets searched along these parameters and the corresponding video sequence gets played out. Where did a team transition? When did they attack on the right, when through the middle? When were the team outnumbered? All those moments can be defined mathematically. Instead of manually searching through videos for hours on end, analysts will leave computers to do that menial work and focus on more productive tasks instead. It's likely that they will extract ever more complex insights from ever more complex numbers. But there's one important part of football where the use of data has already become decisive.

SCOUTING THE DIGITAL SPACE

The best scouts are suddenly being talked about and command transfer fees, just like top players. One of them is Sven Mislintat, who moved from Dortmund to Arsenal. But we'll also meet an outsider with amazingly insightful data profiles.

FOOTBALL'S NEXT HERO

In the last few years, the scout was cast as football's last great romantic figure: a lonely man on a never-ending journey in search of talents that others have misjudged. Author Michael Calvin joined *The Nowhere Men*, as his book referred to them, on provincial pitches in England, writing the 'unknown story of football's true talent spotters'. Over in Germany, Ronald Reng dedicated a whole book to the story of the largely unknown scout Lars Mrosko – *Mrosko's Talente*. Both works were named 'Football Book of the Year' in their respective countries; both painted a picture of a world of impassioned men, toiling in a job that earns them little respect and not much more money. Their reward comes in the form of their judgement being proven right – when they had foreseen an unknown player rise up to develop into a star.

Roughly at the same time, four, five years ago, there also emerged the narrative of the super scouts. They were the faceless men behind a success story, secret club-builders, adept at serially spotting talents.

One eventually famous example was Steve Walsh. Spending relatively little money, Leicester City's Head of Recruitment had assembled the key players in the Foxes' 2016 championship-winning team: Jamie Vardy, Riyad Mahrez, N'Golo Kanté and Christian Fuchs. Vardy was bought from third-division Fleetwood Town. Walsh chanced upon Mahrez, a €500,000 winger in France's second division, having wanted to scout another player there. The Austrian full-back Christian Fuchs was signed on a free from Bundesliga team Schalke 04. Kanté, another find from France, cost €9m. After winning the league with Leicester, the combative midfielder was sold to Chelsea for more than three times that sum to win the Premier League once more. Two years later, the incredibly humble native of Paris lifted the World Cup with France to become a global superstar.

A few months after Walsh had been hailed as a genius, it was Luis Campos' time to receive the plaudits. The Portuguese scout had unearthed many of the players who went all the way to the Champions League semi-final with AS Monaco in the 2016–17 season. Campos had left Real Madrid four years earlier, having worked as a talent and tactics scout for José Mourinho. In his first season at Monaco, the club owned by Russian oligarch Dmitry Rybolovlev, Campos spent the princely sum of €160m on established star players such as James Rodriguez and Radamel Falcao. AS finished runners-up in

Ligue 1 but the following season, the money for investments dried up. The club now made a net profit of €50m in the transfer market, and in 2015–16, they even set a new record for player sales in a single year. Monaco received €180m in transfer fees and spent €110m on new recruits.

Overnight, the Côte d'Azur club had turned into a footballing stock exchange where highly talented players were bought and sold on for huge profit. The team's transient nature at first didn't impact their performances: Monaco scored 107 goals to win the championship for the first time in 17 years in 2017. They broke their sales record soon after: Kylian Mbappé was transferred to Paris Saint-Germain for €180m. Campos, too, left the club to join OSC Lille.

Ramón Rodriguez Verdejo, commonly known as Monchi, is another member of the super scout league. The former Sevilla professional was hired by the Spanish club as sporting director in 2000 but his main expertise was to develop players whose potential had been misjudged by other clubs. Dani Alves was one of those. The Brazilian was sold for nearly €30m more than Sevilla had paid to Esporte Clube Bahia for his services. Signing and selling the likes of Croatian midfielder Ivan Rakitic, Colombian striker Carlos Bacca, as well as many others, proved good business, too. With Monchi in charge, Sevilla weren't just a flourishing import-export store, however. The Andalusians were also very successful on the pitch. They won no fewer than five Europa League trophies in ten years.

Sven Mislintat is one of the stars of the industry, too, even if he abhors the 'super scout' tag. The reliably unshaven and unpretentious German is too down to earth for that. A former amateur footballer blessed with modest talent, he was born in Kamen, a town in Dortmund's periphery best-known for its autobahn interchange and was a childhood BVB fan.

For many years, he had done such a stellar job on the fourth floor of Borussia's club offices – situated next to a dual carriageway – that Arsenal paid a seven-figure compensation to the Bundesliga side for luring him to the Emirates in November 2017.

His Dortmund office was sparsely decorated. A large, tidy desk with a computer monitor, a TV on the wall and a picture on the opposite wall. The most eye-catching thing was the view across the road towards the stadium, a few hundred metres away. Next door was Sporting Director Michael Zorc's office and a few steps further, the scouting department's.

Sven Mislintat is a legend in the European scouting community. Who else would have thought about foraging for players in the Japanese second division in 2010? That's where Mislintat found Shinji Kagawa. He pushed the club to sign the 21-year-old Japanese attacking midfielder on a free from Cerezo Osaka. Two years later, the fans' favourite and double German championship-winner transferred to Manchester United for €16m. That's the stuff every football scout's dreams are made of.

Kagawa wasn't a one-off, either. During the ten years that Mislintat worked for BVB, the club boasted the most successful transfer policy of all German professional clubs. It's instructive to look at their net transfer spend – the difference between money spent on new signings and the fees received for player sales – in relation to the development of players' market values. The comparison is based on estimates by transfermarkt.com. Determining a player's market value is not an exact science, but the website's figures provide reasonably accurate guidance.

Between 2012 and 2017, the squad values of all but a few Bundesliga sides rose, but they fell for some who were relegated. The reduction of value at Werder Bremen and Hamburger SV, who didn't go down in those years, hints heavily at bad transfer policy. Some clubs mainly increased their team's values by spending money on transfers. VfL Wolfsburg, for example, had a positive net spend of €138m for transfers but only increased the value of the squad by €135m over the same space of time. FC Bayern, too, overspent in that respect, whereas RB Leipzig invested aggressively but also created plenty of value in the process.

The table overleaf should not be seen as a mere reflection of successful scouting. Sporting directors and coaches need to be on the same page before players are bought; ideally, the club will also have a strong sense of the kind of football they want to play and choose their players accordingly. In addition, coaches who develop and improve players create plenty of value, too.

As ever, the element of luck shouldn't be underestimated. Kagawa, for example, was being looked after by the player agency of Thomas Kroth, who had specialised in Japanese professionals early on. Kroth, a former Dortmund player whose office is based in the city, has traditionally close ties with Borussia. It was he who tipped off Mislintat about Kagawa's potential. On watching video footage, the BVB scout's interest was sufficiently piqued to fly to Japan to see him play in person. Upon his return, he wouldn't stop pestering manager Jürgen Klopp, Sporting Director Michael Zorc

	Club	Transfer balance	Market value 09/12	Market value 09/17	Market value development	Market value development + transfer balance
1	Borussia Dortmund	38	210	392	182	220
2	1. FC Köln	18	25	106	81	99
3	Bayer 04 Leverkusen	25	130	189	59	84
4	TSG 1899 Hoffenheim	44	87	120	33	77
5	Hertha BSC	11	37	90	53	64
6	SC Freiburg	31	46	73	27	58
7	Mainz 05	21	45	72	27	48
8	RB Leipzig	-148	6	189	183	35
9	Borussia Mönchengladbach	-34	89	157	68	34
10	Eintracht Frankfurt	-18	45	84	39	21
11	FC Augsburg	-12	41	57	16	4
12	SV Werder Bremen	10	82	72	-10	0
13	FC Schalke 04	-14	152	155	3	-11
14	VfL Wolfsburg	-41	116	143	27	-14
15	VfB Stuttgart	6	94	64	-30	-24
16	Hannover 96	-32	77	49	-28	-60
17	FC Bayern München	-236	416	581	165	-71
18	Hamburger SV	-85	109	69	-40	-125
	Average	-23.11	100.39	147.89	47.50	24.39

* all in million euros

Source: transfermarkt.de / Stand: 1.9.2017

and club boss Hans-Joachim Watzke to sign the player, even though they found themselves unable to get a real grip on his potential from watching the videos. The quality of football played in the Japanese second division was so modest that they couldn't quite imagine what Kagawa might be capable of in the Bundesliga. 'The way players challenged for the ball (there) was more reminiscent of volleyball than football,' Michael Zorc, Mislintat's superior, said. Jürgen Klopp, too, was derisive of the mooted transfer. 'How should I explain to a Japanese player from the second division that he doesn't play for us?' he scoffed. But when Kagawa trained with the team for the first time, Klopp became immediately excited.

Kagawa had been the Japanese second division's leading goalscorer with 27 goals in 44 games. That sounded pretty impressive but posed a question that often arises with international transfers. How did the performance in one league compare with that in another? Would a pacy winger from division two be as dangerous in the top flight? Could a Norwegian keeper be expected to be as good in the Premier League as he had been in his own country? And how much should Japanese second division goals count for in German football?

Sporting directors and scouts are constantly faced with the problem of extrapolating a player's ability across different leagues, as football has become a global game. One company has done a lot to contribute to that convergence of knowledge: Wyscout, from Chiavari in northern Italy. Their data bank contains 40,000 players from 250 competitions from all over the world, and clients can access videos from 220,000 games. Each week, another 2,000 games are added. Wyscout's video material comes pre-tagged. Clients can therefore search a player's footage with the use of keywords such as shots, tackles or passes. Any sporting director or scout using the tool can instantly procure a first impression of a player – even if he's based at an obscure second division club in Japan.

Wyscout was founded in 2004 by Matteo Campodonico, a former economics analyst who had worked in a bank's strategy department. In its early years, the firm changed its name and business model a few times until they settled upon becoming a scouting tool in March 2008. Initially, Wyscout was offering statistical information about players and DVDs that would be delivered by courier. Half a year later, it was no longer necessary to send out videos; clients could now watch them on the company's website. Since 2010, the year they stuck with Wyscout as a name, the entire platform has been digital.

Wyscout is by no means the only provider in this area. A similar service has long been offered by English firm Scout7, who were absorbed into OptaPro in 2018. US-based STATS and InStat from Russia also belong to the better-known firms that specialise in that area. Opta also cooperate with American firm TruMedia on marrying data with video sequences. The overall aim is to produce the most extensive and best-tagged video material, which joins up with the most in-depth data sets possible.

A club like Borussia Dortmund get offered about 2,500 players per season. Many of those are at best good enough to play in the fourth division, for the Black and Yellows' second team. But even those must first be culled from the list of possibles. Thankfully, that's done quickly enough with the help of videos and data. Sharp agents can no longer make an average player look like a world-beater on a self-compiled DVD featuring a thumping soundtrack. If an interesting player becomes available, the scouting departments of most clubs in Europe's top leagues are capable of putting together an electronic dossier in the space of 24 hours, and it will include the most telling data as well as a video with all relevant scenes from a minimum of three games. As a result, scouts have avoided countless needless trips to watch contenders in action.

Mislintat decided early on, however, that he wouldn't solely rely on the steady improvement of technological solutions commercial providers offered in terms of digital scouting. He wanted to compete in the global market for players with international elite clubs, which was seemingly impossible.

In Dortmund, Mislintat coordinated the work of ten scouts, quite a big team compared to many German clubs, but almost laughably small in relation to the size of the departments of regular Champions League contenders. The top teams in England, Spain and Italy employ up to 50 talent spotters each. Manchester City, to name but one, employ specialist scouts for Scandinavia, African youth football, and the leagues in Japan, Korea and China. With their army of locally-based experts, those types of clubs never miss out on a prospect.

Mislintat needed to figure out a different way.

MATCHMETRICS AND THE SOBIECH PARADOX

The big day went really well – at first. It was February 2013, and Sven Mislintat was presenting to his bosses a project called Matchmetrics that he had worked on for about a year in his spare time. Dortmund's head scout had joined forces with a sports scientist who had long attempted to statistically record football games, and an IT expert. Ironically, it was Manchester City who had brought the three of them together. The Premier League side had run a competition in 2012, promising to reward the most interesting insight gleaned from a data set of City games they had made available to the public. Nothing of note really came of the contest but Michael Markefka had been inspired enough to crunch the numbers. The former law student had previously worked in an art house cinema, but his main interest lay in coding – and in football. When his cinema jointly hosted an event with Dortmund, he approached Mislintat with a view of introducing him to his ideas about data analysis. He was interested. Six months later, they were pitching the fruits of their labour to the most important men in Germany's second biggest club.

With the help of intelligently used data, they wanted to sift through the vast array of global players more easily. The key, as they saw it, was to marry event data for players with the position of those events. They divided the pitch into 100 squares and assigned them different values of importance. Winning a tackle in the six-yard box was obviously more important than in the centre circle.

The same was true for completed passes and of course shots on goal, as we have seen with Expected Goals and Daniel Link's Dangerousity model. Mislintat and his colleagues calculated the values for their 100 squares based on historic game data and developed an algorithm that was supposed to come up with one definitive number for a player at the end.

In effect, it was a player index. The idea itself was not new. Back in 2009, engine oil company Castrol had sponsored the eponymous index run by FIFA that Arsène Wenger had helped to develop. At the time, media companies started using data providers to collate their own indices, to tell their reader who had played well or badly. They felt a seemingly objective figure might appear more convincing than the subjective opinion of a reporter. But an index is wholly dependent on the weighting of the underlying data. The algorithm at its heart betrays its author's view of football. Different indices can therefore be as disparate as the player grades in the newspapers. On top of that, most indices suffer from the problem that their numbers aren't weighted according to the location of the events on the pitch.

Dortmund's bosses were at first suitably impressed by the presentation. But all of a sudden, Mislintat and his men lost the room. 'Everything went well – until we showed them our top XI,' Mislintat recalled. One of the players in the 'team of the season' the system had picked was Lasse Sobiech, a former Dortmund youth player as it happened, who had been loaned out to relegation contenders SpVgg Greuther Fürth after getting some game time at FC St. Pauli in Bundesliga 2. Sobiech was undoubtedly a solid player – but certainly not an outstanding talent. Sporting Director Michael Zorc and CEO Hans-Joachim Watzke were aghast. How could this system have identified him as one of the best centre-backs in Germany's first division?

Mislintat, too, was aware that Sobiech wasn't an elite defender. But he only realised later why the algorithm had thrown him up. That year, Greuther Fürth were defending very deep and allowed their opponents to cross the ball more often than any other team in the top flight did. Sobiech, tall and good in the air, headed away a large number of those crosses and was accordingly awarded top marks by the system. Mislintat's development team had omitted to scale a player's actions in relation to his team's. If a team like Fürth had a combined 1,000 defensive actions and Sobiech was responsible for 200 of those, his performance amounted to a fifth of the defensive output. At FC Bayern, conversely, Jerome Boateng might have only had 50 defensive actions but they could well represent a quarter of all relevant interventions, since Bayern defended much higher up the pitch and didn't let their opponents put much pressure on the defence in the first place. For strikers, it was the other way around. As one might suspect, Bayern forwards had many more opportunities to get on the ball than those tasked with scoring for Freiburg or Mainz.

Without that vital adjustment being a part of the model, the presentation floundered badly. Mislintat and his team were looking for an investor that would help them complete a project they had worked on for the best part of 12 months, but BVB's bosses didn't think much of funding a program that classified Lasse Sobiech as a top Bundesliga defender. How was such an obviously deficient system supposed to help find prospective players in Spain or even Chile, where the players were far less known? Mislintat contacted other clubs in Germany and England. But no one was willing to invest. Where did they go from here?

The failed pitch laid bare one of football's structural problems. Professional clubs all over the world are besieged by start-ups keen to sell them mooted innovations and a supposed competitive edge – training equipment, nutritional concepts, physiological or psychological treatments, software for data analysis. But no club official is in a position to properly assess whether all those dietary supplements, gym machines or computer programs bestow a real, decisive benefit. Clubs flush with money under the spell of the social proof dynamic therefore tend to buy what everyone else is already buying. Nobody wants to be seen to be missing out on the latest trendy gadget. But later on, quite a few of those expensive acquisitions – including highly-paid specialists – become just as quickly forgotten again. As much as it's great to work as a data analyst at a Premier League club, there's a good chance no one actually reads your reports and findings.

One of the things Mislintat took from his failed attempt to sell his idea was the importance of making his findings visually appealing. He and his team had not been disheartened by rejection and had continued to work on their Matchmetrics start-up. They hired a statistician and a young data visualist from Berlin who produced an attractive front end that even won a design award. 'The moment it looked this good, everyone suddenly wanted it,' Mislintat said. 'No one had been interested before when the very same stuff had been on an Excel sheet. A club's sporting director, seeing it on his iPad, needs to immediately understand what's going on. Now, that's exactly how it works.'

Until 2019, Matchmetrics' founders decided on a strategy of exclusivity. In any given territory, only one club could buy their software. Now it's open for everybody, but the first club in any given country still has the chance to buy exclusivity in its territory. A confidentiality clause precludes Mislintat from naming his clients.

At Dortmund, he had a special agreement with the club: he would use the systems for his work but only a limited number of BVB employees were able to access the data. When he moved to London, Borussia Dortmund had to make new arrangements.

WORKING THE DIGITAL FILTER

It was fascinating to witness Mislintat's program, a sort of real-life football manager tool called Scoutpanel, in action. When I visited him in the spring of 2017, he simulated the search for a left-sided wide defender to demonstrate the system's capability.

The profiles of 1,300 players from all over the world popped up, construed by data brought from providers such as Opta and refined by his own algorithm. A first filter, setting a minimum of 200 minutes played, culled 300 names. Next up: age, 16 to 23 years. Thirdly, the position. 'Defensive Left-Winger' was the super-category that included both 'Left Wing-Back' and 'Left Full-Back' profiles.

The number of hits was reduced drastically once more as soon as Mislintat added qualitative filters. One of them defined a total value, the sum of all performance indicators. In addition, we picked a particularly high 'Take On' rating for one-vs-one actions. 'Shoots' stood for a player's ability to finish off moves, and when top marks for crosses were requested as well, only a handful of players remained. One of them was Raphaël Guerreiro, whom Borussia had bought from French club FC Lorient for €12m at the start of the 2016–17 season.

There was also a player from Belgian side KAA Gent on the shortlist, but how did Mislintat compare performances in Belgium with those in Germany? 'We factor in the performances of the respective leagues in European competitions,' he explained. The lowest multiple was 0.7, the highest 1. Mislintat, though, often turned off the country filter. He was worried he might miss out on talents otherwise.

The best possible rating for a player is ten. A player who constantly performs at this level in a lower league would only be rated a seven by the system, a little better than average. 'I want to leave it up to my subjective appraisal whether a Dutch player with top marks in his league will be able to adapt to the Bundesliga. That's a skill that's not located in the feet – but in the head.'

I found the 'Stability' metric especially interesting. A player who performs consistently at a high level scores highly for Stability. You might call it the Philipp Lahm rating: the former Bayern Munich and Germany captain hardly suffered a bad game in his entire career.

Very young players who display low Stability but fluctuate between average and top-class performances catch Mislintat's eye. 'If he's still young, we might make him into a world-class player. That's the thinking behind it,' he said. Ousmane Dembélé had come to his attention in this manner very early on. Mislintat had suggested Borussia should go for the French winger one year before the then 19-year-old moved from Rennes for €15m. He was sold on to Barcelona only 12 months later, for a partially performance-based fee that could yet rise to €147m.

The index produced by the software varies according to the input of specifications. The total rating is made up from a plethora of subcategories that all come with their own grade. It's not that easy, navigating this world of numbers. Some defenders rate highly for defensive work because they win plenty of tackles but they might be less adept at making interceptions. Their profile could be that of a player who's good in one-vs-one situations but more limited in his reading of the game. It's important not to look at the raw stats in isolation. You have to join the dots. In the end, data is like a language with its own semantics and idioms. Not everybody is as fluent in it as Mislintat and his Matchmetrics colleagues are.

It's not just about finding overlooked talents or underrated players, however. Avoiding costly mistakes in the transfer market is almost more important.

Portuguese midfielder Renato Sanches makes for an interesting case study. FC Bayern were very proud to have signed the supposed super-talent for €35m from Benfica before Euro 2016, where he won the award for the best young player. Sanches is a conspicuous player, not least because of his long dreadlocks that remind people of Ruud Gullit. He takes on many players, passes the ball well and immediately gets noticed by the crowd. He is an example of football's availability heuristic: Sanches does many things on the pitch that people will remember positively.

According to the Matchmetrics index, his defensive actions were appalling for a holding midfielder, however. He was nearly a total failure when it came to shielding the back four.

Sanches has struggled to assert himself at Bayern. His loan to Swansea City was a bit of a disaster as well; he's best remembered for mistaking an advertising board for a team-mate there. Bayern might have been more hesitant to buy him if they had known how poor his defensive contributions rated. Alternatively, they could have decided to play him in a more advanced role, to bring the best parts of his game to bear and mitigate his weaknesses.

There has been a lot of talk about big data in all walks of life in the last few years, football included. A lot of it is pompous nonsense or hot air: especially if the amount of data in question isn't really big at all. Matchmetrics captures roughly 23,000 players in 51,000 games, with 2,500 events for each match. Not quite big data but big numbers for football. They formed the basis of Borussia Dortmund's outstanding transfer policy.

Crucially, Mislintat is not a data nerd, his affinity for technical solutions notwithstanding. A sports science student, he had started scouting games for BVB in 2006 as a freelancer. He was appointed scouting coordinator 12 months later. Initially, the plan had been for a former Borussia player to become head scout but he never arrived. Dortmund were engulfed in a financial crisis that threatened the club's existence; there wasn't much money available for scouting. Mislintat was tasked with managing four scouts who were all over 50 and far more experienced. 'I openly told them that I had to get to know the way they were working,' he said. He told them that he was an analyst, capable of evaluating a player's quality in a technical sense, but that he didn't consider himself a scout. The head scout was taught scouting by his scouts, in other words, and together they became one of the biggest success stories of German football.

One member of Mislintat's former team, the ex-Bundesliga coach Heinz Redepenning, is in his seventies now but he continues to travel abroad for games in Europe. Nicknamed 'Destroyer', he's notorious for his severe verdicts on players and attention to minute detail: he takes note of players spitting onto the pitch or chewing gum. 'If he says we should sign a player, there's really no need to send someone else for a second look,' Mislintat laughed. But he also worked with a guy in his late twenties, versed in the technical jargon of modern coaching. 'We have a great blend of very different sets of eyes, educational backgrounds and footballing experience.'

Once a player was earmarked as a real contender, all the scouts were sent to watch him, each one employing their own criteria and viewpoints. Fishing out great talents from an ocean of data and then having them viewed by a burly coach – Jürgen Klopp – was a process that the marketing department might have dreamt up.

After the success of Shinji Kagawa, scouts were listened to at Dortmund. In many other clubs, they remain peripheral figures, destined to hunt for talents in great solitude. Many sporting directors or managers prefer to rely on their network of agents as far as signing new players is concerned.

'It should never be just Moneyball. But it shouldn't be totally devoid of maths, either – you'll only have subjective opinions otherwise,' Mislintat said. Sometimes, scouts needed to recognise issues that cannot be expressed in numbers as well. A player having the misfortune of playing in the wrong team, for example.

Take Julian Weigl. He was clearly a great passer in midfield but he rarely touched the ball. His side, second division TSV 1860 Munich, preferred to play out long balls from the back. 'We had to notice his qualities in the few moments he actually played the ball.

He was outstanding in scanning the situation. Before he received the ball, he would have his head up three times and look over his shoulder, which made it possible for him to play it straightaway.' Weigl moved to Dortmund for €2.5m in 2015 and was a big success in his first season at Signal Iduna Park.

The most refined algorithm will not be able to detect a player's scanning ability, only humans will. They need to get a sense of who this player really is, down there on the pitch; they have to understand his motivation and his fears, too. But it would be absurd, in this day and age, to look for players without the use of digital pre-sorting facilities.

Moving to the Emirates meant that Mislintat ironically came full circle. 'When I started out, Arsenal had been my personal benchmarks club,' he said. He had wanted Dortmund to do what the Gunners' manager, Arsène Wenger, had specialised in: the signing of highly talented players and their development into big stars.

THE WORLD'S BEST DATA
- MADE IN LAOS

When Arsenal bought American Data firm StatDNA in December 2012 for £2.165m, the deal was shrouded in extraordinary secrecy. The firm's name wasn't even mentioned in the club's annual accounts; it only appeared as an acronym: AOH-USA LLC.

Registered in Chicago, AOH stood for Arsenal Overseas Holdings. The man who had driven the purchase and was responsible for the Chicago connection inside the North London club wasn't even allowed to talk about his work to his fellow Arsenal employees. 'The people in my office didn't really know what I was doing,' Hendrik Almstadt says. The job title on his business card was wilfully obscure, too. 'Football operations'. That could be anything.

Almstadt lives in one of London's most spectacular flats – if you're a fan of Arsenal, that is. It's situated on the top floor of Highbury's former West Stand, now converted into luxury housing. Almstadt's balcony looks out over the courtyard, where the pitch used to be. The other side of his flat comes with a fine view as well: you can spot the Emirates Stadium through the windows.

Almstadt hails from Bremen in northern Germany. He left aged 21, with no idea that he would one day work in football, let alone on a secret mission at one of the biggest clubs in the world. Almstadt studied at the London School of Economics and then worked for three years in investment banking for Goldman Sachs in Frankfurt. He obtained an MBA from Harvard Business School aged 29, moved to General Electric and then once more to an investment fund in London. When his fund lost quite a bit of money during the financial crisis of 2008, he had to look for a new job. 'I asked myself: What am I going to do with my life?'

Almstadt was 35 at the time. After a period of introspection, he figured out that what he really wanted to do was to go into sports. Ideally football. He applied for a position at Arsenal, was hired in 2010 and reported to then CEO Ivan Gazidis.

At first, his was a typical job in sport business. Almstadt was in charge of selling tickets and VIP boxes, and he planned the club's pre-season tours. One day, however, Gazidis asked him to cast a financial expert's eye over Arsenal's squad's composition. No problem, Almstadt said. 'You can look at a squad like a portfolio. It contains 30 assets with different profiles.'

Gazidis found Almstadt's purely analytical approach and the resulting report intriguing enough to let him present them to Arsène Wenger. 'At the end of the meeting, Arsène folded up the paper and put it in his pocket. That was a sign: he had accepted my findings.'

Almstadt's responsibilities evolved: he moved from commercial and business into sports management. He was mainly tasked with making Arsenal's transfer spend and wage bill more efficient. Most importantly, he was supposed to help the club avoid signing costly flops.

There were two examples of costly mistakes at the time. One of them, Marouane Chamakh, a free transfer from Bordeaux, had scored 11 goals in his first 22 games in 2010 and hit the net in six Champions League matches running. But that autumn, his performances went downhill. The Moroccan striker came off the boil and was reduced to being a bit player before going on loan twice. He was finally sold to Crystal Palace for just over £1m three years later.

South Korean forward Park Chu-young didn't even have a good start at Arsenal. Following his last-minute £5m move to London from AS Monaco in 2011, the former Asian Young Footballer of the Year only played for seven minutes in the Premier League. After a series of loans, he left the club out of contract three years later and turned up again at Al-Shabab in Saudi Arabia, where he didn't do much better either.

In both cases, Arsenal had not paid huge transfer fees. But the total cost of wages, sign-on fees and agency commissions still amounted to roughly £34m.

Almstadt was able to show Wenger that data from StatDNA would have flagged up both deals as problematic well in advance. The numbers showed that Chamakh mostly had a low Expected Goals rating at Bordeaux, as he had been taking shots from improbable positions. His good run at the beginning of his short-lived Arsenal career had been nothing more than a 'hot streak', as they say in poker. He had simply been lucky. The system's evaluation of his Bordeaux performances also suggested serious technical limitations which led to him not contributing much in open play. Park's stats cast severe doubt on his ability to play at a club of Arsenal's quality, too.

Having seen Almstadt's presentation, Wenger conceded that he wouldn't have signed either player if he had been privy to the data beforehand. The Frenchman sanctioned the acquisition of a company like StatDNA.

If their numbers could prevent the signing of only one flop in the future, the cost of buying them would have been more than offset by the money Arsenal had saved. The club decided to take over StatDNA. 'The company is an expert in the field of sports data performance analysis, which is a rapidly developing area and one that I, and others, believe will be critical to Arsenal's competitive position,' Gazidis told *The Guardian* in 2014. 'The insights produced by the company are widely used across our football operations – in scouting and talent identification, in game preparation, in post-match analysis and in gaining tactical insights.'

StatDNA was an especially attractive proposition considering they didn't just provide the usual game data. Founder and CEO Jaeson Rosenfeld was also the co-founder of Digital Divide Data, a social impact business dedicated to creating sustainable jobs in the world's poorest countries. Digital Divide Data employed 500 people in Cambodia and Laos, providing part of the workforce for StatDNA.

Eighty men and women in the Laos office work on the technical analysis of football games. They codify every match sent to them in great detail and log classic match data such as shots, passes and tackles – but at a level of granular detail that other companies rarely provide – for reasons of cost. There are other parameters. Did a player use his better foot to shoot? What was the goalkeeper's position? The Expected Goals value calculated there has long been far more precise than most models, as the number of defenders between shooter and goal as well as pressure on the shooter are being taken into account. The laborious nature of the work restricts the number of games that can be codified. But that's not a problem for Arsenal: a few rare exceptions aside, the club is only interested in players from the top five leagues anyway.

Almstadt and his staff kept on adding new categories that could enhance the search for players. One of the metrics they relied on a lot was called 'Pass Value'. It measures the impact of a specific action on the pitch – like a pass – on the probability of a goal being scored. Each player is then assigned a 'Value Creation' grade. It's interesting to see that attempts to quantify performances tend to throw up similar ideas. Daniel Link had developed a comparable metric called Action Value for calculating Dangerousity, as we have seen before.

Arsenal tried to align their wage structure with performance levels as objectively as possible. The quality of attacking players is relatively easy to calculate, by way of looking at their output. But the further you go back on the pitch, the harder it gets to do the same, as we've seen before.

Arsenal and StatDNA tried to develop new data sets for defenders to tackle that problem. A look at the usual numbers would not have shown up Per Mertesacker as a must-buy in 2011. The German centre-back, at Werder Bremen at the time, didn't win an extraordinarily high number of tackles. He didn't intercept a huge number of balls, and his percentage rate for headers won was far from spectacular, too.

But the Laos team learned to identify and categorise 'Defensive Errors'. A mistake could be being too slow, getting caught out of position or having the wrong body shape for attacking the ball.

Applying that filter, Arsenal could automate a part of the preliminary search and flag up quietly solid contenders who would have otherwise been missed – like Mertesacker, for example. They also developed new parameters for goalkeepers, as the existing data was seen as unhelpful. But when Mislintat worked with it, he got the impression that this concept tends to undervalue defenders who like to go for physical encounters with their opponents.

Arsenal spend $2m a year on high-end analytics. They're likely to be one of the clubs with the most advanced data in international football. The scale of the investment didn't put off Arsenal's American owner. Stan Kroenke owns the NBA team Denver Nuggets, the Colorado Avalanche (NHL) and the Colorado Rapids in MLS. He's also the co-owner of the NFL franchise Los Angeles Rams. Investing in data comes naturally for him, and he's friends with Billy Beane, the star of *Moneyball*, as well. 'I was always interested in Moneyball,' Kroenke said in a talk at the 2016 Sloan Sports Conference in Boston. 'One of Billy Beane's heroes happened to be our manager at Arsenal, Arsène Wenger. Arsène has an undergraduate degree in economics and has always had that analytical thing going on. Player analytics is something that goes across these different teams.'

Beane, incidentally, had started to be interested in football. Since 2015, he's been working at Dutch club AZ Alkmaar, run by the former Major League Baseball pro Robert Eenhoorn, on adapting his baseball ideas to the game. He's also part of the consortium that took over second division Barnsley. The group is headed by Chinese businessman Chien Lee, who already owns OGC Nice, where Lucien Favre used to coach.

Almstadt is still amazed today that one of the most famous managers in the world was talking transfers with him. 'I benefited from the fact that Arsène likes numbers. He listens to people who don't have 50 caps, too.' Wenger didn't want the public or even the people in the club to know that Almstadt was doing work for him. The club's scouts knew, however. The fact that Wenger undoubtedly valued Almstadt's input made them take him seriously, albeit grudgingly. 'They didn't accept me as part of their group,' Almstadt says. Maybe they felt under pressure by the bald-headed numbers expert, or they simply didn't appreciate his very confident manner, a vestige from his days in the City.

The wide availability of complex analytics didn't turn Arsenal into a purely data-driven club, however. Sometimes, the data would identify an interesting player, like Kostas Manolas, playing for Olympiacos. But the Greek defender failed to convince the Arsenal scouts and instead moved to AS Roma in 2014, where he became a regular. On the other hand, some transfers allegedly fell through due to the data. Frenchman Antoine Griezmann, who wasn't signed from Real Sociedad, was apparently one of them but the final decision, in any case, didn't lie with the scouts but always with Arsène Wenger.

Nevertheless, 'the analytical process has already become an automatism at Arsenal,' Almstadt says, looking back on his time at the Emirates. The people in charge there now had more than the gut feeling and genius of a great coach to fall back on. This development towards a more analytical approach continued with the hiring of Sven Mislintat – at first.

Almstadt was keen to implement his ideas in a more dominant role and left Arsenal in 2015 for a tumultuous year as Aston Villa's Sporting Director. His experiences didn't differ too much from those Chris Anderson had at Coventry. He didn't have to pay the bus driver or make sure the kit man had enough washing powder but he repeatedly clashed with manager Tim Sherwood in a power struggle. Sherwood found allies in the local tabloid press who regularly criticised the 'bloke from Harvard' but in the end, both were fired. Almstadt moved on to work for the PGA Tour and later followed his former boss to AC Milan, where Gazidis had taken over as CEO in the autumn of 2018.

There is no question Almstadt's work paved the way for Sven Mislintat's move from Dortmund in 2017. The club were even willing to part with the highest transfer fee a head of recruitment has ever attracted. Mislintat arrived at a club in transition. Only six months after he'd started working there, Arsène Wenger left the club after 22 years at the helm. Gazidis soon called time on his decade at the Gunners, too.

In his first two transfer periods, Mislintat pushed through the signings of three players he knew from his Dortmund days. Goalscorer Pierre-Emerick Aubameyang was an immediate success and became Arsenal's best goalscorer straightaway. Sokratis, a solid Greek defender, too, established himself in the first XI, while Henrikh Mkhitaryan arrived from Manchester United in a swap-deal for Alexis Sánchez. The player exchange reduced Arsenal's wage bill and replaced one player who was past his best with a reliable performer. Those were all safe transfers in the sense that they held little risk. The same was true of buying German keeper Bernd Leno, who took over from Petr Cech in goal before too long.

Mislintat was aiming higher, though. He wanted to take the club back to its player-developing roots and discover talents with the potential to grow in the Arsenal shirt. Midfielder Lucas Torreira from Uruguay exemplifies this strategy. Mislintat found him thanks to a feature in his software called 'Similar Players'. It follows the logic of Amazon's algorithm: 'Clubs who like this player might also be interested in these ones.' Eager to add more resilience to Arsenal's midfield, Mislintat checked players with a similar data profile to the Frenchman N'Golo Kanté. The system proposed Sampdoria's

Torreira. 'I knew him, and I had also noticed him doing well before,' Mislintat said. But without looking at the stats, he might not have thought of the South American. Torreira instantly became a firm favourite with the Arsenal supporters after delivering a man of the match performance against Tottenham in their 4–2 North London derby win in 2018.

The club's fans also took an instant liking to Frenchman Matteo Guendouzi, a signing from second division Lorient. For once, the energetic young midfielder's arrival had nothing to do with data analysis but instead came about courtesy of some old-fashioned scouting, not unlike that of Julian Weigl. Mislintat saw in the 19-year-old qualities that cannot easily be measured in numbers: courage, strength of nerve, enthusiasm and leadership.

In his 14 months at Arsenal, Mislintat proved that his way of doing things worked in the Premier League. Arsenal's newly appointed Director of Football, Raul Sanllehi, however, decided to put more trust in his network of agents as far as recruitment was concerned. Mislintat saw this startling development as a signal. His contract was terminated by mutual consent.

THE TRANSFER EXCHANGE RATE

There can't be many transfers in professional football that still go through without anyone looking over the player's numbers. The question is no longer whether data gets consulted – but how good it is, how layered and to what extent it guides the recruitment process. Most clubs are rather tight-lipped on this subject and very few are as outspoken as Fulham were after their promotion to the Premier League in the summer of 2018. 'I'm thrilled to announce that Fulham FC has signed André Frank Zambo Anguissa. André's great data profile, top scouting reports and his sterling reputation confirm his world-class talent. He's been one of our top targets,' club co-owner Tony Khan wrote. The American was just as gushing about the arrival of Calum Chambers from Arsenal: 'I'm very pleased to announce that Calum Chambers has joined Fulham on loan. Calum is a versatile defender and the combination of his strong data profile and positive reports from our scouts confirm that he's a tremendous talent.'

Khan's official title at Fulham is Vice Chairman and Director of Football Operations. His familiarity with player stats isn't all that surprising, given that he's also the co-owner of the Jacksonville Jaguars in the NFL, a sport with a long tradition of analytics. In addition, he owns TruMedia, the aforementioned sports analytics company that works with many leagues and clubs in baseball, American football, football and cricket as well as big media companies such as ESPN.

A whole raft of English clubs are now being owned or part-owned by Americans, including Manchester United, Liverpool, Arsenal, Crystal Palace, Millwall, Barnsley and Coventry. They are presumably especially keen to implement data-driven or at least data-supported decision processes.

In some cases, specific transfers also point to a club's strong affinity with data. When Brighton & Hove Albion were promoted to the Premier League for the first time in 2017, the Seagulls bought a player from the Bundesliga: Pascal Groß. Few people would have heard of the midfielder in England before, and even in Germany there hadn't exactly been a queue of suitors. Groß had played for Ingolstadt, an unfashionable club founded by the merger of two even smaller teams in 2004, based in the city of car-maker Audi. In their second season in the top flight, they had been relegated again without anyone paying too much attention.

But Pascal Groß had been the player who had provided the most assists for shots on goal – not just for Ingolstadt, but in the whole of the Bundesliga. Only four of the 98 attempts he had lined up for his team-mates had found the net but that was chiefly down to the quality of the Ingolstadt strikers: his Expected Assists were nearly twice as high as the goals scored.

Player	Team	Shot assists	Assists	xA
Pascal Groß	FC Ingolstadt	98	4	7.63
Emil Forsberg	RB Leipzig	94	19	7.81
Vincenzo Grifo	SC Freiburg	71	8	5.63
Ousmane Dembélé	Borussia Dortmund	63	12	10.73
Thomas Müller	FC Bayern	60	12	9.96
Kerem Demirbay	TSG Hoffenheim	60	8	6.35
Sebastian Rudy	TSG Hoffenheim	60	7	5.01
Markus Suttner	FC Ingolstadt	53	5	6.33
Julian Brandt	Leverkusen	51	8	7.91
Max Kruse	Werder Bremen	50	7	5.53

Source: OptaPro

Groß attracted the attention of a few clubs whose scouting was predominantly data-based. Brighton, too, had become aware of his numbers, their recruitment analyst Elliott Williams told me at an analytics conference. Williams, who moved to RB Leipzig in 2018, politely declined to share more information on the process, citing confidentiality. But in an interview with *11FREUNDE* magazine, Groß recalled his astonishment at the technical report the English club had compiled on him. 'During negations about the transfer, Brighton's scout suddenly put a 50-page dossier on the table. What I can do, what I can't do… they knew everything about me. I was impressed.' Brighton also didn't mind that supporters were likely to be underwhelmed by the signing of an unknown German player from an unknown relegated team in Germany. As a newly promoted Premier League side, they would have been able to spend much more on transfers.

Making smart, inexpensive deals saves money that is better spent on wages. As we have seen, that's a more profitable allocation of your resources. Groß, bought for a mere £2.7m, turned out to be an immense bargain. He immediately became a regular on the south coast. He played in all 38 league games, scored seven goals and made eight assists.

Brighton & Hove Albion making this kind of left-field deal was not a coincidence. The club, remember, is owned by professional gambler Tony Bloom, who's likely to have the same numbers-driven approach to transfers that his old rival Matthew Benham follows at Brentford.

The recurring question that surrounds the movement of players across international borders is the portability of their performance levels. There is an incalculable human factor – players have to adapt to leaving their home and settle in a different country – but also one of analytics. What extent of their qualities can players such as Kagawa or Groß transfer into a new league?

When FC Midtjylland signed Finnish pro Tim Sparv from SpVgg Greuther Fürth in the summer of 2014, Sparv quickly realised that he didn't owe his move to his agent making the right phone call at the right time or to a scout who had seen him on a good day. Sparv, it turned out, was the first player signed on the recommendation of Benham's model. The program's international club ranking valued the performance quality of a decent Bundesliga 2 team such as Fürth as highly as a Danish top team. The Franconians were even rated better than some clubs in the lower third of the Premier League at the time. There was no point trying to get a Premier League player to sign for Midtjylland, short of heaping tons of money on him, but a comparable player from Germany's second division could be lured to Denmark with the promise of winning trophies and playing in European competition.

In 2018, football consulting firm 21st Club found that players from Ligue 1 were on average 17 per cent more expensive than players of a similar level from other leagues, like Switzerland, for example. In other words, there were bargains to be had. 21st Club talks of a 'football exchange rate' when it comes to international comparisons between leagues and clubs. You don't need your own data sets and complex rankings to get an overview of a club's or a league's quality level. A website like clubelo.com offers useful guidance. They list the Elo values (a concept transferred from chess for evaluating players relatively to each other) of 614 European football teams ranging from Barcelona at the top to bottom side San Marino's SP La Fiorita.

This is how the league rankings looked in January 2019:

Liga	Club Elo Points
La Liga	1,736
Premier League	1,709
Bundesliga	1,680
Serie A	1,634
Ligue 1	1,580
Russian Premier League	1,547
La Liga 2 Spain	1,520
Jupiler Pro League Belgium	1,478
Bundesliga Austria	1,477
2 Bundesliga Germany	1,460
Swiss Super League	1,458
Süper Lig Turkey	1,452
Ukrainian Super League	1,447
Eredivisie Holland	1,424
Serie B Italy	1,403

Source: Club Elo

This table provides a decent overview of the balance of power in European football. A club's scouting department can strategically pick leagues that fit their own playing level.

21st Club noted that three times as many Serbians as Hungarians were playing in the big leagues, even though their national divisions were roughly on a par. It could be that Serbian players are more skilful and therefore prone to heading abroad earlier in their careers, which hurts the chances of their home clubs competing internationally. But the discrepancy might also be down to the fact that there are a lot of Serbian agents and club officials working in European football in contrast to just a handful of Hungarians. The data tells us little without context and proper interpretation.

PACKING PLAYS

When I met Stefan Reinartz again in autumn 2018 to learn how Packing had developed, he came up with a remarkable line. 'I've spent a lot of time over the course of the last six months figuring out what it is we were really doing here and what the data was actually telling us,' he said. It sounded a bit like the onset of an existentialist crisis. But Reinartz questioning himself had in fact produced an interesting answer.

'Traditional data is good at capturing the skill set of a player; ours is good at quantifying his performance,' Reinartz said. Knowing that a player is capable of many sprints, of playing good passes in the final third of the pitch or of taking many shots from good positions makes it possible to produce a portfolio of individual skills. But that doesn't tell you much about the player's contribution to the game and to his team's collective performance. Reinartz and his team at Impect wanted to ensure that Packing could do precisely that.

In Germany, almost every football fan had heard of Packing. A few people had come across the term abroad as well. But what was the business case for their program? That was another important question. German state broadcaster ARD's use of it during the Euros in 2016 had helped to build the brand but proved a one-off. After Mehmet Scholl stopped working as a TV expert, Packing was no longer deployed. Some coaches, namely Thomas Tuchel at Borussia Dortmund (and also at Paris Saint-Germain), worked with Packing in their game analysis but it hadn't quite found wide-scale acceptance as a tool.

The muted response showed up one fundamental problem of data analytics in football: most coaches spend so much time working with their teams that the added value of having your own game translated into numbers isn't all that high.

Sporting directors and heads of recruitment, on the other hand, are hungry for useful data that boosts their ability to make more informed decisions in the transfer market. Talking to club officials, Reinartz realised that most of them preferred to see one single number, to get a rough idea of a player's footballing worth. Packing provided an abundance of new parameters such as bypassed defenders, passes received or players brought back into the game by interceptions but making sense of them all was a circuitous process. What's more, many other data services (STATS, for example) had started offering their own indices as well. Sven Mislintat's Scout-panel software, too, shared the same approach.

In response, Impect set out to produce something unique: their proprietary, exclusive data. Reinartz's aim was to consolidate all of their numbers into one absolute figure that would be beyond reproach – like the objectively measured values in other sports. 'We had to figure out one thing: what does performance mean in football?' Reinartz said. He had put that question to many coaches and club officials, and most of the answers had been surprisingly trite. 'Players playing well,' someone said. Another popular answer: 'Players doing what I tell them to do.'

In other sports, performance is much easier to define. A 100m sprinter's excellence is measured in seconds. A high jumper's skill is expressed in metres, a weightlifter's power in kilograms. Football's measures of success are goals scored and goals conceded. But that doesn't tell us much about one individual player's contribution to his team's ability to score or defend.

Reinartz and his colleagues looked at their Packing numbers and tried to figure out how much a player increased his team's goalscoring probability with his shot, killer pass or brilliant run – and how much he reduced the probability of a goal being conceded. Essentially, they recalibrated the existing data. To what extent did the different parameters increase a team's chances of finding the net and to what extent did they reduce their chances of conceding? Daniel Link had asked himself the same question in his bid to calculate Dangerousity, even if his data base had been different.

A defender playing the ball past two strikers into midfield increases the goalscoring probability by an average rate of 0.5 per cent. If his pass is received in front of the opposition back four, the probability goes up by nearly 5 per cent. The cumulative effect of these actions over the course of 90 minutes can be surmised in one value. If it's 0.2, it stands for a player adding 20 per cent to the probability of a goal being scored. A defender who's not that good in his build-up play can still rate this highly, too, if he scores from set-pieces every fifth game. A player's passing ability and the goal threat he carries are both taken into account.

'We haven't built an index but a model,' Reinartz explained. The value of each player produces a ranking for six different positions: centre-back, right side of defence, left side of defence, defensive midfield, attacking midfield and striker. Two examples of the 2018–19 season in the Premier League illustrate the concept.

Liverpool's Roberto Firmino is unsurprisingly revealed as very strong 'playing' forward. His profile shows him being great at receiving balls in front of the back four (bypassed opponents receiving) and very good at producing through-balls that split the back line (bypassed defenders).

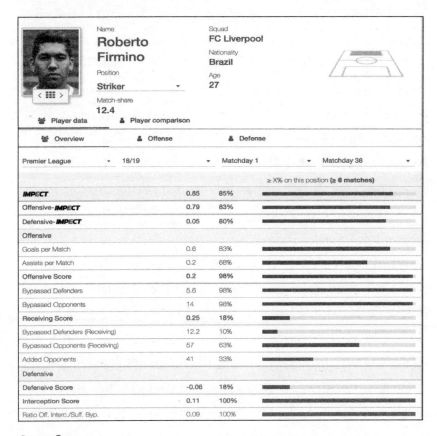

Name		Squad		
Roberto Firmino		**FC Liverpool**		
		Nationality		
		Brazil		
Position		Age		
Striker ▾		**27**		
Match-share				
12.4				

👥 Player data   👤 Player comparison

👥 Overview		👤 Offense		👤 Defense	

Premier League ▾	18/19 ▾	Matchday 1 ▾	Matchday 38 ▾

			≥ X% on this position (**≥ 6 matches**)
IMPECT	0.85	85%	
Offensive-*IMPECT*	0.79	83%	
Defensive-*IMPECT*	0.05	80%	
Offensive			
Goals per Match	0.6	83%	
Assists per Match	0.2	68%	
Offensive Score	0.2	98%	
Bypassed Defenders	5.6	96%	
Bypassed Opponents	14	96%	
Receiving Score	0.25	18%	
Bypassed Defenders (Receiving)	12.2	10%	
Bypassed Opponents (Receiving)	57	63%	
Added Opponents	41	33%	
Defensive			
Defensive Score	-0.06	18%	
Interception Score	0.11	100%	
Ratio Off. Interc./Suff. Byp.	0.09	100%	

Source: Impect

By comparison, Callum Wilson (AFC Bournemouth), a more orthodox goalscorer, excels in making deep runs beyond the defence himself (bypassed defenders receiving).

Name			Squad		
Wilson			**AFC Bournemouth**		
Position			Nationality		
Striker	▾		**Ireland**		
			England		
Match-share			Age		
18.3			**26**		

👥 Player data   👤 Player comparison

👥 Overview	👤 Offense	👤 Defense

| Premier League | ▾ | 18/19 | ▾ | Matchday 1 | ▾ | Matchday 38 | ▾ |

			≥ X% on this position (≥ 6 matches)
IMPECT	0.83	83%	
Offensive-***IMPECT***	0.82	88%	
Defensive-***IMPECT***	0.01	28%	
Offensive			
Goals per Match	0.5	70%	
Assists per Match	0.3	83%	
Offensive Score	0.09	55%	
Bypassed Defenders	2.8	60%	
Bypassed Opponents	4	33%	
Receiving Score	0.45	78%	
Bypassed Defenders (Receiving)	17.7	80%	
Bypassed Opponents (Receiving)	49	33%	
Added Opponents	33	85%	
Defensive			
Defensive Score	-0.04	57%	
Interception Score	0.05	20%	
Ratio Off. Interc./Suff. Byp.	0.04	23%	

Source: Impect

Impect makes it possible for scouts to configure individual search templates. Those searching for a purely defensive enforcer in midfield might be happy to look past a relatively low Offensive-Impect while those who need a deep-lying playmaker certainly won't. 'In the data-based search for players, many fire a shotgun. We are the sniper's scope,' Reinartz says.

There's also the option of comparing player profiles or to check whose profiles would make for a good partnership. Have a look at N'Golo Kanté and Paul Pogba, World Cup winners France's two central midfielders. Pogba's skills are predominantly on the left side of the radar based on data from the performances in Russia, Kanté's are mostly on the right. Put together, they make for the ideal player in front of the defence.

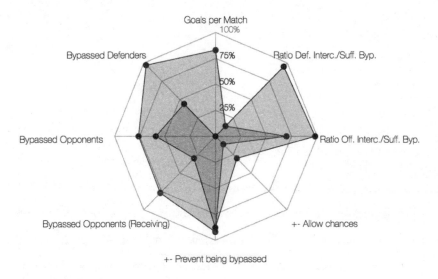

Source: Impect

One of the recurring issues with data-based research is the frequent use of averages. Players can be quite up and down in their performances. Mislintat's Matchmetrics software, you'll recall, includes a Stability parameter that takes note of such variance, and Packing recognises the problem as well, as we can see with a closer look at FC

Augsburg's Philipp Max. The left-back attracted a lot of attention in 2018. Many Bundesliga clubs as well as scouts from England came to see him play, and something very unusual happened. Opinions were extremely divided. Some went home shrugging their shoulders, wondering what all the fuss was about, others were thrilled by what they had seen. Impect stats ranked him the fourth-best Bundesliga player in his position in 2017–18 but they also revealed why experts couldn't agree on his quality.

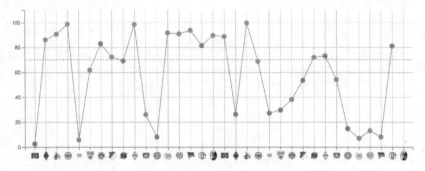

Source: Impect

The dotted line shows his comparative rating: he was better than 65 per cent of left-backs in the Bundesliga. More interestingly, however, he had also played ten games in which he'd been dramatically below his best and ten games where he'd been absolutely outstanding. His performances were hugely inconsistent. But Max was not a youngster who might have been forgiven such volatility – he was already 24 years old at the time. That was probably the reason he continued playing for Augsburg in the following season.

As mentioned before, Impect had opened a new office in the Philippines and started providing Packing numbers for the Premier League,

Spain's La Liga, the Dutch Eredivisie, Belgium's top flight and the second divisions of Germany and France. The plan is to broaden their offering further in the next few years. Reinartz is convinced that far less money will be wasted on bad transfers in the future, even if it weren't for the model he helped develop. 'In ten years, we won't see anyone getting it badly wrong in factual terms,' he says.

Reinartz also believes that Packing will make it possible to digitally analyse squads before too long. 'We're hopefully not far away from being able to simulate the theoretical impact of playing a different player. Most people are mistaken in their belief that good players are good at a lot of different things. They are not. They're extremely good at doing a few things and can't do some others well at all.'

GOALIMPACT: CHARTING A PLAYER'S UNSEEN NET EFFECT

In the summer of 2001, the Dallas Mavericks basketball team signed the virtually unknown center, Evan Eschmeyer, from the New Jersey Nets. He had been on $400,000 per year, but at Dallas, he was given a six-year deal worth a total of $20m. This was basketball's equivalent of Liverpool buying a Huddersfield reserve player and awarding him Mohamed Salah-type wages. As it turned out, Eschmeyer never really made it at Dallas. Two years and a bad injury later, he was released before his contract had expired. But what was it the Mavericks had seen in him? And how could they have overestimated him this much?

In 2005, the Houston Rockets had to cut their roster after the summer training camp, as they did every year. The axe fell on a rookie called Chuck Hayes. He was signed by NBA Development League franchise Albuquerque Thunderbirds. A series of injuries led to Houston re-signing him six months later. Hayes played much more often than expected and became part of the first team as a power forward in the following season. His stats weren't overly impressive, with the exception of one: whenever Hayes was on court, the Rockets were defensively stronger and conceded fewer points.

No one could quite explain why that was the case. In basketball, as in football, it's tricky to quantify defensive work. Hayes went on to stay for seven years in Texas and played a total of 11 NBA seasons with more than 600 games and more than 11,000 minutes on court.

A few years later, when Evan Eschmeyer had almost been forgotten, Mavericks owner Mark Cuban explained why he had been a flop: they had vastly overvalued his plus-minus data. The metric's concept is easily grasped – it looks at the net points won or lost during a player's time in the game. You don't need to land any shots to attain a value of +15; it's enough that your team scored 15 points more than the opposition while you were on court. Cuban, an early adopter of stats-based recruitment, had noticed Eschmeyer's fantastic plus-minus rating but he couldn't live up to it at Dallas, in contrast to Chuck Hayes who made his teams better every time he played, over the course of a decade.

Football, too, grapples with the challenge of finding the type of player that doesn't register highly in existing data because his type of game is hard, or maybe even impossible, to measure. How can the contribution of a player who acts like a 'glue', in the words of their manager, be measured – someone who brings the whole team together in inexplicable ways? How can humility and industriousness be calculated? Is there a way to mathematically comprehend the special talent of someone who prevents an opposition pass being played or a tackle from happening by being in the right place at the right time very often?

'This player who always wins the 50-50 balls, barks defensive instructions at his team-mates and hunts down the opposition – the classic stats don't reflect his value. But plus-minus does,' Cuban said. Was there a way of applying that logic to spot those hidden champions in football?

Jörg Seidel, an executive at an energy company in Hamburg, would probably be too careful to get involved in any debate about football's deeper secrets. But he's at least mildly interested in the game. Sometimes, he'll even have a match on in the background, while he's on his computer tending to his algorithm. He's never heard of some of the players who feature in his index, let alone seen them play. Seidel is much more keen on handball, the game he used to play himself. But his lack of knowledge and indeed interest in football didn't stop him from winning a prediction game a group of his friends had run during Euro 2004. He had developed a mathematical model similar to the plus-minus rating, not unlike the statistical patterns banks use to distinguish between good and bad debtors when approving loans. His job has taught him to crack complex problems with the use of algorithms and computers.

The triumph as a tipster encouraged him to develop his model further. He wasn't interested in a player's running stats, the number of passes he played or how many shots he'd taken. His Goalimpact index took a leaf out of the plus-minus metric: all he needed were the team sheets including the substitutions and the timing of the goals. Calculating a footballer's net impact is less clear-cut than in basketball due to the higher number of players on the pitch, far fewer substitutions and most of all, the low-scoring nature of the game.

'I can tell that a player is good but I can't say why,' Seidel said. He has effectively reversed the regular analytics method of deducing a player's performance from data. 'I can prove that a team scores more goals and concedes less if a certain player is on the pitch,' he says. The precise nature of the player's involvement is not important in this context. All that matters is the bottom line; quite literally: his net effect.

Seidel's results are perhaps most readily comparable to golf handicaps or the Elo rating system, which calculates a player's skill level in chess. He would never claim that Thomas Müller (Goalimpact value of 195 in 2017) was a better player than Karim Benzema (190). But his model sees Müller as a slightly more valuable player when he's on the pitch for Bayern than Benzema is for Real Madrid.

Seidel needs a player's data from a minimum of two seasons to make meaningful calculations. He's included 320,000 players from over 200 leagues worldwide, including many competitions that even the biggest data providers don't cover, such as the Venezuelan league, the Conference North in England or Scotland's League Two. Over the years, Seidel has tweaked his algorithm to weight the strength of a league and of its teams, as well as the age of the players. A 21-year-old player does worse, on average, than a 23-year-old, and professionals tend to hit their maximum performance levels at 26. The model even takes into account the relative age effect for youngsters: players born in the second half of the year are at an advantage when they come up against those born in the first six months.

'It's statistics. Luck can therefore influence the position in the ranking,' Seidel said. Some players might simply be fortunate to be part of a team on a winning run. Gareth Bale, on the other hand, had probably little to do with the fact that Tottenham didn't win the first 24 league matches he featured in at the beginning of his career. Spurs, coached by Harry Redknapp, were notoriously flaky at the time.

But if a team always wins or always loses with a certain player on the pitch, it's probably not entirely down to coincidence. I found it strange that the model rated Mario Götze in first place, Lionel Messi in fourth and Cristiano Ronaldo only in 38th in winter 2016. But Seidel proposed a different reading. 'I have hundreds of thousands of players in my data set. If the superstars show up in the top 50, that's good enough for all intents and purposes.' He was right, of course. More importantly, his purely mathematical system that rated all those unsighted players didn't make the mistakes of one reliant on an element of visual judgement. 'Human perception suffers from a series of defects. We overvalue actions – players who dribble or score goals. We overvalue playing time – "he didn't play, he must be bad". And we overvalue attacking play,' Seidel said.

When Sadio Mané moved to Southampton from RB Salzburg in 2014, some experts wondered whether the step up to the Premier League was too steep. But Seidel had already pinpointed the Senegalese forward as a prospect for any club in Europe's top five leagues.

The opposite was true of Tiemoué Bakayoko, Chelsea's €40m flop bought from Monaco who was loaned to AC Milan after only one season at Stamford Bridge. According to Seidel's calculations, he was never a player of Premier League class.

Goalimpact has proved surprisingly good at predicting the performances of teams as well. Ahead of Germany's semi-final win over Brazil at the 2014 World Cup, the hosts' starting XI had an average rating of 128; that of Joachim Löw's side was 154.8.

The Goalimpact rating also reflects the work of managers. 'Pep Guardiola has beaten the model's prediction so often, it's safe to assume that he does indeed get more out of his teams than the sum of their parts. The same goes for Christian Streich at SC Freiburg,' Seidel explained.

Such striking predictions would make Goalimpact interesting for professional gamblers, too, but its core business is the scouting of players. The first enquiry came from an English club, in 2004. The man on the phone said he was following Seidel on Twitter and that he would like to know more. The gestation of a Goalimpact deal can take a while. One Polish first division team got in touch at roughly the same time as the English club but then only called back two years later. 'They said to me: "You were right then." And then they wanted to buy information.' Seidel didn't reveal the club in question nor the identity of his other clients. 'But when we started the cooperation, they were fighting relegation in Poland. Now, they're contenders for the championship.'

Many English clubs, from Premier League down to League One, take his data. One of the few sides who openly admit to working with him are Shandong Luneng of the Chinese Super League.

The fees Seidel charges are dependent on the club's league. A German fourth division club only pays a token licence fee but Goalimpact will receive a sell-on fee if a player bought on Seidel's recommendation is later sold on for profit. The latter hasn't materialised yet but the terms have been contractually agreed. Higher-level clubs unwilling to structure deals this way pay a flat rate.

There are different kinds of enquiries. Small clubs who are offered a player by an agent consult Goalimpact for an objective appraisal. First division teams are more likely to use Seidel's model as a search engine: Who are the best centre-backs valued up to €2m and out of contract soon? Seidel believes there are still bargains to be had. 'According to our algorithm, there are many good players in the German fourth division, for example, who have perhaps simply been unlucky to be stuck at that level.'

No club should buy a player on the basis of one sole number; Seidel is the first one to admit that. Individual performances always need to be seen in the context of the team. Concrete observation must exclude the possibility that a player was overrated by statistics, as had happened in the case of Evan Eschmeyer. The sample size had been too small to take such an expensive punt on him.

Mark Cuban is still adamant that plus-minus ratings can help the evaluation of players, however – especially those who have both major strengths and weaknesses. 'What do I do with a player who nails six out of ten shots but is useless in defense?' he says. 'And what about the great defensive guy who can't dribble at all and can't shoot either? The most experienced basketball heads find it extremely hard to answer those questions by simply watching a player. How do you weigh up advantages with disadvantages to see what it says on the scales? You have to count.'

Goalimpact also attempts to anticipate players' careers. Applying the model retrospectively makes for interesting results. Cristiano Ronaldo, five-time Ballon d'Or winner, was rated a future top club player as a teenager, but he exceeded expectations in extreme fashion, constantly, year by year.

In the illustration below, the solid line charts the Goalimpact value, and the thin line is the prediction of the value's rise. In his first five years, Ronaldo was projected to become one of the 500 best players in the world. At the age of 22, both the forecast and his actual value shot up dramatically. And when he moved to Juventus from Real Madrid in 2018, Goalimpact still rated him among the top 20 in the world.

Source: Goalimpact

The charts of two players with similar projections but different career developments are also intriguing. The model expected Mesut Özil to become one of the best 1,000 players in the world but he in fact became a top 30 and top 50 player.

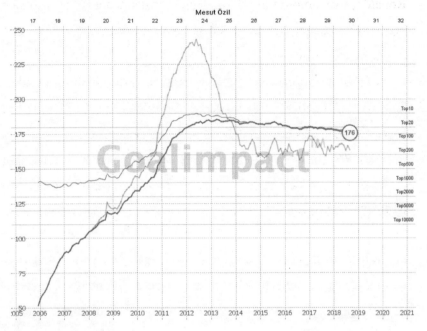

Source: Goalimpact

The initial projection was based on nothing more than his games for his club's youth team and the youth national teams. Another player who had been tipped to become a great by many experts would have had a similar forecast by the model. Unlike Mesut Özil, who turned out an overperformer, Bojan Krkic developed in line with expectation or slightly below, however.

Source: Goalimpact

The performances of players aged 16 or 17 can give you an indication of their career trajectory but no guarantees. Talented youngsters can get lucky and receive the right mentoring in a conducive environment or they can get coaches who don't recognise the player's talent. Severe injuries have put paid to many promising careers, while others suddenly underwent a huge footballing growth spurt. Nineteen-year-old Zlatan Ibrahimović was forecast to be a mere top 1,000 player by Goalimpact but he made it all the way to the top ten.

For the German version of this book, published in spring 2018, I asked Seidel who will be a world-beater in ten years' time. He named a Canadian I had never heard of: Alphonso Davies. The winger under contract at Vancouver Whitecaps had an estimated market value of €450,000 according to transfermarkt.com at the time, and

Goalimpact predicted that he'd develop in a way that would make him worth a multiple of that in no time. A few months after the book was released, German giants Bayern announced that they had bought Davies for €10m in January 2019.

The U17s player with the highest Goalimpact right now is Eddy Salcedo, touted as the next wunderkind in Italy. He plays at Internazionale on loan from Genoa, and the Milanese club have an option to make his move permanent for €15m. In the summer of 2018, 16-year-old Salcedo played his first friendlies for the senior team. Will he be the next global superstar?

COGNITIVE
FOOTBALL

The history of football is one of acceleration. Clubs want their players to develop faster minds. Personality profiles may contribute to a more efficient working culture within football clubs.

THINKING FASTER

Sebastian Rudy lifts his head and notices a lot of space opening up in front of him. The Hoffenheim player hesitates for a moment in disbelief. But there really is no opponent from Leipzig to worry about. Rudy has already run past one. Another one is surprisingly retreating, instead of challenging him. And a third opponent drifts out to the right. Go on then! By now, Rudy has taken the ball 25 metres up the pitch and almost reached the centre circle. He passes the ball to Kerem Demirbay on the left. The midfielder with the startlingly spindly legs takes control of the ball with his left foot. Keeping his head up, Demirbay plays a long ball forward, deep into the heart of Leipzig's half.

Since the start of the counter-attack, exactly 6.7 seconds have passed and every bit of it is choreographed. All players understand the runs they have to make. Striker Sandro Wagner vacates the centre in order to make room for Demirbay's pass and drag an opponent with him. His attacking colleague Andrej Kramaric dashes to the left side, while Nadiem Amiri powers forward on the right. Hoffen-heim's coach Julian Nagelsmann has a word for this attack pattern, when the ball is played from the centre to the wing and back to the centre again – a 'zig-zag-opening'. Once Amiri receives the ball from Demirbay on 9.2 seconds he immediately passes it on to Kramaric. The counter-attack is still on track as the Croatian striker follows the ball to the left side of the six-yard box and puts in a low, first-time cross. Amiri finishes off the 12.9 second move with an easy tap-in from close range. It's one of the finest attacks of the Bundesliga season 2016–17 – and a goal bristling with stories.

In the days leading up to the match in Leipzig, I had spent some time at Hoffenheim's training ground in Zuzenhausen, observing the drills and instructions of Julian Nagelsmann. The 29-year-old had saved the club from relegation and was on course for delivering their best Bundesliga finish to date: fourth spot. After playing their first-ever season in the Europa League, Hoffenheim qualified for the Champions League a year later.

Nagelsmann belongs to that group of coaches who walked through the door Christian Heidel had opened for them in Mainz, when he promoted Thomas Tuchel from youth coach to first team manager. Having captained 1860 Munich's youth teams, Nagels-mann was forced to retire from playing aged 20 due to several injury problems. Tuchel appointed him opposition scout for the U19s of FC Augsburg. Nagelsmann, a business school student at the time, accepted the offer. Aged 22, Nagelsmann became U17 coach at Hoffenheim; three years later, he led the club's U19s to the German championship. They would have promoted him to first team coach the following season but he was still busy doing his pro coaching course then. From close up, Nagelsmann's approach to football training was highly exciting. I witnessed a coach who had conceived an astonishing amount of ideas.

Usually, the training pitch featured different drill stations. On my first day, I saw more than 20 players getting crammed into an area the length of half a football pitch but just 15 metres wide. The narrow playing field constantly forced them into one-vs-one situations and into adopting a certain passing game logic. A different drill was set up so they would play the first ball into wide areas, over and over again. And at the end of the morning session, four goals suddenly appeared on the pitch. Two of them were proper football ones, the other two were the size of ice hockey goals. A small goal was placed opposite a big one at the other end of the pitch, which now resembled a parallelogram and saw players constantly switch the flanks with long diagonal balls.

The teams were obviously busy focusing on the complex tasks. Some of the drills didn't just look odd, they also came with some peculiar additional rules such as restrictions on certain passes and special conditions that had to be met before a shot on goal was permissible. Defender Benjamin Hübner, a new summer signing, later told me it took him weeks to get to grips with it all. Once the players left the pitch, you could tell the training session had not only challenged them physically. 'We want their heads to spin during training,' explained Jan Mayer, Hoffenheim's sports psychologist.

Nagelsmann's brand of football is based on 31 principles. 'The players probably can't list them all. But once I stop training and ask them what we are currently working on, they can name that particular principle,' he said. Those 31 principles are Nagelsmann's trade secret. He has only spoken about a few of them publicly. Here's one: Nagelsmann prefers to force the opponent into playing a poor pass rather than win the ball in one-vs-one situations, which are subject to too many random outcomes for his liking. 'Our goal is to always use an interception to have an advantage of pace over an opponent that's fanned out and positioned widely,' Nagelsmann declared. In other words: He wants to catch the opponent off guard, as his team did so brilliantly in the build-up for their delightful goal against Leipzig.

The coach also demands that passes are played diagonally rather than squarely or vertically. This allows for more angles and more depth – the prerequisites of the zig-zag move in Leipzig. He asks his players not to pass the ball first time, as that would increase the chance of a bad pass. That's why Demirbay controlled the ball with his first touch, well enough to be able to play a precision pass to Amiri. But in crucial moments players are of course free to ditch the principles – just like Amiri and Kramaric did when they combined with first-time passes before finishing the attack.

Those principles hardly reinvent football. But they are conveyed in interesting ways. Striker Sandro Wagner, who later joined FC Bayern, said: 'It was new for me to have a coach who takes a modular approach to football. He takes a complicated game, takes it apart into different sections, rehearses those and then puts it all back together, step by step.' Nagelsmann is also one of the few Bundesliga coaches who makes real tactical changes during matches. He sometimes reshuffles the formation several times and moves players around.

Standing in Nagelsmann's office, you quickly realise that he's unfairly categorised as a so-called 'laptop' manager in Germany. Yes: he has a laptop. But there are also pieces of paper everywhere. He likes to take notes and files his training plans in bulky, old school ring binders. He might be a theoretician as well as a passionate tactician, but Nagelsmann also said: 'Football is a players' game and not a coaches' game.' He doesn't think of players as pieces that he moves back and forth on the pitch in a tactical chess game on Saturdays. He's more of a player-coach who can't play any more, but would still very much love to. He's close to his team, not just in terms of age. 'Football is not meant to be a tactical battle for coaches!'

Different coaches come with different priorities and have different qualities. Nagelsmann is first and foremost a teacher of football. He wants his players to learn constantly, even the older ones, and prepare them for the Bundesliga – in general terms, as well as for each and every game. In order to make it work, he draws up a curriculum in which every day of training and every drill serves a specific idea. Tuesday is 'education day', dedicated to deepening the understand of his principles. Training sessions on Wednesdays are closed to the public and used to specifically prepare for the upcoming opponent. On Thursdays, players attend a video analysis session in the morning, followed by a full XI-vs-XI test game – again behind closed doors. Fridays see a much lighter training session during which smaller details are addressed.

Ahead of the match against Leipzig, Nagelsmann had carried a tactics board onto the pitch and explained to his players how the opponent could be caught off balance. He wanted to take a different approach than usual, to utilise the wings more and operate with long balls. Those tactics ran in parts contrary to his usual doctrine. He chose the team's exercises accordingly. They were designed to get the players to make the right intuitive decisions on the pitch rather than cast their minds back to what they had seen on the tactics board. 'The development of training drills for one specific area is a very creative task which I enjoy a lot,' Nagelsmann said. He never wants to do the same drill twice with a team, which is why he's already archived hundreds of exercises. If he has come up with a nice new form of exercise you can see it in his face as he enters his office, radiant with joy.

Following Hoffenheim's qualification for European football, the players were amazed to find a giant video screen installed next to the training pitch in Zuzenhausen. The new tool was meant to relay the contents of Nagelsmann's footballing philosophy even faster. He could immediately show them what he wanted them to do or what had gone wrong. Speeding up the process was especially important as the burden of extra matches meant that there would be even less time to prepare for upcoming opponents in detail.

Time is an essential factor in modern football, every way you look at it. If a coach of a team involved in European competitions creates elaborate match plans tailored for every opponent, he needs to find a time-efficient method of communicating them to his players. Nowadays, the quality of a player is also judged by how quickly he can understand and implement the things his coach asks of him. Time during a match is especially important because there is so little of it. The history of football could be told as the vanishing of time. 'Control, look around and pass', a method taught to players in the past, has become a 'look before you receive the ball' and the control and pass sequence has merged into one moment.

BRAIN APPS AND VIRTUAL REALITY

Jan Mayer, who has been working as a sports psychologist at Hoffenheim since 2008 and looks after youth players as well as the professionals, feels that the main difference between playing in the youth academy and for the first team is one of pace. 'All of the young players training with the seniors for the first time say the same thing: "Oh, that's fast!"' Youth development must therefore follow one clear objective: Players need to learn to think very fast, consciously. On the pitch, they basically need to be on autopilot, like we are when driving a car, not deliberately thinking whether we're switching from second into third gear or how to operate the clutch. But pure instinct in itself is also no longer enough, as there's a match plan to implement.

'We want to speed up the processes inside the brain. Many athletes are too slow in that regard. But you can train and improve them,' Mayer explained. That's how Hoffenheim's goalkeepers, including number one Oliver Baumann, as well as defender Benjamin Hübner, came to be sitting on the first floor of the training centre, playing what looked like a normal computer game on tablets.

Mayer was one of the developers of the app. It aims to improve conscious thinking: perception, understanding and decision-making. The goalkeepers are especially keen on this type of cognitive conditioning, and they show up twice a week. Some of the outfield players are regulars and others are not. Youth players are scheduled to come in for a tablet session once a week.

The brain apps have been programmed by SAP, the software development company co-founded by club patron Dietmar Hopp. It sounds like a no-brainer (pun unintended) but the company and the club only started working together systematically in 2016. Some of the previous sporting directors and coaches thought brain exercise, and such like, was a total waste of time, but Nagelsmann is a huge fan. Mayer admits that there was a lot of 'fiddling around and tweaking' involved over the past couple of years. Cognitive research is still a relatively new field in sports, and there are few scientific findings so far.

That's why the German Football Association (DFB) set up a 'cognitive group'. Mayer is one of its members, alongside Hans-Dieter Hermann, the national team's sports psychologist. Other members include Gerd Gigerenzer, a renowned psychologist specialised in the study of risk, and DFB Head of Analytics, Christofer Clemens. 'Perhaps psychology and analytics will become joined up together much more closely than we currently anticipate,' said Clemens.

At Hoffenheim, they use various ways and means to work towards this day. On the training ground, to the right of the main structure, there's a building that offers a glimpse of what the future may hold. It's the realm of Rafael Hoffner, coordinator for sport and innovation. The key feature is the Footbonaut, a training facility which only exists in three other places on the planet – at Borussia Dortmund, in Kazakhstan and in Qatar. I first met Christian Güttler, inventor of the Footbonaut, in 2007 when he was working on his prototype in an old car warehouse of the Stasi in East Berlin. It had taken an eternity to convince clients of the Footbonaut's use. Hoffenheim had one installed in January 2014.

The Footbonaut looks like a cage. Its playing field, 14 by 14 metres in size, is surrounded by 64 square target areas. A player training in the Footbonaut sets up in the centre and is served balls by one of four distribution outlets, capable of hitting passes with a speed of up to 100 kilometres per hour. As the ball heads for the player, the frame of one of the target areas lights up, to signal where the pass needs to be played to. Accuracy and time needed to complete the course are logged to measure a player's rate of improvement. There are multiple ways to vary the rhythm of the Footbonaut's 'passes', their speed and even their trajectory. Players can refine their first touch but the machine also hones their situational awareness and helps them make quicker decisions. All of Hoffenheim's teams come to practise here once a week; only the first team don't have regular sessions. But players can still use it on a voluntary basis. Many do. The goalkeepers, in particular, love working with the device. It's also of great use to players recovering from injury, who want to regain their high level of ball control and get many touches on the ball without running the risk of opposition contact.

The Footbonaut isn't the only training device installed in this hangar-type building, though. There is also the Helix, a 10 metre wide and curved projection screen with a curious back story. It was developed for SAP's global video conferences, meant to make participants feel as if they were really sitting in the same room with each other. It didn't quite work as intended, however, and the device ended up in a dusty basement before someone at the club came up with the idea of utilising it as a training device. It trains the memory through Multiple Object Tracking. Four blue and four red players are projected onto the screen, with one of them in possession of the ball. Two red and two blue players, as well as who's in possession of the ball, need to be memorised. All players are then set in motion and the person doing the exercise is tasked with keeping his eye on their runs. For the untrained eye, this is incredibly difficult – you lose track of the situation after just a few seconds. But you also get the feeling that the exercise could help players make sense of the intense chaos unfolding on the pitch in real life.

The training regimes in this building are monitored by a number of scientific studies. More than 50 students work on their theses here, ranging from bachelor to PhDs. 'We aspire to having everything we do here scientifically substantiated,' said Mayer, who is an honorary professor at University Saarland in Saarbrücken.

Amazingly, they have found one system of tests which they now believe can distinguish between good and bad footballers: the Vienna testing system. The device for it can be found in an adjacent room. It puts a player's reaction times to the test, measuring how quickly they can push red, blue or differently coloured buttons and how quickly they can pick up on sounds. A total of 350 reactions are checked, in as little time as possible. The best footballers need 0.5 seconds for one correct answer; worse ones take 0.8 seconds. On the pitch, this 0.3 of a second makes the difference between good and outstanding players.

Hoffenheim combine the results of the various tests and calculate the so-called 'ExF-Score', an evaluation of the brain's executive functions. But this is also about developing the player. And it's an important aspect, as time on the training pitch is so limited. Exercising the brain, not the body, will become a more significant part of training regimes.

Virtual reality is likely to come into play, too. At a DFB conference in Frankfurt, Ben Kappner, Head of Analytics at Arsenal, demonstrated how the club are employing the technology. 'Our assumption is that virtual reality can help improve cognitive functions,' he explained. Arsenal cooperate with Beyond Sports, a company from the Netherlands that also works with Ajax and the Dutch FA. Players are not shown regular match footage but a first person angle from down on the pitch. 'The way we see football bears little resemblance to what players experience on the pitch,' Kappner said.

From an educational point of view, VR opens up the spectacular possibility of a player reliving a specific situation in 3D on his data glasses. What did he see? What should he have seen? Was he positioned poorly and missed something? The demo was impressive, but the technical implementation is far from perfect. The players don't look real, a bit like the pixelated figures that populated early football simulations. VR is not ready for the immediate future, but it will be in a few years' time, at the latest. The theoretical possibilities are already hugely exciting. Christofer Clemens believes that one day match preparations could take place in the virtual world. 'You could put players in situations that may occur 20 times during a real game. I couldn't just tell the players that the opponent will press with three players up front. I could get Hummels and Boateng to see what that feels like in the simulation.'

Kappner also talked about 'Gamification', the application of typical elements of video game playing. Arsenal experimented with it to make the use of VR more fun. They did not reach a final conclusion during their early trial phase. But real-life football and its video game counterpart are moving towards each other in rapid, unstoppable fashion.

BLUE PLAYERS

Football is played by humans. And these humans are not just vessels filled with abilities of the motoring or cognitive kind. They are not just good in the air or come with special skills of anticipation on the pitch; they are not only pacy or blessed with special talent for controlling a ball. Footballers also have distinct characters and certain ways of interacting with their team-mates and coaches that are no less important for achieving success than the ability to ping a 50m diagonal pass.

Upon my return from my trip to Midtjylland, I spent some time thinking about the club's methodical approach to the human dimension of the game. They didn't just look at performance stats but worked with personality profiles. Not just the players and coaching staff, everyone in the club – kit men, officials, secretaries, even the sales assistants in the club shop – had undergone a personality test. Results were visualised with the colours red, yellow, blue and green. They all represented a basic type.

I am rather averse to such personality examinations for several reasons, especially in the workplace. They are often the manifestation of a creepy corporate culture, where multiple-choice questionnaires take the place of respectful interaction. Clubs in many countries work with them, mostly in the youth academies, but occasionally the professionals are profiled as well. The way the Danes did it I found appealing, however. There were no 'good' and 'bad' profiles, for starters. Every basic type had positive as well as negative attributes. At the training ground, they were written in Danish and English on the wall:

Red Type	
On a good day	On a bad day
Determined	Tough
Goal-oriented	Arrogant
Demanding	Dominant
Powerful	Harassed
Result-oriented	Impatient

Yellow Type	
On a good day	**On a bad day**
Inventive	Hectic
Spontaneous	Thoughtless
Enthusiastic	Superficial
Seek contact	Unstructured
Visible and talkative	Uninhibited

Blue Type	
On a good day	**On a bad day**
Exact	Cool
Methodical	Skeptical
Systematic	Slow
Disciplined	Unyielding
Detail-oriented	Dissociated

Green Type	
On a good day	**On a bad day**
Loyal	Defeated
Harmonious	Hesitant
Understanding	Evasive
Considerate	Gullible
People-oriented	Touchy

For my own orientation, I labelled the four types – which never exist in pure form – as fighter (red), artist (yellow), engineer (blue) and social worker (green), before speaking with the coach and several players about this system. Kristian Bach Bak, the captain who had originally been one of the greatest sceptics as far as the innovations at the club were concerned, told me he was 'totally red'. I was not surprised to hear that Bak had been quite hostile to taking part in the personality tests and the sessions with a mental coach that came with it. But things changed. 'At the beginning I wondered why I should be talking to him about how I behaved,' Bak told me. But he quickly realised that it truly helped him to not only improve his performance, but also made him better at interacting with his team-mates. 'I learned a lot about myself, and I had to learn to keep calmer sometimes. I got frustrated too quickly. It was a huge step for me.'

Having a better understanding of yourself, and of your positive and negative characteristics, is probably beneficial to every human being. Those who are critical of themselves for being hectic and superficial sometimes, might be more lenient in their self-appraisal once they realise that they're also spontaneous and imaginative. If you are proud of being able to tackle life's challenges methodically and systematically, however, you should perhaps also realise that others might perceive you as cold and unapproachable.

For Bak, it was about staying true to the positive aspects of his 'red personality' as a fighter, while also being aware of his negative aspects and managing to keep them under control. This insight also helped him relate to his team-mates. A special trait of these person-ality profiles was the fact that FC Midtjylland had made all results public. They printed out radar charts that revealed how distinct each colour was for each player. That level of transparency, I realised in Denmark, can contribute to everyone's better appreciation of their co-workers' different personalities, which in turn makes for a better working atmosphere. But that requires a very careful handling of the personality profiles. It was obvious that Midtjylland knew what they were doing.

Shouting at another 'red player' on the pitch was fine, Bak explained to me. But a 'yellow team-mate', a more creative player, might be disheartened rather than encouraged. 'I now know if I should address a team-mate in a forceful manner, or differently. It's made me a better leader.' Finnish international Tim Sparv, who moved to Denmark from Germany, is a fan of the personality profiles as well. 'I was totally amazed to receive 24 pages of a detailed evaluation of myself, from a test that only took 20 minutes.' When we spoke, I soon found myself wondering which of the colours dominated for him. I couldn't help myself and had to ask. Sparv laughed and said: 'I am blue. Very organised and very focused. But I struggle to improvise.' Sparv then explained to me how a 'blue player' would always stick to the plan of the coach. But if the plan doesn't work out and things become chaotic on the pitch, he struggles more than 'yellow colleagues', who are more likely to come up with a creative solution.

Glen Riddersholm, the coach at the time, even had his own test results hung up on the wall of his office. His diagram showed a three in both yellow and blue, a five in green and a six in red – the highest possible value. He explained to me that his was a rare combination of traits. 'If I were red only, I might be one of those coaches who are only good at what they do when things run smoothly. They lack emotional intelligence.'

There are vast numbers of personality tests and they have been used in football for a long time. In early 2012, some German papers carried an interesting story. 'Players of Hannover 96 need to conduct a sex test,' their headlines screamed. It was nonsense, of course. Hannover players had been asked to fill in a questionnaire that contained 128 statements, including sentences like: 'I am what you could call sexually rampant', 'I want all the sex that I can get' or 'I have a lot of erotic fantasies'. Players could then answer on a scale of -3 (never true) to +3 (always true). The questions are part of a personality analysis called the Reiss test, developed by the American Steven Reiss. Its results are supposed to give an indication of a human's main motivation, whether that's a search for a sense of community, the striving for approval, for money or perhaps for sex. 'Every player needs different conditions to perform at his top level over a long period of time. I need to pay attention to that. Every player must get the sense that his individuality is being taken into account,' Peter Boltersorf explained. The motivational consultant has worked with manager Mirko Slomka and for various clubs for many years.

As coach of Mainz 05, Thomas Tuchel also made use of psychological surveys to get a better handle on his team. The personality test his players were subjected to was specifically designed for athletes and came with a 30-page evaluation. 'We didn't just want to individualise training content, but also the way we addressed our players,' Tuchel explained to me back then. Some of the players needed to be egged on with a bit of reverse psychology, sentences such as 'I am keen to see whether you can do this' or 'there is no way you can get this done'. Others needed clearer instructions as to what and how they were supposed to do things. But there were also players, he said, who maybe just needed to be calmed down and hear a word of encouragement. 'I want to know who needs to have an occasional conversation about his family or his hobbies. How can we help a certain player and give him this feeling of "the coach knows what I'm about"?' Tuchel said.

He had a player in his team whose main incentive was money. I thought this was unsettling, but Tuchel explained to me that such a clear motivational profile didn't make life difficult for him. The player wanted to have maximum success to receive all the bonuses. He wanted to play well so that he could one day move to a club where he could earn even more money. If that was clearly the case, a manager knew how to handle the situation.

Tuchel's aim back then was to create conditions for better social interaction. 'This is the next step of the refinement process,' he said. 'We have basic values, defined by me, and the team do live and breathe them. But, after five years, communication needs to develop further.'

He also tested himself and the result was type AP1 – 'a security-minded creative'. He read out a few lines about the aspects of his personality he needed to work on. Sometimes he was too controlling and thus too authoritative. He had a tendency of being a perfectionist but at times was too indulgent, as well. When the conflict with Borussia Dortmund's club board escalated in 2017, I remembered another thing that Tuchel had read out that day: 'If you do not pay attention, you will simplify things in a radical manner. You tend to get carried away and become too contrarian, rather than stay in control with [the aid] of intuition.' But there was a flip side to this particular coin. On a good day, Tuchel is also an enthusiast overflowing with ideas, and with a nice line in self-deprecating humour.

Following my visit to Herning, Rasmus Ankersen, the Chairman of FC Midtjylland and Technical Director of Brentford, gave me a lift to Copenhagen. He spent a long time on the phone at first, and I started wondering about the match I had just watched. Midtjylland had won 1–0. But truth be told, it had been a rather poor performance against a side from the relegation zone. When Ankersen asked me how I felt about the match, an answer came to mind that had showed how much I was still thinking about those personality tests. 'It felt to me as if there had been too many blue players in the team,' I said. Of course, the red fighting spirit of Kristian Bach Bak and others had also been very much in evidence; the team had also exuded some green qualities on the pitch, they had helped each other out. But the most distinct impression had been that of a team slavishly working through a pre-defined list of tasks, without any sense of innovation. They were focused and committed, but devoid of special ideas. Blue, in other words. Ankersen laughed. There was a general lack of yellow players in the side, he said; they only had two of those and both had been injured for the game. The blue players had indeed been in the majority.

FUTURE
STRATEGIES

Strategies from London and the art of assembling a professional team; how to be successful the Finnish way; football as science fiction.

A GAME OF STRATEGY

The meeting room of 21st Club is decorated with references to extraordinary success stories in football, and as the firm is located in London, many of the events in question revolve around English football. Geoff Hurst's hat-trick in the 1966 World Cup final features here, alongside the sensational title-winning season of Leicester City and the 'Invincibles' of Arsenal, who won the Premier League without losing a match.

These achievements are remembered in an unusual way, however. 'Chances of Geoff Hurst scoring a hat-trick during a World Cup final: 2 per cent,' the text says. Another line states that a team could be expected to complete all league games without defeat once in 18,000 seasons. The year before they won the league, the probability of Leicester City getting relegated had been rated 85 per cent.

Even the disastrous 2014–15 season of Borussia Dortmund gets a mention. That kind of collapse only happened in eight out of 1,000 seasons, it says here.

21st Club is an unusual consulting firm. Their name reveals their mission. What would we do if we were the 21st Club in the Premier League? 'Our basic idea is not to spend more money than our rivals, but to invest in intelligence instead,' revealed Blake Wooster, a former trialist at Cardiff City and Hereford United who later studied sports science. After his graduation, he worked in data analysis for Prozone for nine years before teaming up with Rasmus Ankersen, to develop the idea of 21st Club in 2013. The search for investors led them to David Sheepshanks. The former CEO of Ipswich Town and Chairman of the Football League currently serves as head of the FA's National Football Centre in Burton. 'We are fully convinced it's possible to be successful by applying intelligent decision-making processes. There are many contentious terms out there like big data and analytics, but we believe it is much more about the principles of decision-making and about strategies,' Wooster said. In the topsy-turvy world of football, where plans often don't go beyond the next weekend, long-term schemes for sporting success and strategic development are often given short shrift.

The boutique company, which operates from an office near Smithfield Market, published a brochure outlining its ideas for a more tactical approach. It's called 'Changing the Conversation', as 21st Club want football to be talked about in a different way. Eighty short chapters, most of them not longer than a single page, ponder a multitude of questions regarding strategy, planning, talent scouting and performance. Which countries should clubs be targeting for scouting? What is the age structure of successful teams? Which player of the squad should be earning the most money?

Many of these deliberations and a vast number of accompanying calculations have been compiled by Omar Chaudhuri, the company's Head of Football Operations. The Brazil-born economist studied data analysis before joining Prozone. His blog, in which he dismantled common myths in football, served as an entry point to his new job. Just as he had done at Prozone before, he now develops new metrics for 21st Club that evaluate player performances. He has also constructed his own model for Expected Goals.

In the summer of 2018, Red Star Belgrade contacted 21st Club as part of their search for new players. They brought a list of players that had been recommended to them by agents. But Chaudhuri suggested a player for the Serbian club from a league that few clubs were considering in their quest for talents. Dutch player Lorenzo Ebecilio had somehow ended up playing in Cyprus for APOEL FC, and the data showed that he was doing very well. Red Star took a closer look at the player, signed him, and Ebecilio would later feature in the Champions League after Red Star had surprisingly qualified for the competition.

Most of the time, though, Chaudhuri's job is less to do with data scouting and more about answering fundamental questions. This one, for example: How do you quantify the value of a single player in relation to the overall success of his team? 21st Club's model predicted that Lionel Messi or Cristiano Ronaldo would add 15 points to a relegation candidate in one of Europe's top five leagues. Such flights of fancy aside, a similar question should be asked ahead of every transfer. How many points will the player contribute during the season? Delving deeper into this conundrum, you realise that individual players are nowhere near as influential for the overall performance of a team as the game's superstars, in particular, are believed to be. It makes more sense investing in the depth of the squad rather than to spend large chunks of money on a single star player.

After Philippe Coutinho had joined Barcelona from Liverpool, 21st Club examined how the loss of star players had affected teams in the past. 'We found that the points penalty was at worst around 0.1 points per game – around two points over half a season or four points over an entire year,' Chaudhuri revealed. In this context, a study of transfers in the top five European leagues between 2010 and 2018 was just as telling. Only 56 per cent of the new recruits became regulars. Star signings, in other words, often don't meet expectations.

Their combination of data analysis and studies of strategic questions has gained 21st Club entry to club's boardrooms. They often talk directly with directors and even with owners. This has partly to do with the fact that investors like to get an independent opinion on what the proper football men at their clubs tell them about the somewhat peculiar business practices in the game. These people, hugely successful in their original line of work, are also used to strategic assessments and have found that this approach is lacking in football.

Chaudhuri investigated whether a club desperate to clinch promotion to the Premier League should rather invest in defensive or offensive players. And: What needs to be done once promotion is actually achieved? 'My head is spinning at times, but it is very interesting to find answers to these questions,' he told me. Chaudhuri has spent time at Ajax debating how the challenges faced in the domestic league differ from those encountered on the European stage. Ajax are far superior to many of their national competitors, but, their 2018–19 Champions League campaign aside, they tend to be rank outsiders in most matches in UEFA competitions. What does it mean for a squad's composition and tactical deliberations when you are demolishing opponents on weekends but worry about not getting demolished in midweek?

In football, the team creating the better quality of chances only end up winning the game two thirds of the time. Better teams are thus served best by games with many goals: 21st Club's analysis showed that superior sides won 75 per cent of games with more than 2.5 goals. Games with fewer than 2.5 goals were only won in half of all cases by the better teams. Clubs who dominate their leagues, such as Ajax or Celtic, should play a risky attacking game. But in Europe, where they were inferior to most opponents, they were better off adopting a more conservative approach.

21st Club also developed software for contract management capable of simulating changeable situations. How many funds would be freed up at the end of the season when contracts expired? What would the financial consequences of getting relegated be? In addition, they also offer an evaluation of coaches and help clubs to find the right man. They analyse the playing style favoured by the different managerial candidates. They look at how willing a candidate has been to nurture young talent in the past. And they can identify the type of coaches who have previously done better with the resources at their disposal than expected. 'We also look at the candidates that our clients usually haven't considered. Some of them may have achieved better results than they should have,' declared Chaudhuri.

Advanced data analysis isn't even necessary most of the time. Applying the rule of thumb helps as well. Smaller clubs can consider a much larger pool of potential new signings than top teams do. For Manchester City, Juventus or FC Bayern, only about 300 to 500 players are real contenders. But a club at the level of Wigan, for example, can chose from about 3,500. A smaller club's chance of gaining quality is therefore much higher. On the other hand, the Wigans of this world find it much more difficult to carefully consider possible signings than bigger clubs with access to far greater resources in that regard.

Omar Chaudhuri and Blake Wooster have scoured all of Europe for clubs who have attained a strategic advantage. Dinamo Zagreb, to take one, have produced a remarkable amount of first team players, thanks to their exceptional work with young talents. Olympique Lyon returned to the group of elite clubs in France by committing to their youth development. Borussia Dortmund's recruitment process is similarly impressive. During his research, Chaudhuri found an interesting pattern. Many good ideas are born from a crisis: 'Almost all of them started doing this after they had run out of money.'

It's a great observation. Creativity excels when other means are exhausted. Sven Mislintat only became the head of Borussia

Dortmund's scouting department and had a hand in the club's renaissance because BVB had been nearly broke. Would a flourishing club have entrusted this important position to a surfer-type sports science student without any experience? Would Christian Heidel have come up with the idea of promoting his over-the-hill centre-back Jürgen Klopp to the position of head coach if the club hadn't been in a desperate relegation struggle? And would FC Midtjylland have been open to new ways of club management if there hadn't been major financial problems when Matthew Benham came calling?

But it's easy to be led astray from successful paths. Wooster and Chaudhuri had long been admirers of Southampton and their managerial appointments. Nigel Adkins had led the club from the third division to the Premier League. He had been succeeded by Mauricio Pochettino, Ronald Koeman and Claude Puel. 'We are impressed by their managerial strategy,' Wooster told me during my first visit. 'They have changed coaches even though their results were decent, and lost a few they would have preferred to keep. When we visited them, Sporting Director Les Reed had a folder on his desk which read "Champions League ready" – it was their strategy for the year 2020. That was in 2015. They were planning five years ahead.' But things didn't go according to plan in Southampton. Their coaching appointments stopped working out, some of their transfers backfired and when Les Reed was sacked in November 2018, the Champions League was a mere afterthought for a Saints team battling relegation.

OPPOSING THE NEW

In the autumn of 2018, at a conference dedicated to sports data in Switzerland, Chris Anderson – the man who had wanted to be Billy Beane – gave a presentation called 'Football doesn't play Moneyball'. He talked about an interesting aspect which had proved an obstacle to that model.

The potential investors Anderson and David Sally had spoken to about buying a club often got nervous at one particular point of the discussion. Although the idea of approaching the business of football in a different, more strategic and data-based way did appeal to them in principle, when things became more concrete, they got cold feet. Owning a club exposes an investor to a much higher level of public interest than for most corporate takeovers. Broadcasters talk about it, newspapers report on it and the internet bursts with all sorts of comments because many people, perhaps even millions of them, care so much about the club. 'They didn't want to embarrass themselves. So they wanted football people instead,' explained Anderson. Handing over the keys of the club to a couple of odd American academics appeared too risky a proposition in their eyes. If anything went wrong, it would reflect on the owners' judgement.

In his book *The Structure of Scientific Revolutions*, American philosopher of science Thomas S. Kuhn described how new ideas only achieve acceptance once they are no longer considered new – regardless of how sound they might be. There's a similar dynamic at play with regard to the uptake of new technical products. Their process of gaining prevalence is informed by five groups of varying size, and at different times. Innovators lead the way, followed by early adopters. Then there's the early majority, the late majority and eventually the laggards. The number of innovators (2.5 per cent) and early adopters (13.5 per cent) is relatively small, which is also down to the previously mentioned phenomenon of social proof. Working with advanced data for scouting, using personality profiles for squad composition or having players train with brain apps is all new stuff. For it to go mainstream, it mustn't feel new any longer.

In 2016, Michael Lewis, author of *Moneyball*, published a book called *The Undoing Project*. It tells the story of Daniel Kahneman and Amos Tversky, two psychologists from Israel. Kahneman had received the Nobel Prize in Economic Sciences in 2002 and is the author of the book *Thinking, Fast and Slow*, a copy of which was given by Brentford owner Matthew Benham to all of his staff as a gift. *The Undoing Project* begins with a chapter about Daryl Morey, the general manager of the Houston Rockets. It describes his struggle with the cognitive biases of human thinking. Lewis wrote: 'This hunger for an expert who knows things with certainty, even when certainty is not possible, has a talent for hanging around. It's like a movie monster that's meant to have been killed but is somehow always alive for the final act.'

Thanks to Kahneman's research we know how shockingly poor experts are at making predictions for the future. They often do worse than simple formulas. A famous example is the question whether a relationship will last. One attempt saw psychologists interview couples extensively and make predictions of their future life together. Another one merely consisted of a survey that asked how often couples had sex each week and subtracted the number of weekly disputes from that amount. The latter results offered much more accurate predictions than the one the experts had come up with.

As in all walks of life, predictions are made constantly in football. Which tactics will work best in the next match and who are the players that will implement them most effectively? The whole process of scouting and recruitment is essentially a prediction of how well a player or a coach will function at a club. The investors that sat with Anderson and Sally in an expensive London restaurant were also overcome with the hunger for an expert who'd guide them on these questions. They wanted people who had been involved in the football business for years and knew all about it. They wanted certainty. And even if they sensed that the football people couldn't offer that certainty, they didn't want to expose themselves to getting publicly hammered for passing up on experts. The monster is alive.

Many experts in football – coaches, officials or chairmen – were football professionals themselves at one point. It is an advantage for them to have experienced many potential issues themselves, no doubt, but their previous roles might also increase their difficulties in reaching sound conclusions and making accurate predictions. As players, they had learned to appreciate the absence of doubt as a strength. A player who questions his own performances will not necessarily play with a sense of freedom. In difficult times, it often helps to pretend that there's no crisis at all. A seasoned coach with decades of experience once told me he preferred working with players who were 'a bit blunt'; not out-and-out stupid, but not too self-occupied in an overly complicated manner either. But things that may have worked for players might be bad for managers or officials tasked with making carefully considered decisions.

Football's culture is such that it's hard to overstate the degree of courage Rasmus Ankersen showed on 11 December 2016. Midtjylland had just suffered a 2–1 defeat against Danish top flight heavyweights Bröndby. The loss in Copenhagen was their third in a row, leaving the provincial club ten points adrift of the leaders in second place. Supporters and the media had been calling for the head of coach Jess Thorup, Glen Riddersholm's successor, for quite a while. One of the major sponsors had even called Ankersen and told him that the extension of their contract with the club was conditional on Thorup being sacked. 'But everyone who worked closely with him saw the coach in a positive light,' Ankersen told me. This was not just true of himself, owner Matthew Benham and Sporting Director Claus Steinlein – the players felt the same way, too.

After the game, Ankersen went to the mixed zone and defended the coach in front of the journalists. He didn't do so by rolling out the usual supportive phrases, however, but by mentioning Expected Goals and a thing Ankersen called 'the table of justice', the club's own calculations which had Midtjylland 15 points below the expected haul from their performances. Thorup was probably the first coach who kept his job thanks to Expected Goals as opposed to real ones. The same happened with the aforementioned Ben Olsen at D.C. United in Major League Soccer.

Ankersen's comments caused a stir. 'I explained the concept and I don't have a problem speaking about it in public, either, because I'm fully convinced. The majority of people made jokes about it, but some took an interest, too.' A Danish business magazine wrote an article called 'The war of numbers in football' outlining Ankersen's strategy. Before publication of the article, the journalists had questioned economic experts and found that it was perfectly normal to look at underlying performance indicators. 'This led to a real debate. By now, I would say that Expected Goals get more mentions in Denmark than in any other European country. It has gone completely mainstream, even amongst those who initially criticised and mocked me,' Ankersen said.

Before he had gone out to back the manager, there had been an internal debate inside the club as to whether or not it was right to stick with him, however. 'The right decision can also be the wrong one,' Ankersen mused. Public pressure by fans, media and sponsors could have become so strong that the club on the whole could have been damaged. But their faith in Thorup was eventually vindicated. The following season, he led FC Midtjylland to the Danish title.

FOOTBALL, BLOODY HELL

In August 2018, I received an enthusiastic WhatsApp message from Ankersen: 'We look very dangerous this season. Smartodds rating has us as the best team in the league now.' Brentford had recorded two victories and two draws at the start of the season and were in fourth place. As mentioned, the team plays a different style than most competitors in the league, less physical and more cultured than many of their competitors. It was fun watching their matches. And it seemed as if the small club from west London had a decent shot at getting promoted to the Premier League.

Ankersen and his colleagues at Brentford were following the advice of the company he had co-founded: 21st Club. The club still had one of the smallest budgets in the league, and the aim was to overcome that disadvantage with a smarter use of resources. A specific footballing strategy – including a guaranteed amount of training time for dead balls – was a big part of that. Data, too, had a role to play, naturally, especially in relation to the signing of new players. An experienced German player agent told me he had never received such detailed enquiries for one of his clients than those Brentford had requested. He felt that made the club appealing – it indicated a high level of dedication to the players.

Ankersen and company took a bold step in 2017: they gave up on youth development. This might sound crazy at first, but it made sense. Their competitors had snared many of their best youngsters, without paying significant transfer fees. One U16s inter-national joined Manchester United, one U17s international signed for Manchester City, and they each only brought in £30,000 in compensation. After getting rid of their youth teams, Brentford attempted to turn the tables to benefit from the academy work of their competitors. The idea was to sign players coming through the ranks of Premier League clubs, those who didn't stand a chance of getting into the first teams there. In addition to signing those fringe players, Brentford started recruiting young players from bigger clubs on loan. 'We no longer consider the bigger clubs as enemies as we did in the past. We now see them as partners,'

Ankersen explained. Brentford also started a B team and put together a match schedule for them.

Yes, they made mistakes, too. The data suggested they should appoint Marinus Dijkhuizen, the manager of Excelsior, a small club in the Dutch top flight. It soon became apparent that Dijkhuizen was out of his depth at a much larger foreign club, however, and he was let go after just a few months in charge. Ankersen and the sporting management had perhaps become victims of their own unique approach.

On the other hand, Brentford were very successful. It had been 62 years since the club had last managed three consecutive seasons in the second division. Now they were an established member of the Championship, a league with gigantic economic differences, and they had managed four top ten finishes in a row.

But when they nurtured faint hopes of getting promoted in the summer of 2018, the force of fate came crashing down on them. First, a key player sustained a serious injury. Then head coach Dean Smith left the club. He had a release clause in his contract that Aston Villa triggered. As a child, Smith had been fan of the Villa, and his family still lived in Birmingham. Much higher wages might have influenced his decision to leave for the Midlands, too.

Smith informed the club of his desire to go at 5pm. Five hours later, the club released a statement regarding his departure. In sudden need of a head coach, Brentford promoted Smith's Danish assistant Thomas Frank. But those were negligible inconveniences compared to a subsequent tragedy. On the eve of their game at Queens Park Rangers in November 2018, Brentford's Head of Football Operations Robert Rowan, the man responsible for compiling the Bees' fantastic player dossiers, passed away at the age of 28. Rowan had joined the club in 2014 after sending applications containing scouting profiles of players to clubs all over the country.

At Griffin Park, his boundless enthusiasm and easy-going personality had made him the man who held everything together. He was 'the glue', Ankersen wrote in a moving obituary on the club's website. Following Rowan's untimely death, any thoughts of a promotion appeared preposterous and, at times, it looked as if the club might even get sucked into the relegation battle. In the January transfer window, their highly talented central defender Chris Mepham joined AFC Bournemouth for £12m. The Welshman had arrived at Brentford as a 15-year-old on a free transfer from Chelsea. Despite this loss, the club managed to steady the ship in the second half of the season.

FC Midtjylland, too, had been successful in the transfer market. In the winter of 2017, the Danish team had sold Norwegian striker Alexander Sörloth for €9m to Crystal Palace, having signed him for €400,000 from Groningen just six months earlier. They also received €8m from Belgian heavyweights RSC Anderlecht for Bubacarr Sanneh in 2018. The Gambian striker had cost only €200,000 when he was signed from a small Danish club a year before. Both transfers constituted spectacular commercial successes for the club, and one would naturally assume they were both down to their advanced data scouting. But that wasn't the case for either of them. Both players had been recommended to the club by their scouts, the old-fashioned way. The data had actually thrown doubt on one of the signings. The fact they received such large sums for the pair of strikers wasn't just down to their performances having markedly improved but also as a result of fortuitous circumstances. The coaches at both buying clubs really wanted the players and both club owners felt that they had to grant them their wishes to keep them happy.

Tim Sparv, the Finnish international playing for FC Midtjylland, occasionally writes articles and publishes them on his website. His reflections on life as a footballer are always worth a read. He sees things differently from your regular professional. At the end of 2017, for example, he wondered why Midtjylland had returned to their winning ways following a rather disappointing run. The Danish media had decided that their switch from 4-3-3 to 3-4-3 had made the decisive difference. 'Since the tactical change we've only lost once so inevitably people tend to dedicate our good form to the new formation,' he wrote. 'An easy and tangible explanation delivered by players, staff, supporters and media.' Sparv didn't actually disagree. The mood in the dressing room had improved as a result of the switch, the team were once more playing entertaining, attacking football and the defence had become more solid, too.

But his mind was occupied with something a little more fundamental. 'I always find it interesting to read about why some teams are more successful than others. What are the reasons behind a team's positive results? Have they done something differently? What's been the secret formula? I always want it to be something that enlightens me but I'm rarely satisfied with the explanations I get. It's like everyone wants it to be because of a tactical change, an in-form attacking player or the new coach/manager. I feel we're not asking the right questions when we always end up with the same answers.'

He listed all the things that had changed in the three years he had played at Midtjylland, which didn't make for terribly exciting reading. At first, there had been no breakfast at all. Then, a rather poor breakfast had been served, now it was outstanding. Thanks to the new staff in the kitchen, they now also enjoyed a tasty lunch every day. In the dressing room, players could make use of a Jacuzzi and an ice bath. They had an artificial pitch for training, which was helpful during spells of bad weather and when they prepared for opponents who played their games on a plastic surface, which is permissible in the Danish league. The club had added training pitches, enabling them to train on good surfaces, which in turn reduced the likelihood of injuries. The physiotherapists were thus free to treat players with massages and other therapy. 'I want to believe that a team's success is a result of small improvements during a longer period of time. In my mind there's no such thing as a quick fix, in this case a change of system. Unfortunately it's always "sexier" to talk about this than about marginal gains.'

I called Sparv to find out more about the situation in Midtjylland and the club's use of data. 'We still talk about statistics. But I really thought it would play a bigger role. It's possible that the real revolution is taking place one level above,' he told me. But perhaps, Sparv simply no longer noticed how ubiquitous the numbers had become at his club. In the same breath, he told me that Lars Knudsen, an assistant coach who's exclusively tasked with working on the team's attacking game, had discussed their crossing statistics with him. Knudsen had told them where goals were most likely to be scored; a practical application of Expected Goals.

Despite his failure to find a definitive explanation why Midt-jylland had been so successful, Sparv was satisfied. 'This is still a well-run football club,' he said.

But were FC Midtjylland the most modern club in the digital wonderland – or did they simply install a couple of ice baths, serve better croissants, build new pitches and get incredibly lucky in the transfer market? When I brought up Brentford and their Danish sister club in a meeting with the sporting director of a major English club, he shrugged his shoulders. 'Well, they have it easy,' he said dismissively. At Brentford, the relatively small group of fans meant there was no external pressure, he explained, whereas every decision at his club would be debated at great length by the media and the fans, which made it incredibly hard to stay calm.

Smaller clubs do enjoy the luxury of relative tranquillity, that much was true. But whether they're rank outsiders or corporate behemoths, all clubs have one thing in common. At the start of a season, they all embark on a journey into the unknown, fraught with unpredictable difficulties and turbulences. The next crisis is never far away, and it takes a lot less than the tragic death of an important staff member for things to go awry. Injuries to key players, unex-pected departures of players or the coach, or just a string of bad luck in front of goal can lead to everything falling apart in no time.

Sir Alex Ferguson is responsible for one of the best football quotes of all time. Following the historic victory of Manchester United over Bayern in the 1999 Champions League final, he exclaimed: 'Football, bloody hell!' His team had snatched a last-minute victory in a match that they had seemingly lost. That's the greatness of football, a game of fate. It's possible to describe the sport's history as the relentless attempt to get to grips with its capriciousness. And that's precisely the reason why working in a systemic, structured way is so important. It helps you keep your head when destiny calls with bad news.

GHOSTING AND PREDICTIVE ANALYTICS

It took me a while to understand how it worked, but the name itself had me hooked immediately: 'Ghosting'. Hoang M. Le was on stage at the Sloan Sports Conference in Boston, an animated football match showing on the screen behind him. It was a rather primitive animation that turned players into colourful dots who dragged a trail behind them when making a run. They bore an unfortunate resemblance to sperm under a microscope. However, it was interesting to see that they were not on their own on the screen. They had shadows, or rather: ghosts. Those ghosts were smarter than the players, because they always moved to the best possible locations, Le declared.

At first, I didn't understand how the ghosts knew what they were doing. Which information had the programmer fed them, whose tactical instructions were they implementing? Then it dawned on me: Le and his colleagues from the California Institute of Technology had similar thoughts to Daniel Link when he had developed the concept of Dangerousity.

Data-Driven Ghosting is also concerned with probabilities, in this particular case the avoidance of goals. The scientists had fed match data into the computer and taught it how teams were defending. The

277

program now compared events of real matches with the lessons it had learned from games past. Looking at the arithmetical average actions of previous matches, the defender in a comparable situation would not have waited at the edge of the box, but instead attacked the player in possession. A different situation would have seen the defender man the post in order to stop the striker from pouncing on a rebound. For football and its 22-player mayhem, this was an early-stage concept; football science fiction, if you will.

But in basketball, a game of ten players on a much smaller playing area, Ghosting was already a functioning tool. The Toronto Raptors invented it in 2014 and have been using it ever since.

In the future, will we experience simulations of football games akin to those already widely established in Formula 1? During races, 200 experts constantly monitor data and simulate consequences of potential decisions. What will happen during a pit stop? What impact would a premature change of tyres have, or a modified telemetry? A car has hundreds of sensors – in the engine, gearbox, suspension and pretty much everywhere else – beaming out valuable information. Football players are not machines you can attach sensors to, but computer programs of the future could handle certain parts of match analysis in real time. Many deliberations take the form of 'what-if' relations that are not too dissimilar from chess. If you send out three defenders against a team with just one striker, a computer can simulate the consequences. If a team is defending with a high line, they will leave space behind. If they're defending deep and narrow, there's space on the wings. All of that isn't really complicated but still much harder to compute than chess, because the pieces also happen to be running, passing and shooting. There won't be a 'Deep Blue' football coaching a team to victory, but as a helpful tool it's easily conceivable in the near future.

Coaches equipped with headsets and receiving information from video and data analysts during matches is not an unusual sight any more. Analysts are positioned in the stands and will send video clips down to the bench, outlining where spaces are not being properly utilised and other tactical problems that might have come up. One day, we might see them simulate what would happen if the tactical formation was changed or if one player were to be replaced by a different type. Coaches deal with exactly those questions all the time during a game. Right now, they're conferring with themselves and with their assistants, but soon they might consult the simulation expert in the stands.

It may sound speculative at the moment, but in general terms, predictive analytics will become more important than descriptive ones. Managers will still want to understand why a match took a certain course: But it's much more significant to find out what needs to be done to win the next match – or the one that's still going on. The ability to correctly assess the current performances of a player will likewise remain relevant but the evaluation of his future potential is much more critical. Whoever will crack this problem will gain a momentous advantage.

Clubs have consequently started their own research labs, mostly behind closed doors. Liverpool hired Ian Graham as Director of Research in 2012. With the help of a handful of highly qualified co-workers, he has been producing statistical models predicting the outcome of football matches and conducting performance analysis of players. He holds a PhD in physics from the University of Cambridge. Manchester City and FC Bayern have set up similar departments.

It's increasingly difficult to find out exactly what they are working on because clubs are rather secretive in this regard. The attainment of advanced knowledge has become a part of the competitive struggle.

FC Barcelona, remarkably, have taken a different route, however. Having established the Barça Innovation Hub (BIH) in 2017, the club not only runs its own version of a sports university, but also explicitly encourages the exchange of knowledge. There are conferences on technology, coaching and nutrition, and the Barça Innovation Hub also cooperates with universities and selected companies. An investment fund worth €125m will enable BIH to invest in start-ups and existing companies dedicated to technology and sports. The club have already developed a tracking system which is used by all clubs in the Mexican Liga MX. In cooperation with FIFA, they are also working on the global standardisation of data collection. Club President Josep Maria Bartomeu labelled the BIH as 'the most important project' of the club. The global exchange of knowledge is being conducted in a thoroughly open manner. Even arch-rivals Real Madrid were invited to learn what Barcelona are working on.

Given these efforts, it does not come as much of a surprise that the first-ever football research paper to be honoured as best contribution at the Sloan Sports Conference was submitted by Barcelona. This represented a remarkable breakthrough in 2019, coming exactly two years after my visit to Boston when football analysts from all over the world had still been very much on the sidelines. The paper was titled 'Decomposing the Immeasurable Sport: A deep learning expected possession value framework for soccer' and built on the ideas of Daniel Link. The term Dangerousity was no longer used. It was replaced by 'Expected Possession Value' (EPV), a phrase that had already been in use in US sports for a good few years. Applying this metric, one is able to assess whether a particular action increases or decreases the chance of a goal at any given moment of the game. Once EPV is available in real time – which is currently not possible due to the huge amount of data to be processed – match analysis and performance evaluation are likely to change quite radically.

The research paper is also noteworthy for the people who wrote it. Barcelona's Javier Fernández co-authored it with Luke Bornn (Sacramento Kings) and Dan Cervone (Los Angeles Dodgers), two renowned analysts in basketball and baseball.

Sander Ijtsma, a surgeon from Groningen who developed the Expected Goals Plots and has been part of the global data community analysing football in new ways for years, told me we were witnessing a golden moment of openness with data and concepts. 'I believe that everything will vanish behind closed doors,' he added; clubs and associations were likely to buy the best ideas and take them out of circulation in no time.

Teams like Liverpool and Bayern are going down that path; Barça's Innovation Hub holds out the chance of a different route. There can be no doubt, however, that the different worlds of knowledge are drifting apart at high pace. While the bigger clubs increase their myriad advantages through the funding of cutting-edge research, the smaller ones are still at the stage where they're trying to understand what all these numbers are useful for. The data revolution in football is gaining momentum – but at the same time it's not. It all comes down to being able to apply mathematically-gained insights in a system prone to irrationality and knee-jerk decisions.

Over the course of 2018, US baseball fans were once again reminded of the Moneyball story when the Oakland A's finished the regular season as the fourth best team, despite having only had the fourth-lowest team budget of the 30 clubs in Major League Baseball. They recorded 97 victories – the best result since that legendary season of 2002, that Michael Lewis had chronicled in his book. Obviously, the A's were still capable of pushing the envelope. Billy Beane was still a part of it, too, even though he wasn't much involved in everyday operations as Executive Vice President of Baseball Operations. In an interview with a German website, he said: 'Generally speaking, we need to make ends meet with less experienced, younger players. In a way, we need to be the Borussia Dortmund to New York's Bayern Munich. That is our approach.'

In baseball, as in basketball and American football – ice hockey is limping behind somewhat – it's absolutely taken for granted that all clubs use data to analyse the performance of teams and the potential of new signings. In baseball, that approach went mainstream in 2004, at the very latest. That year, the Boston Red Sox won their sixth World Series and ended a trophy drought dating back to 1918 – with the help of analyst Bill James, who had been a huge influence on Billy Beane.

But what about the football version of Moneyball? In the autumn of 2018, Chris Anderson travelled to Switzerland to give a presentation with an altogether more optimistic title: 'The war has been won, a kind of Moneyball is already going on.' It's true – if you reduce Moneyball to the topic of data. The field has become highly competitive: big data companies, such as Opta or STATS, are merging into larger units in an effort to dominate the industry for years to come. The combination of data with videos and special services is becoming standard, too. Wyscout, formerly a provider of raw videos only, now adds their own proprietary data. There are also the start-ups, like Impect with their Packing product, Goalimpact or Sven Mislintat's Matchmetrics. Ted Knutson transformed his website Statsbomb into a company called Statsbomb IQ that offers tailor-made analysis and also collects data. A host of brand-new companies are vying for clients for their various ideas. Some start-ups are likely to fail over the next few years, whilst others will thrive or be bought out.

But the Moneyball story needs to be read correctly, as Omar Chaudhuri has insisted for quite some time. 'The irony of Moneyball is that it is a story, and the Oakland A's management hated stories,' he wrote in his blog for 21st Club in 2018. In Michael Lewis' book, and even more so in the Hollywood movie, everything was reduced to the conflict between archaic scouts with outdated beliefs and a new generation led by Billy Beane, who challenged the decades of institutionalised knowledge and came out on top. 'The irony, however, is that this period of history about fighting against narratives has itself become a narrative – about the power of data in sport,' Chaudhuri wrote.

It's a valid point, because the Moneyball story is much more complex than the bite-sized version of it that's being mostly told and retold today. 'The reasons behind the Oakland A's success were complex and manifold, and not simply about the use of data. There was cultural change, management change, an ability to learn, critical thinking, luck, and so on,' Chaudhuri continued.

THE POETRY OF A PERFECT PASS

Sometimes I ask myself why I find all these things so intriguing: Ghosting, Expected Goals, blue players. I am wholly incapable of writing computer programs and I lack what you may call a scientific background. In school, I dropped physics and chemistry classes as soon as I was allowed to, and everything I learned in maths class has long been forgotten. Technology never really fascinated me, neither in the form of engines nor computers. They are tools but I don't really care how it is they help me. But the digitalisation of football? I found that hugely interesting from the outset – because I want to understand the game better.

The longer I dedicate my time to it the less I am satisfied by most explanations and stories. It almost feels to me as if there is a constant fight over the best and coolest narratives. Sometimes the change of systems is seen as crucial, at other times it might be the new approach to fitness training or that fine new striker from France. Do players sleep better and have the proper diet – eating more carbohydrates or less? Could it be key that the coach has finally taken drastic measures or that he has shown more empathy in the dressing room?

That team spirits are high or that the team finally has a star player setting an example with regards to having the highest of ambitions? Or that the club is perfectly set up digitally and is making Moneyball a reality in football – somewhere in the middle of nowhere in Denmark, in a secret laboratory in Liverpool or at the sparkling university of FC Barcelona?

After marvelling at the concept of Ghosting at the Sloan Sports Conference, I saw NFL star Cris Collinsworth make an appearance. Now in his late fifties and working as a TV pundit, he was a five-time Emmy winner for his broadcasting. Collinsworth was in decidedly good mood when he insisted that outsiders, in particular, had constantly been coming up with new ideas in his sport: 'Twenty per cent of my information is taught to me by people who have never worn a helmet in their life. I think that's great!'

In helmet-less football, too, there is a new universe of information, potentially capable of delivering a couple of additional percentages. And it is no coincidence that this book is full of career hoppers, rule breakers and underdogs who never graced the football pitch, at least not at the highest level. I like their stories because I like the people behind them but that's not all: I hope that their stories will be told for a good time longer, for football needs more of these headstrong characters, to get one over on those who have more money but less imagination. And I hope for their sake that they will meet people with the generosity of spirit and curiosity of Cris Collinsworth. But no computer will ever replace a coach or a sporting director.

Ignorance makes people overestimate and underestimate the possibilities of digitalisation at the very same time. My view of the sport has permanently changed. These days, I wonder whether a team's lack of goalscoring opportunities is down to the attackers drawing too few passes in dangerous areas. After games, I look at Expected Goals and perhaps even at xGplots, if they are available. Maybe the rising and falling EPV numbers will soon accompany my football viewing, too. Data tells a story of the game – not *the* story, but often a new and better one than the one we have all become used to.

Football will continue to be in need of a lot of new thinking, such as the Packing concept Stefan Reinartz concocted. But when he talks of his former team-mate Toni Kroos, he almost sounds lovestruck. For two years they played together at Leverkusen and Reinartz is still totally in awe of the completely unfazed and almost flawless way Kroos distributes passes on the pitch – at Real Madrid, for Germany or back in the day at Leverkusen. 'You can recognise one [of] his passes blindfolded, by their sound,' he says. Kroos strikes the ball so cleanly that it rolls flat and smoothly across the pitch, and for his team-mates, receiving one of his perfectly weighted passes is so easy as to be a pleasure. That's exactly the scope needed to understand football in the 21st century. We should know the amount of bypassed defenders and keep our sense of wonder for the poetry of a perfectly timed pass.

FURTHER READING

There aren't many books that take a deeper interest in football data analytics. Recommended reading: David Sumpter: *Soccermatics*; Chris Anderson/David Sally: *The Numbers Game* and by Simon Kuper and Stefan Szymanski: *Soccernomics*.

The best source of information on the subject is the internet. A good starting point for further exploration is statsbomb.com, a blog that publishes excellent writers such as Ted Knutson, Colin Trainor, James Yorke, Dustin Ward and Euwan Dewar. Good analysis and new ideas are also found on OptaPro's website. Twitter is the community's digital talking shop.

ACKNOWLEDGEMENTS

My heartfelt thanks go out to all who generously gave me their time to answer questions and who proved informative and open throughout: Hendrik Almstadt, Chris Anderson, Rasmus Ankersen, Matthew Benham, Omar Chaudhuri, Christofer Clemens, Simon Cuff, Ian Graham, Heimir Hallgrímsson, Jens Hegeler, Michael Henke, Sander Ijtsma, Nicolas Jover, Katja Kraus, Peter Krawietz, Ted Knutson, Daniel Link, Jan Mayer, Daniel Memmert, Sven Mislintat, Marco Neppe, Michael Niemeyer, Himar Ojeda, Stefan Reinartz, Michael Reschke, Jörg Schmadtke, Kai Peter Schmitz, Jörg Seidel, Tim Sparv, Daniel Stenz, George Syrianos, Colin Trainor, Hendrik Weber, Blake Wooster.

I would also like to thank everyone I met while researching features for *11FREUNDE*, first and foremost Julian Nagelsmann. Parts of the story about his work at Hoffenheim informed two chapters of this book; the same is true of a piece on Midtjylland.

This book would not have been possible without the support of my *11FREUNDE* colleagues. Many thanks for that, especially to editor Philipp Köster, who readily created the necessary conditions for this project.

I want to also express my heartfelt gratitude for ideas and support in myriad ways to: Jonas Boldt, Jan Distlmeyer, Christian

Frommert, Jens Grittner, Uli Hesse, Michiel de Hoog, Günther Janssen, Fabian Jonas, Lukas Keppler, Saskia Kirf, Hans Krabbe, Cornelius Kreusser, Olaf Meinking, Thomas Pletzinger, Josef Schneck and Kurt Thielen.

Many thanks to Matt Phillips of Blink, without whom there wouldn't have been an English edition, and the same can be said of my agent, Nick Walters, and everyone at David Luxton Associates. Thank you for looking after me and this book in such a professional and caring manner.

I'm especially grateful to Raphael Honigstein for his excellent translation. I was already a big admirer of his, and I couldn't have wished for a better person to help me bring this book to a new audience.

Helge Malchow being my German editor and publisher for 23 years now is a blessing for me; the fact that he's become a friend, a gift.

Finally, thank you to Birgit!

INDEX